Method of Movement
for Marimba

with 590 exercises

LEIGH HOWARD STEVENS

25th Anniversary Edition

Substantially revised and Expanded

To a few dear friends
without whose sobering influence
the contents of this book
would have been
"Filled to the Brim" with clichés,
confused by flaws of grammatical,
not well laid-out,
and generally contaminated by
the author's obscure sense of humor.

Contents

CHANGES OR NEW MATERIAL HERE ☞

Preface

Through this book the author attempts to shed bright light into one dark corner of the marimbist's art: the mechanical principles of good technique.

The technical demands of solo marimba literature have become complex in recent years. Although B-flats and F-naturals (etc.) are no more difficult to strike today than they were ten years ago, marimbists are now expected to strike more of them, further apart on the instrument, and in less time. Today's problem then is not so much striking individual notes or groups of notes as it is **getting to** those notes. The author believes that this is the area in which traditional methodology is inadequate to the demands made of the marimbist by contemporary music: efficiency of movement. This is the area that **Method of Movement** presumes to enlighten.

This book does not deal with the mechanics of pressure strokes, one-handed baroque ornamentation, independent rolls, or any other sustaining techniques. Some students of marimba playing may be disappointed that the author has not fulfilled his dubious mission as purveyor of insights into "advanced" techniques. But when these recent developments have become commonplace and their attractive sheen has been eclipsed by **tomorrow's** advanced techniques, the fundamentals of efficient movement will have retained their intrinsic prestige and burnished lustre. In fact, as the marimbist's art becomes more sophisticated, the player's basic method of movement **increases** in importance.

This text does not discuss **every** aspect of struck note technique; some factors have been ignored because of limitations of space. This book makes no pretense of dealing with the problems of playing other mallet keyboard instruments. The author leaves it to others to decide whether the concepts of this method have application to xylophone, vibes, or other instruments of percussion.

First Part
Method of Movement

1 How To Use the Method of Movement

The student should not attempt to play **any** of the exercises in the second half of this book until **all** of the preceding text has been read. While proceding with the practice of a few of the preliminary exercises, the student should **return** to the text—this time to **study** it. Later in the development of technique the intermediate and advanced student can use the text as a guide to the solution of particular technical problems.

The second half of the book is divided by stroke type into five major sections. There is no reason for the student to study these major sections individually or in order of appearance. In fact, the beginning student might do well to start with the double vertical section and tackle the preliminary exercises in the other sections as he or she feels able.

The exercises devoted to a particular stroke type are divided into subsections. The exercises within each subsection should be practiced in order of appearance beginning with the preliminary subsection; thereafter the subsections may be practiced in any order that seems complementary to the student's other musical studies. The last section of exercises (mixed strokes) should be avoided until a substantial portion of the earlier exercises have been mastered.

The exercises should be practiced in cycles. A given exercise is practiced until either progress on it stops, or the student becomes bored with it and loses the ability to concentrate. The exercise is then left untouched for a period of a few months to a year, and then the cycle is repeated.

The slower metronome mark that appears before a series of exercises is intended to be a guideline for the initial practice of an exercise. The faster metronome mark will probably not be attainable until a given exercise has weathered several practice cycles.

In most of the exercises the rhythms are simple, and the pitches are based on major scales and major chords. The pitch and rhythmic difficulties have been kept to an absolute minimum for two reasons:

1. that the student might focus **all** attention on proper execution, and

2. that the beginning student need not be discouraged from developing technique because of difficulty with reading.

All the exercises are to be transposed chromatically and continuously through the twelve keys. After a short time chromatic transposition will become automatic. It is then, when the student ceases to think about **what** note to strike, that the student can fully concentrate on **how** to strike. Transposition by circle of fourths or fifths is **not** recommended (except for the advanced student), as these transpositions often contain technical problems unrelated to the purpose of the exercise.

The student should remember that profitable practice concentrates on what is **between** the notes even **more** than the notes themselves. This is why mentally focused, **slow practice** pays off: the time **between** the notes is expanded so that one is able to feel and examine the motions in microscopic detail. That the **tempo** is slow (the strokes are separated by time) is no justification for proportionally slowing down the velocity of the shifts, interval changes, or the **strokes themselves.** Each complete gesture should be executed as it would up to tempo, but "thinking space" should be placed **between** the gestures.

II Numeration

The information contained in figure 1 is used throughout this text. The student should become familiar with this identification system before commencing study of section V.

NB: This is the only photograph in MOM that is not my hand. Obviously, I am not that hairy. If you must know why, I was late for the photo session. To all those amateur palm readers who were predicting my early demise and lack of good fortune: Sorry to disappoint.

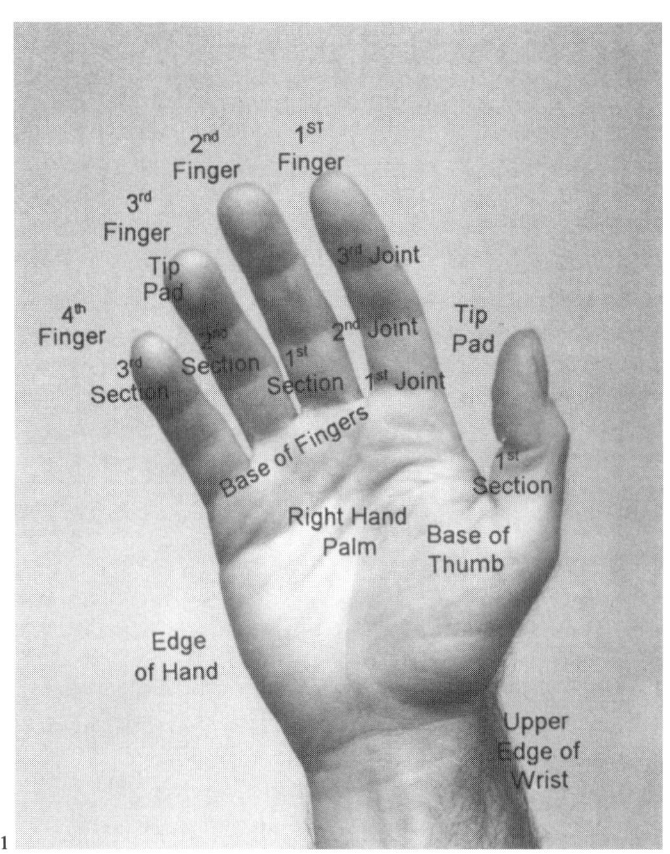

1

The mallet numbering system used in this text is shown below.

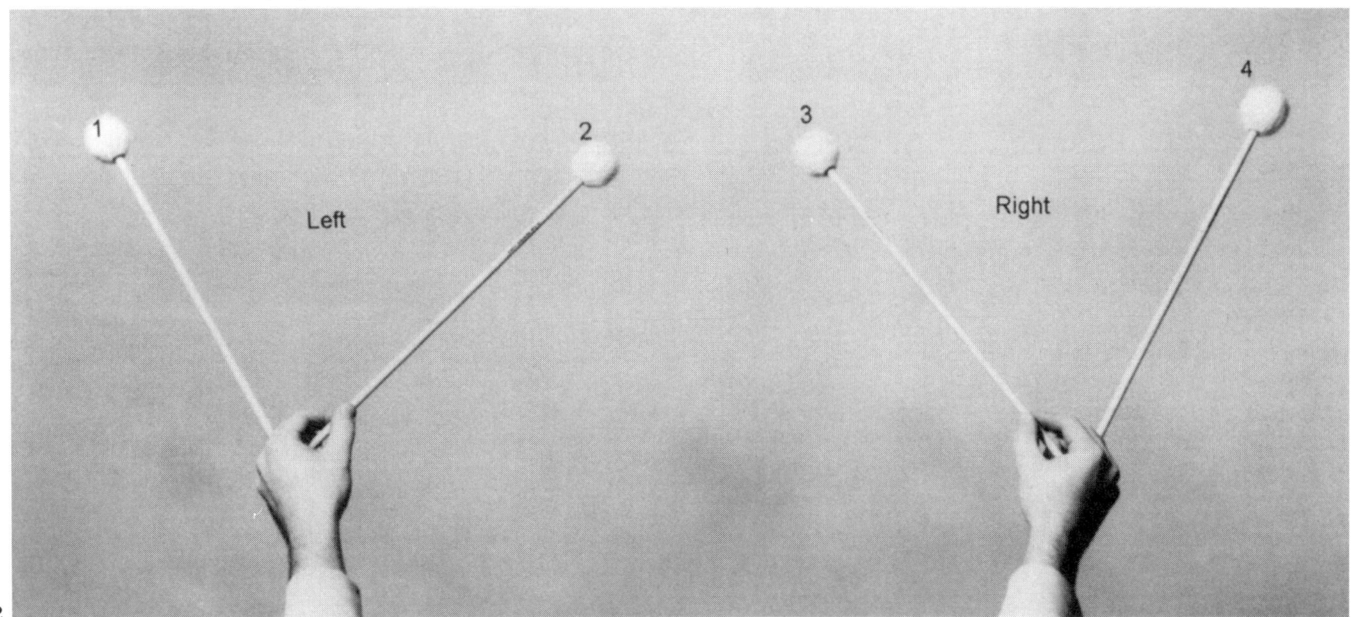

2

III Sticking Permutations

There are twenty-four different single note sticking patterns. These patterns are of three basic types:

1. Those that alternate hands every pitch

2. Those that alternate hands every two pitches

3. Those that start with a single pitch and then alternate hands every two pitches (the first and fourth pitch are played by the same hand).

Table A contains the twenty-four sticking permutations divided into these three categories. The columns within the table are in ascending numerical order. Many of the exercises in the second part of this book can be varied by application of these twenty-four patterns. The order of the pitches changes, but the rhythm remains intact. Some of the exercises in the second part are already written out in sixteen of the twenty-four permutations.

Table A

1	2	3
1−3−2−4	1−2−3−4	1−3−4−2
1−4−2−3	1−2−4−3	1−4−3−2
2−3−1−4	2−1−3−4	2−3−4−1
2−4−1−3	2−1−4−3	2−4−3−1
3−1−4−2	3−4−1−2	3−1−2−4
3−2−4−1	3−4−2−1	3−2−1−4
4−1−3−2	4−3−1−2	4−1−2−3
4−2−3−1	4−3−2−1	4−2−1−3

Once the student has studied the text, mastered all four stroke types, and completed a portion of the exercises in each section, it may be more functionally clear to use Table B. Table B contains the same permutations as Table A, but they are divided into columns according to stroke type. The columns within Table B are in their **natural permutation order**, i.e., the first digit in the first permutation becomes the last digit of the second permutation. The fifth through eighth sticking patterns in each column are the reverse order of sticking patterns one through four.

The student will notice that the first column in Table B is identical in contents to the first column in Table A. These are the single alternating stroke permutations

(see section XIV). The second column of Table B contains the sequential order double lateral stroke permutations (see section XVI). After the pattern has been established it will appear that the sticking order is 1234 or 4321: an inside double lateral is always followed by an outside double lateral, and an outside double lateral is always followed by an inside double lateral.

The third column in Table B contains the mirror order double lateral stroke permutations. After any of the patterns in this column have been established it will be noticed that the hands are "mirroring" one another: the strokes in these permutations will be either double lateral inside or double lateral outside — never one of each.

Double vertical strokes (see section XV) and overlapping double lateral strokes may be introduced into the table by the use of brackets and then applied to the second part for further variations of the exercises. The pattern 1234 might become (12)34: a left double vertical followed by a right double lateral inside; or 1(23)4: a left double lateral outside overlapping a right double lateral inside; or 12(34): a left double lateral outside followed by a right double vertical. In the above cases nothing but the original pitches of the exercises remains intact — both the order of the pitches and the rhythm change: groups of four sixteenth notes are changed into sixteenth note triplets.

The monomaniacal student may continue almost endlessly with this variation process by linking any two or three members of any of the twenty-four permutations.

Table B

Single alternating	Sequential double lateral	Mirror double lateral
1−3−2−4	1−2−3−4	1−3−4−2
3−2−4−1	2−3−4−1	3−4−2−1
2−4−1−3	3−4−1−2	4−2−1−3
4−1−3−2	4−1−2−3	2−1−3−4
4−2−3−1	4−3−2−1	2−4−3−1
1−4−2−3	1−4−3−2	1−2−4−3
3−1−4−2	2−1−4−3	3−1−2−4
2−3−1−4	3−2−1−4	4−3−1−2

IV   General Principles of Marimba Technique

The methodization of efficient marimba technique requires muscles and appendages to be assigned performance tasks best suited to their natures. Large muscle sets are adapted to large, slow gestures, and small muscle sets are adapted to small, fast gestures.

The broad responsibilities are divided as follows:

1. The feet, legs, and lower torso deliver the upper torso and arms to the correct basic area of the keyboard. This lower part of the body also adjusts the angle of the upper torso to the keyboard.

2. The arms move the hands horizontally across the length and width of the keyboard (shifts). When the arms are delivering the hands across the **width** of the keyboard, they may also legitimately make **small** vertical adjustments to compensate for the different heights of the natural and accidental keyboards.

3. The wrists supply the basic motive power to accelerate the mallet heads to the bars. The wrist is also capable of making horizontal adjustments.

4. The fingers adjust the interval spread and are also capable of making mallet acceleration adjustments.

It is generally harmless for a small muscle set to participate in the task of a larger muscle set. For example, the fingers may aid the wrist in mallet acceleration, and the wrist may aid the arm in shifting horizontally around the keyboard. Participation of a **large** muscle set in the task of a **smaller** muscle set is **harmful,** e.g., the arm should not contribute to the vertical acceleration of the mallet heads, and the legs should not make small horizontal adjustments that could be more easily negotiated by the arms.

When two different muscle sets have proportionally difficult tasks to perform in a given period of time, the large/slow muscle set should begin its task earlier than the small/fast muscle set. For example, the wrist begins the acceleration of the mallet heads before any finger contraction is made, and the legs must begin their contribution to a large shift before the arms.

The Marimbist would do well to keep the above principles in mind while studying the general science of movement and solving more particular personal technical problems.

V The Four-Mallet Grip

The three major categories of four-mallet grips are:

Traditional: the shafts of the mallets are crossed in the palm of the hand with the outside mallet shaft under the inside. The grip operates on a spring-tension principle with fingers 3 and 4 supplying the interval closing energy, and the thumb and finger 1 supplying the interval opening energy.

Burton: The shafts of the mallets are crossed in the palm of the hand with the outside mallet shaft on top of the inside. The grip operates on an axle-type pivot principle with fingers 3 and 4 supplying most of the interval opening and closing energy (by pushing and pulling on the shaft of the inner mallet).

Musser: The shafts of the mallets are held in different sections of the hand with the inside mallet being contolled by the thumb and fingers 1 and 2, and the outside mallet being controlled by fingers 3 and 4. The grip operates basically on a horizontal pendulum principle with the interval opening and closing energy being supplied in a number of different ways.

The traditional and the Burton grips are often described as cross-stick or dependent grips because the shafts of the mallets criss-cross in the palm of the hand. The Musser grip is sometimes described as an independent grip because the shafts of the mallets are held in separate parts of the hand and are never in contact with one another.

Although the author has used all three of the above grips (in the order presented) for various lengths of time and has experienced improved facility with each change of grip, he cannot heartily recommend any of them for solo marimba playing. The grip used by this author (around which the bulk of this text revolves) is a **child** of Musser grip, but it does not resemble or operate like the family of Musser grips described in various "Total Percussion" method books. The chief differences lie in the areas of hand position (posture), mechanical operation, and area and method of grasping the mallet shaft. (For a complete description, see section VI, page 10).

From this point in the text the name "Musser grip" and "Stevens technique" will be used interchangeably, depending on context and whether the reference was part of the first edition text, or added in a later edition.

Feeling "Secure"

Burton and Traditional grips give the player the illusion of greater security and solidity because you hold and touch the mallet handles much further up on the shaft. This is similar to a baseball batter choking up on the bat - of course things feel more "secure" when you choke up! But once you have choked up, you have also reduced your reach and leverage. If you use the same mallets when comparing cross-stick to Stevens technique, it is not a fair "apples to apples" comparison. To compare the two systems you must equalize the large interval capability by using shorter mallets with Stevens grip. To really test "solidity of feel", use shorter mallet shafts with Stevens so that the maximum comfortable reach is **identical** to what you can do with longer mallets with cross-stick technique. This usually means trimming 2 to 3 cm (about 1 to 1 1/2 inches) off the ends of the handles. Watch that saw blade! I recommend using this type of shorter mallet handle for the first few months for any player making a change from cross-stick to Stevens. There is nothing wrong with using shorter handles with Stevens Technique all the time, as long as you don't need large intervals! There is no question about it - the feel of the physics in your hand do not lie to you: effectively shortening the mallets by using a cross stick grip, or by actually using shorter mallets and holding them on the ends with Stevens Technique, produces a more secure, solid feel.

Speed of interval change

One of the most basic technical problems faced by the marimbist is opening and closing the interval between the mallet heads. The initial security and firmness offered by the traditional grip backfires on its user when fast interval changes are required: (a) The larger the interval is, the greater the isometric counterpressure that is required of fingers 3 and 4. As this muscle tension increases, speed and flexibility decrease. Quite simply, a technical system based on tension cannot be expected to produce agility; (b) In the case of small intervals (seconds), traditional and Burton grips require the withdrawal of the first finger from the "vee" formed between the shafts to allow the angle to close. Or, it is necessary to twist the wrist and/or the arm so that the shafts are more perpendicular to the bars.

Although the Burton grip is faster than the traditional grip, neither can approach the fluidity that the Musser grip offers to rapidly alternating small to large intervals (i.e., seconds to octaves - ♪'s, ♩=152): (a) No isometric counterpressure is required to open or close the interval; (b) Since the shafts can be made parallel, there is no need to turn the wrist to accommodate a second. The mallet heads can even **pass** the position of a second and cross to each other's position; (c) Because the motion of the mallet heads is initiated at the end of the shaft, the grip maximizes the ratio of mallet head to finger movement: a small finger motion produces a large change in the interval.

Interval limit

At the time of this writing, there are numerous pieces in the solo marimba literature which are virtually impossible to play with traditional or Burton grips because of their limited reach. The degree to which a grip allows the mallets to approach a straight line (opening angle=180°) is a measure of its large interval capability. A crossed-stick grip by definition cannot achieve a 180° angle without uncrossing the shafts. The Musser grip actually permits angles even greater than 180 degrees! (As in the case of the peculiar ability of the Musser grip to cross the inside mallet over the outside, this author is hard pressed to think of a practical application of interval spreads of more than 180 degrees.)

Two other important factors in large interval capability are shaft length, and **where** on that length the mallets are held - **usable** length. With the mallets used by the author, elevenths in the low register and two octaves in the upper register are possible.* More importantly, from such an extreme position, the grip allows the mallets to be flipped quickly and safely back to a closed position.

Wrist maneuverability

Marimbists are usually taught to play the instrument with the palm of the hand flat (facing straight down). This approach is allegedly "more secure" and therefore more accurate. A simple experiment will demonstrate the superior **maneuverability** of an edge of the hand down position: Keeping the palm of the hand facing the floor, move the hand at the wrist from left to right. The **horizontal** arc that the tips of the fingers can describe (about 45°) is a measure of how far the mallet heads can be shifted up or down the keyboard without involving the arm. The **vertical** arc that the hand can describe in this position (about 120°) is a measure of the available stroke height. Repeat the process with the **edge** of the hand facing the floor and the **wrist curved** to the outside. The angles that are possible with this hand position are about 120° and 110° respectively. This basic posture permits the small and fast muscles of the wrist to execute small shifts that the traditional and Burton grips would have to relegate to the slower less agile arm.

One other comparison of wrist maneuverability is worth mentioning. The basic method for opening the interval with traditional grip, and to a lesser extent Burton grip, involves spreading out the thumb and first finger as in figure A. The more these two appendages are spread (the larger the interval) the tighter and more restricted the wrist becomes. So, using traditional or Burton grips, as the interval opens, it becomes increasingly difficult to produce the stroke with the wrist. This is also a problem with Musser grip in the original version used by Musser and his students. I believe this is at the root of the obvious phenomenon that traditional grip players use their arms more than Burton players and Burton grip players use their arms more than Stevens technique players. A fundamental difference between Musser and Stevens techniques is found in this area: In Stevens technique, the first finger and thumb stay together even in very large intervals, making it easier to use the wrist to produce the stroke.

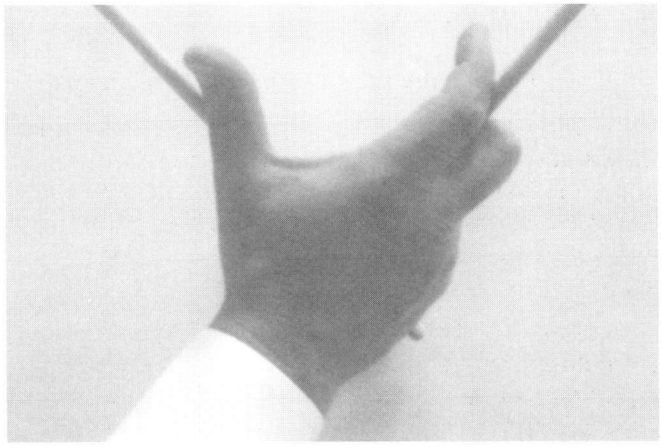

A

Finger control

One measure of the potential agility of a grip is the ability to maneuver individual mallets with the fingers, without the aid of the wrist or interference with the other mallet. Finger control in a crossed-stick grip is very limited because the mallets operate as a unit with the wrist. Independent movement requires delegating more authority to the fingers and lessening the constrictive contact of the shafts with each other and with the palm of the hand.

Generally speaking, since the mallets respond to any wrist or arm motion equally, trying to "voice" strokes dynamically without the aid of the fingers is as successful as trying to wrap mallets while wearing mittens. The only type of advanced finger control available with a crossed-stick grip is the outside mallet 90 degree pivot stroke used by Gary Burton for melody, outlined in his book **Four Mallet Studies.**

This author's adaptation of the Musser grip offers something similar to Burton's pivot stroke but does not require the mallets to be at right angles. More importantly, this grip allows **each** of the four mallets to perform independent strokes **regardless** of the interval opening. The grip also frees the fingers to accelerate the mallets at different speeds - greatly increasing the individual dynamic control of each mallet.

All of these comparisons which point to the superior agility of the Musser grip are moot if the student is not convinced that potential dexterity is more important than initial security. There is no doubt that crossed-stick grips are easier to master because there are fewer possible motions to refine. In this sense one can never "master" the Musser grip. The preliminary instability soon blossoms into freedom of movement. Once freedom of movements is attained, the technical possibilities are endless.

* When this text was written, 5-octave super-wide bar marimbas were only a dream. On the instrument the author performs on today, he can "only" reach an octave in the low end and an octave and a seventh at the top.

VI Holding the Mallets

Outside mallets 1 and 4

Start with the arm hanging at the side — wrist and fin-gers relaxed. Raise the forearm from the elbow until it is parallel with the floor. Turn the wrist so that the surface of the thumb nail is parallel to the ceiling.

Slip the shaft of a mallet between fingers 2 and 3. Rest it on the second joint of the third finger. Now curl fingers 3 and 4 around the shaft until the tips of the fingers just touch the section of palm near the base of the fingers. Adjust the length of the mallet so that only ¼th of an inch protrudes beyond the third section of the fourth finger. The shaft of the mallet should touch the second finger in its first section, closer to the second joint than the first. *

Check the following points before proceding:

1. Fingers should be relaxed — mallet **hangs** in position.

2. Weight of mallet heads should pull up slightly on ends of fingers 3 and 4 — more so on 4.

3. Shaft should lie on top of second joint of third finger and beneath first section of second finger, close to, but not beneath second joint.

4. Edge of hand should face floor.

5. Compare with figure 3.

Inside mallets 2 and 3

Place the end of the mallet handle lightly into the palm flesh 1 to 1 ½ inches beneath the thumb. Set the shaft down on the side of the third joint of the first finger. The weight of the mallet will be distributed like a hanging lever: the end of the handle will pull up on the flesh under the base of the thumb, and the shaft will push down on the first finger. The mallet should be **balanced** in position.

Check the following points before proceding:

1. Fingers and wrist should be relaxed.

2. Position of fingers holding the outside mallet should not have changed (if so, vom anfang!).

3. Inside mallet should **hang** between flesh in base of thumb and third joint of first finger.

4. Compare position with figure 4.

Drop thumb onto handle. Curl joints of second finger so that third section of second finger touches end of shaft. Check over-all position with figures 5, 6, & 7.

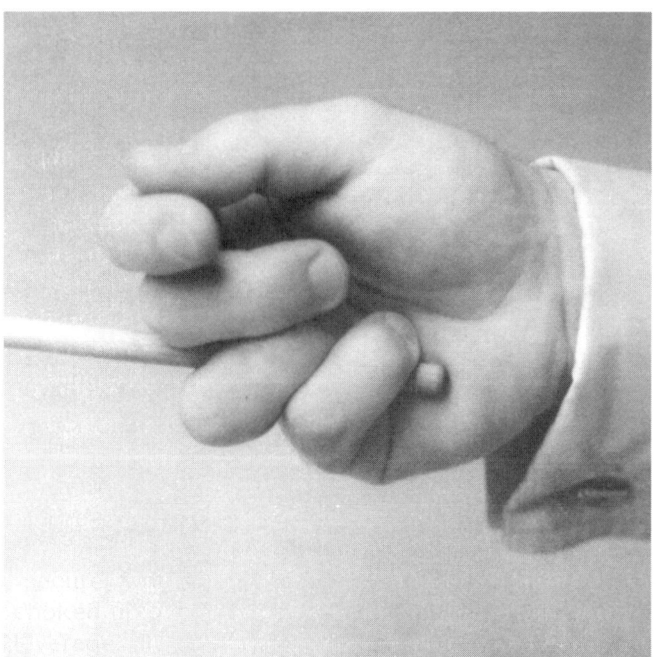

3

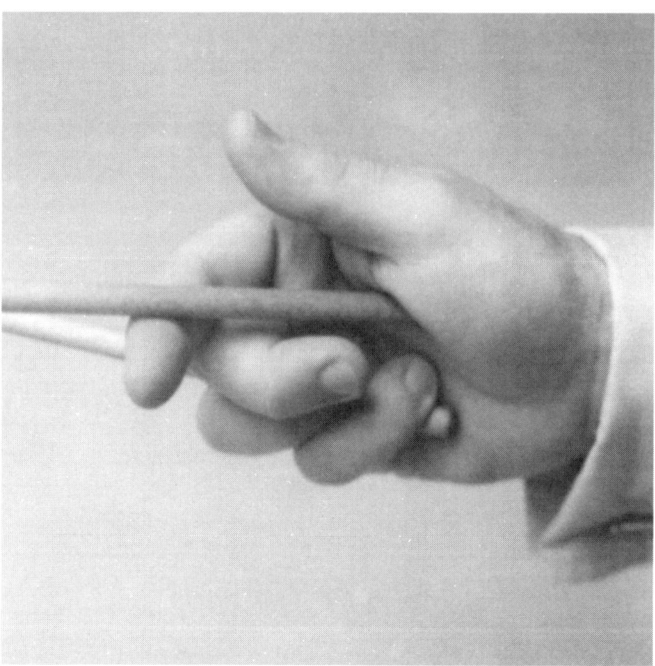

4

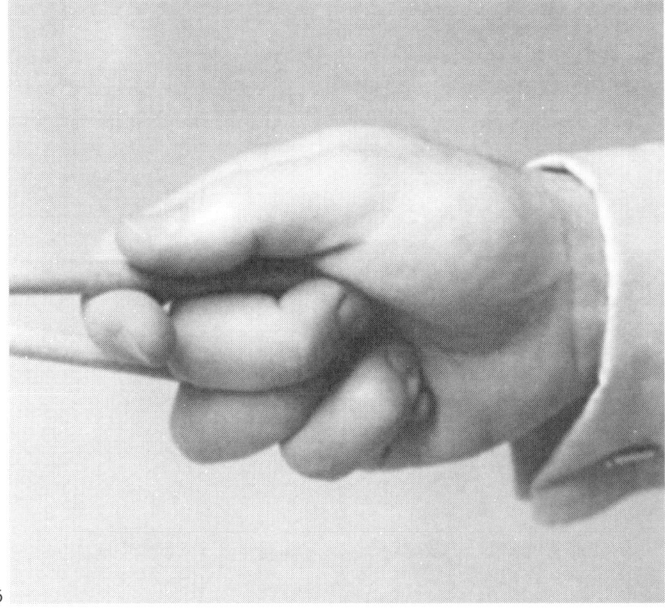

5

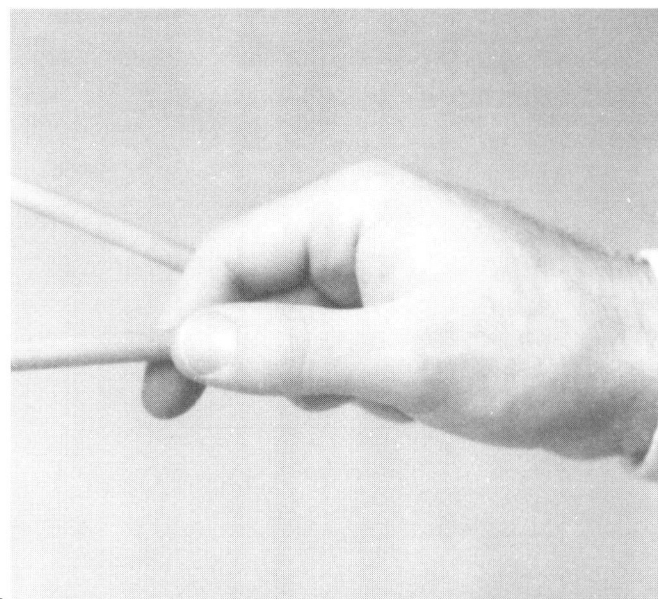

6

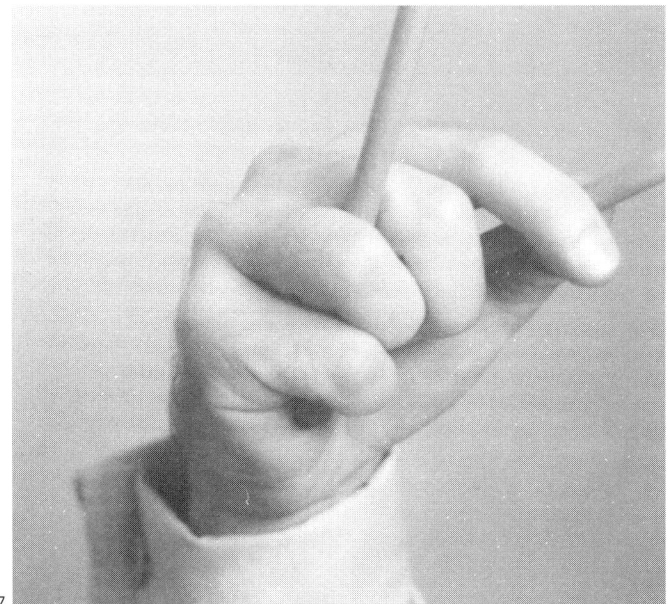

7

Check the following points:

1. Hand and fingers should look graceful, curved, and natural.

2. Mallets should **hang** in hand with both hand and fingers relaxed: expend no more energy than is necessary to keep mallets from falling out of hand.

3. Inside mallet should be ½ to 1 inch longer than the outside. (Of course, this assumes that the student was clever enough to start this section with a matched set of mallets.)

4. Mallet heads should be at the same playing height (distance from floor).

5. If mallet heads are not at the same height, do one of the following:

   (a) Move end of inside mallet **up**, closer to base (first joint) of thumb.

   (b) Curl finger 2 farther into the palm in order to make room for the first finger to be pulled down by the weight of the mallet.

   (c) Pull **down** slightly with fingers 3 and 4 to pull outside mallet head **up**.

6. There should be a natural, open curve between thumb and first finger.

It is highly recommended that in the initial stages of study, the student refer to this hand position description whenever there is the **slightest** bit of tension or awkwardness in holding the mallets. Remember, holding the mallets **correctly** is almost effortless.

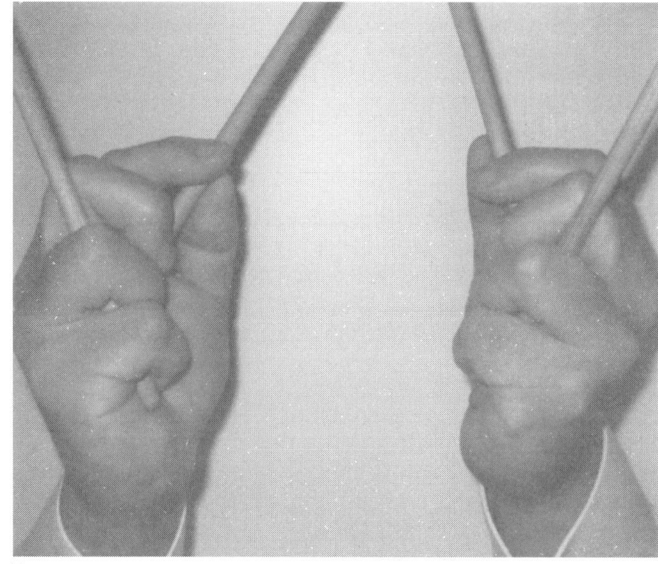

7a

* Position the outside mallet so that it contacts the second finger close to the second knuckle - not centered and never back in the "webbing" between the second and third fingers. Moving the "home position" of the outside mallet to the position shown in figure 7a reduces wobbliness in the outside mallet, allows fingers 3 and 4 to control the mallet with less effort and improves overall control and power.

VII Interval Changes

Problems related to interval changes can plague the first few years of marimba study. To prevent these physical hindrances, it is essential that from the inception of holding the mallets, the student learn to move them correctly. Since the subject is so complicated — and therefore potentially confusing without on-the-spot demonstration and correction — the following is offered only as a guideline of the most critical aspects of efficient interval control.

General considerations

1. Keep the hand and fingers **relaxed** up to intervals of a tenth. Security of movement is a product of coordination, not strength.

2. Tension will negate the superior interval changing capacity of this grip. If the student wants to play with tension, it is recommended that he switch to traditional grip.

3. Hand and fingers should **look** graceful and curved up to intervals of a tenth. A contorted or angular looking hand position is a sure sign of tension. Remember that tension is both a **symptom** of something wrong and a **cause** for further things to go wrong. Get rid of it **NOW** before the muscles can familiarize themselves with the feeling.

4. The muscles controlling the outside mallet are slower to develop than those controlling the inside. One should not be concerned if several months go by with comparatively little of the outside mallet interval changing capacity being used.

Specific considerations

While bearing in mind the above general considerations, the student should memorize the content of the following particulars (**memorize,** not familiarize).

1. The inside mallet will spin slightly between the thumb and the first finger as the interval changes. When the interval is **opening,** the mallet in the right hand will spin counterclockwise; the mallet in the left hand will spin clockwise. The direction of spin will be opposite when the interval is **closing.** See figure 8.

2. The **first finger straightens** as it flips the inside mallet up and out. As the first finger straightens, it moves from its position under the mallet to a position on the side of the mallet. See figure 9.

3. When the mallets are spread to about the position of a third, the hand configuration will be **identical** to the basic "rest" position described in the section on holding the mallets. The inside mallet is **centered** under the thumb and is in a straight line with the length of the thumb. As the interval opens and the mallet spins between the first finger and thumb, the spinning motion will roll the mallet from its central position under the thumb to a position on the side of the thumb. There is now an acute angle formed by the thumb and shaft. See figure 9.

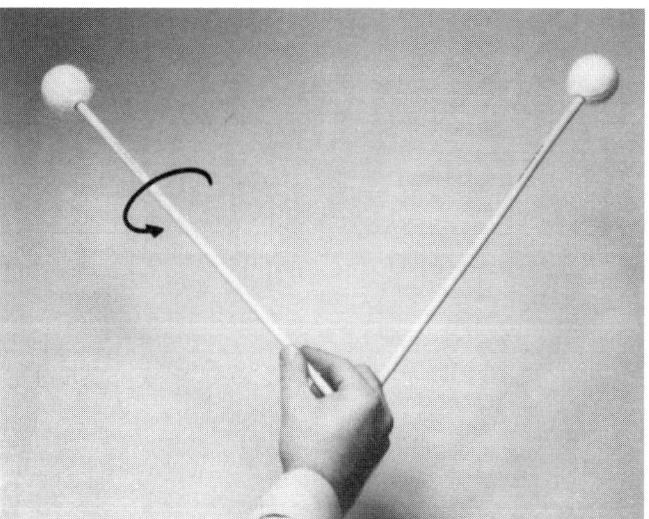

8

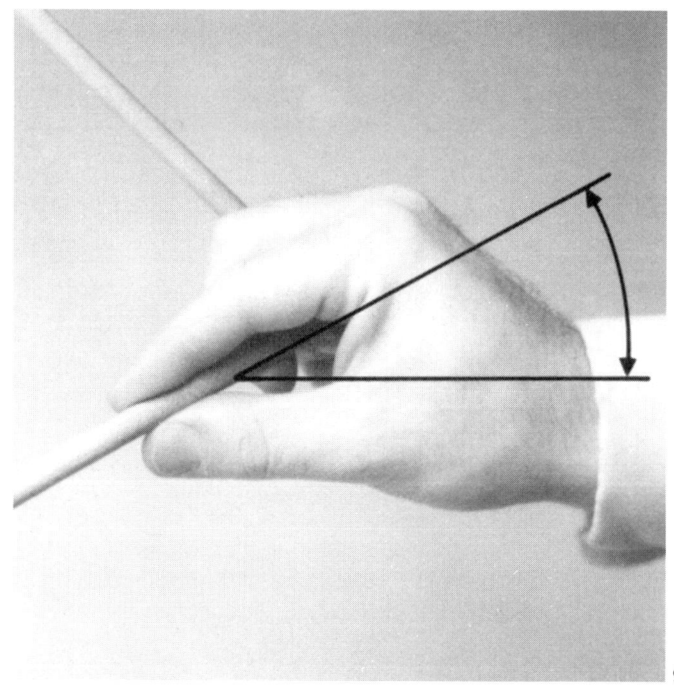

9

4. If the large interval position (partially described in item 3) is to be maintained for an extended period – perhaps a passage in one-handed octaves – then the position of the thumb may be "corrected" by centralizing the pad of the thumb over the shaft. However, the shaft will not form a straight line with the length of the thumb as it did in the position of a third. The thumb merely changes its point of contact with the shaft from the side of the thumb to the pad. This realignment of the thumb is usually unnecessary and should be undertaken only when there are extended large interval passages or when extra support is needed for Neanderthal strokes. See figure 10.

5. The first finger and thumb remain in juxtaposition. The first finger should not curl under the mallet during large intervals. The thumb and first finger work **together**. If the thumb is very long in relationship to the first finger, the student may have to bend the second joint of the thumb to keep it opposite the first finger on large intervals.

6. As the interval opens and closes, the end of the inside mallet will inscribe an arc in the palm of the hand. See figure 11. This path that the end of the mallet travels is a slightly curved line extending from its resting place beneath the base of the thumb (thirds), to the first joint of the second finger (very large intervals).

7. If there is any tendency for the thumb and first finger to change their point of contact on the length of the shaft, the mallet is being held at an incorrect length. If the end of the shaft catches or drags on the flesh of the palm when interval changes are being made, the mallet is being held **too short**. In this case the student should return to a hanging rest position (section VI) and move the end of the inside mallet **up**, closer to the base of the thumb to lengthen the

grip on the shaft. If the student feels that the end of the shaft is not obtaining support from contact with the palm, the mallet is being held **too long**. In this case the student should return to a hanging rest position and move the end of the mallet **down**, away from the base of the thumb to shorten the grip on the shaft.

8. The second finger helps to open and close the interval and is the major means of supporting the end of the shaft in the palm. Points **a** through **d** refer to the operation of the second finger.

(a) The second finger **never** uncurls. Joints 2 and 3 remain bent. The second joint of the second finger strays very little from a 90 degree bend. The third joint of the second finger will vary from about 100 degrees (thirds) to 90 degrees (large intervals). The only joint of the second finger which ever straightens is the **first** joint.

(b) The second finger pushes and pulls the end of the shaft through the arc described in item 6. Most of the pushing and pulling power of the second finger comes from the first joint; that is, the connection point of the finger to hand. As the interval grows larger and the end of the shaft is pulled toward the base of the second finger, the first section of the second finger approaches a straight line with the back of the hand. See figure 12.

(c) Since the second finger is the major means of supporting the end of the mallet in the hand, it is kept in firm contact with the last inch of shaft. The second finger applies more pressure on large intervals and when extra support is needed. The pressure is released when the interval is changed.

(d) The second finger is snapped back into its position under the shaft to help close the interval.

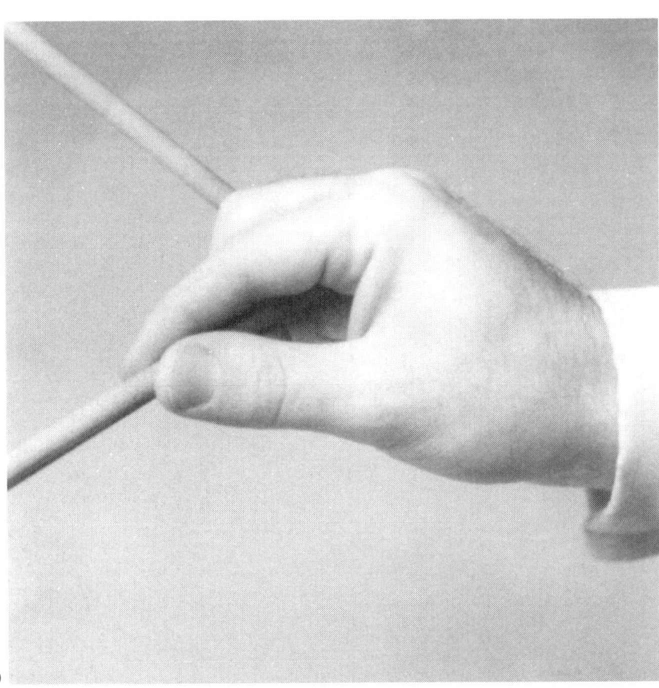

10

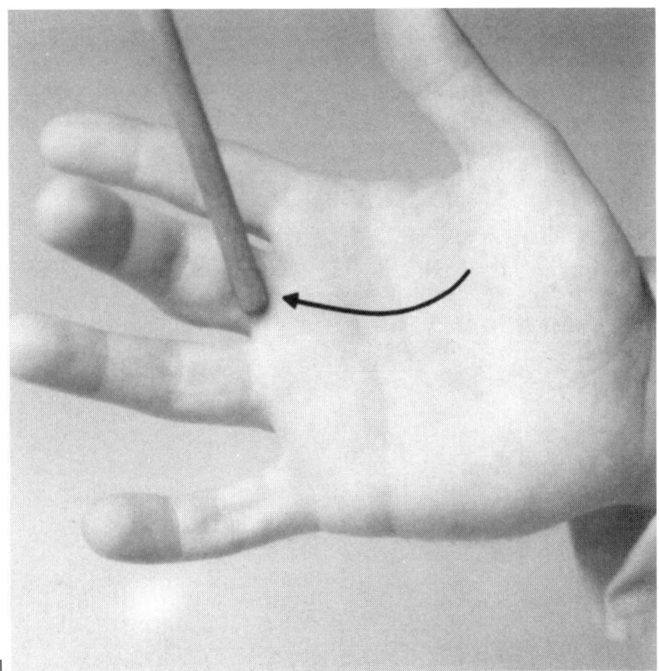

11

9. Except for extreme cases, such as the end of William Penn's 4th *Prelude* (where an octave and a seventh is required), the thumb is never placed between the shafts. Allowing the thumb to go into this "ham-fisted" Neanderthal position completely eliminates all the fine motor control and sensitivity offered by the opposable thumb and index finger combination. It also flattens the hand position, making all inside rotary strokes more awkward. See Figure 13.

10. The outside mallet is moved principally with fingers 3 and 4. Although the first section of the second finger follows along with the outside mallet and remains in light contact, it should not be used to "push" open the outside mallet. The second finger's main responsibility is control and strength of the inside mallet, so it should never uncurl and leave contact with the inside mallet to help the outside mallet.

11. The motion used by fingers 3 and 4 in opening the interval is similar to that of the second finger. The angle formed by the first section of the 3rd finger and the back of the hand approaches a straight line. See figure 14. Note that in the largest intervals, the tip of the 4th finger may pull away from its contact point near the center of the palm toward the base of the fourth finger. However, the back of the first section of the 4th finger does not flatten with the back of the hand like the back of the third finger. Note that in figure 18 there is a very large interval but the 4th finger is still touching the palm and is not "overextended".

12. The muscles which control the outside mallet may be strengthened with the following exercise:

    (a) Attempt to scratch an imaginary itch in the first joint of fingers 3 and 4 with the tips of fingers 3 and 4. See figure 15.

    (b) Repeat until it doesn't itch anymore.

    (c) Although this exercise can effectively strengthen the fingers (or probably harm them if done excessively), in practice, even in large intervals, the back of the first section of the 4th finger does **NOT** flatten with the back of the hand. Note that in figure 18, despite the very large spread of the mallets, the fourth finger is wrapped securely around the mallet shaft and it is tucked firmly into the palm, completely **UNLIKE** the position of the fourth finger in the "imaginary itch" exercise shown in figure 15.

13. Study the large interval position sequence shown in figures 16, 17 & 18.

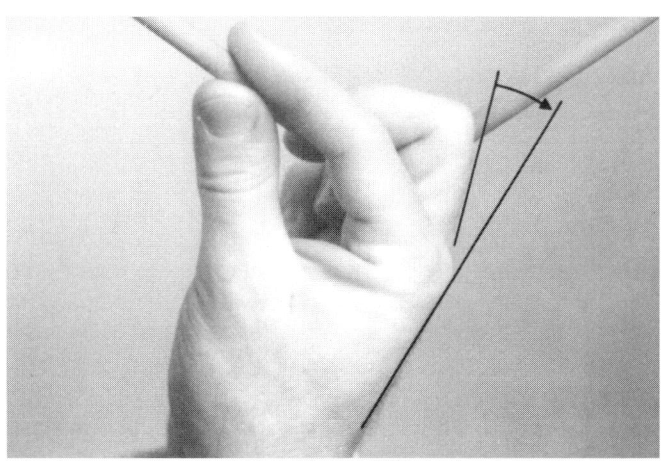

12

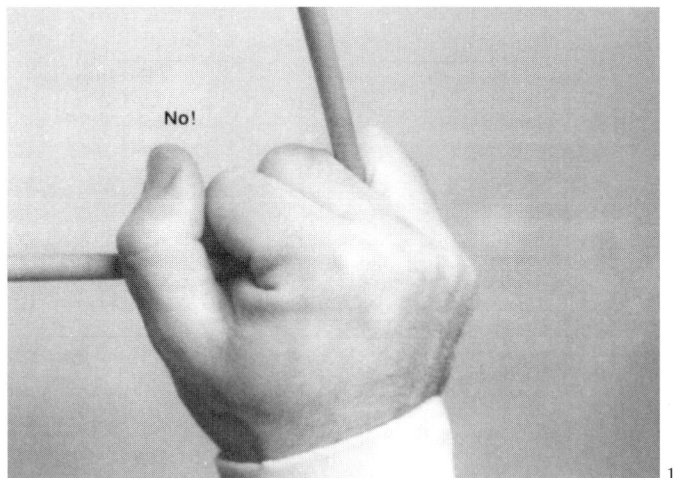

13

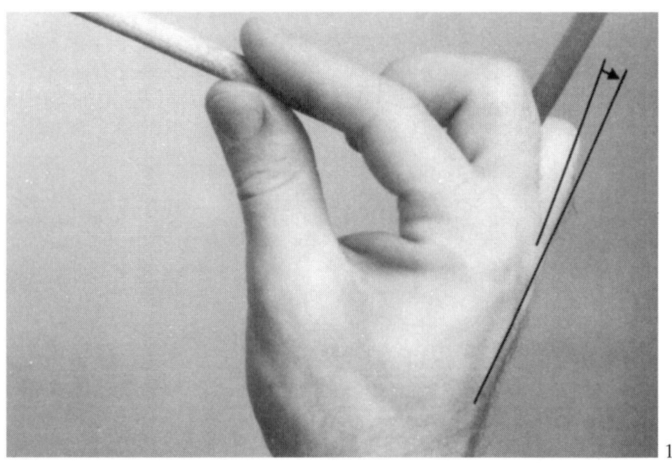

14

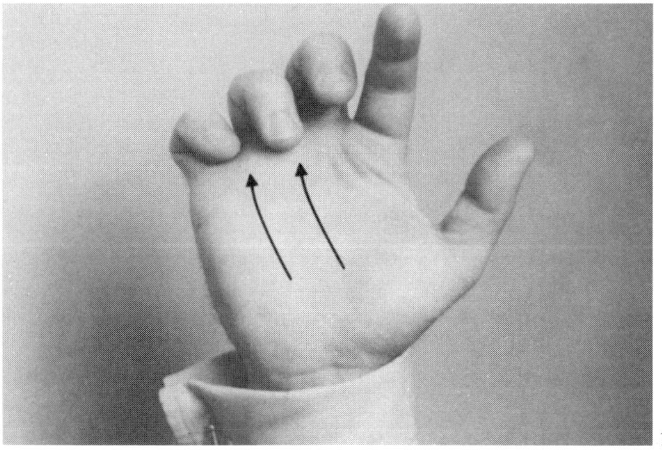

15

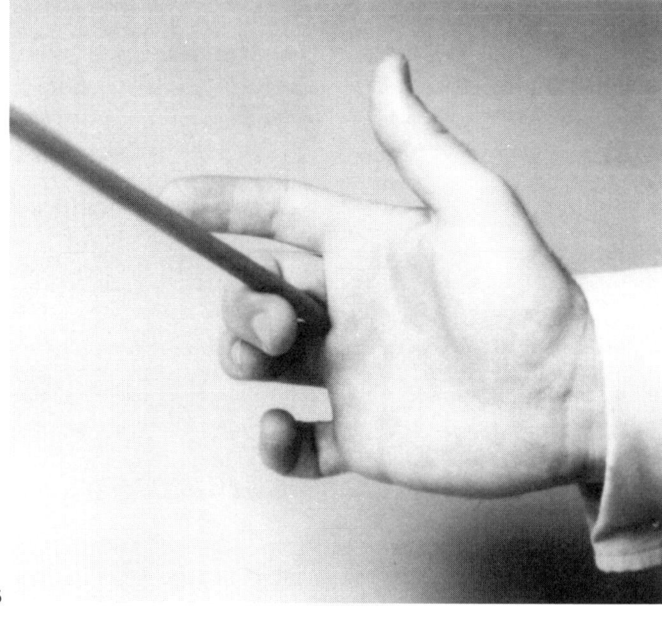

16

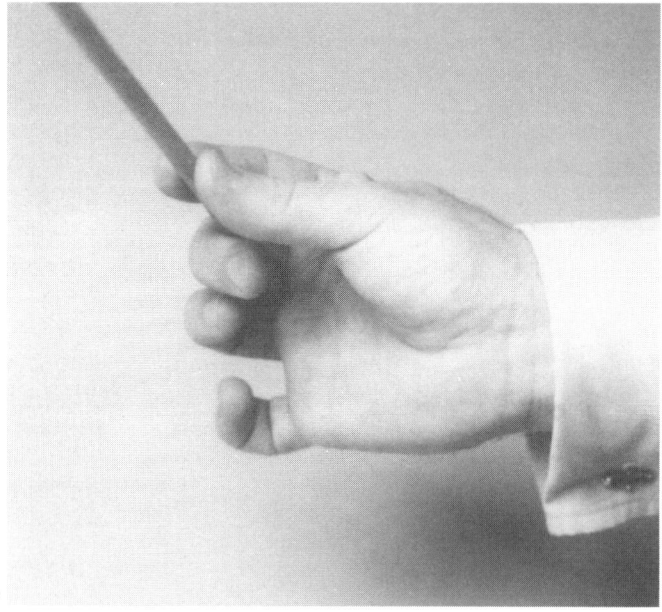

17

VIII Stroke Height

One of the simplest but rarely articulated truths of playing percussion instruments is that soft notes are easier to play with a short stroke than with a long stroke, and that loud notes are easier to play with a long stroke than with a short stroke. If this fact is not obvious, the student should try to play fortissimo first with a one-inch stroke and then with an eight-inch stroke; pianissimo first with an eight-inch stroke and then with a one-inch stroke. In fact, there is a "correct" starting height for every dynamic level. Facile players are able to produce greater volume from a given height than inept players. Hard, dense mallets can produce greater volume from a given height than soft, light mallets.

Although the general rule is easy to understand — louder = higher and softer = lower — it is difficult to refine. What if the starting height of a mezzo-forte stroke with a medium mallet feels "OK" anywhere from three inches to six inches? One should choose the **lowest** stroke height that preserves a natural, smooth acceleration of the mallet heads. If the starting point is too **low,** the stroke will feel pinched and tense. If the stroke starts too **high,** it will feel cushioned and restrained.

Why choose the **lowest** comfortable height? It is easier for a marimbist to hit a "bull's eye" at three inches than at four inches. This one-inch difference does not make playing **much** easier, but it may keep a few of the thousands of bulls' eyes necessary in a performance from sounding like some other portion of a bull's anatomy.

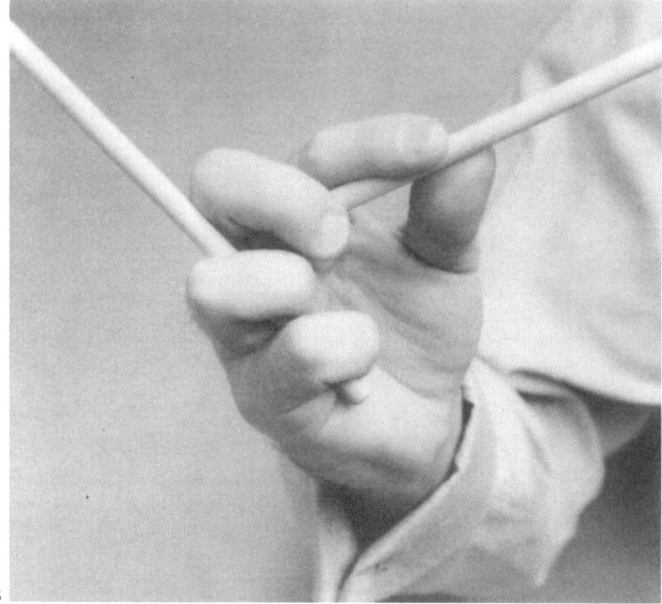

18

Although there is great variation in terminology, the two most often **recommended** stroking methods are:

1. The stroke with preparation (up — down)
2. The stroke with lift (down — up)

Using solid lines to represent the actual stroke, dotted lines to represent recovery, dashed lines to represent preparation, and the left to right axis to represent time, a series of these strokes would be diagrammed like this:

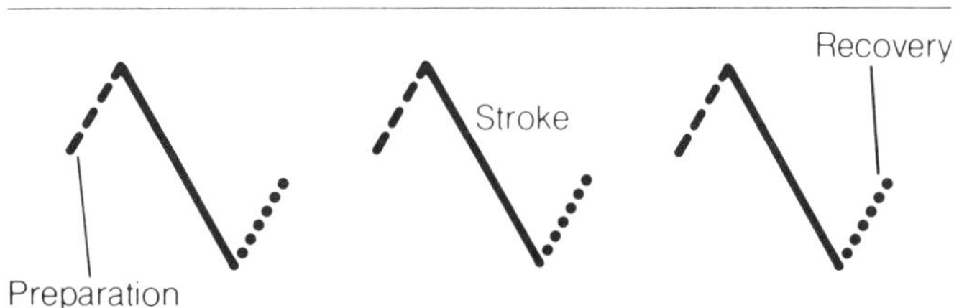

Stroke with Preparation

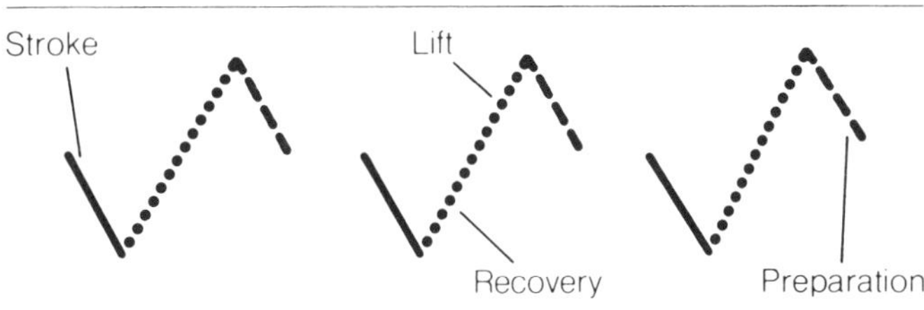

Stroke with Lift

A widely used stroking method is a "synthesis" of the two previous strokes:

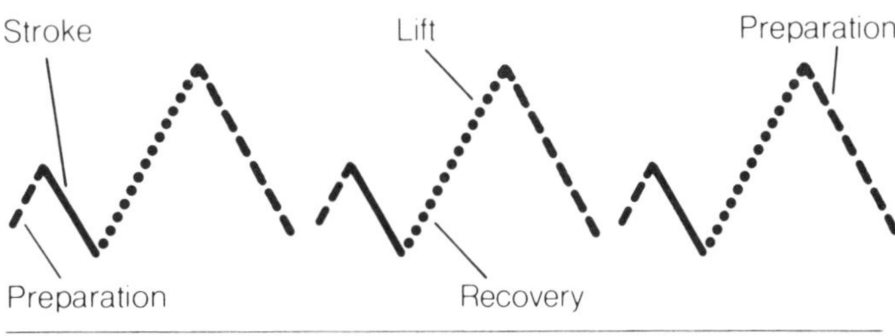

Stroke with Preparation and Lift

The student is encouraged to take a mallet in hand and try a few of each of these strokes — they are difficult to visualize on paper but instantly recognizable when performed.

All three of these strokes **waste motion.** That is, the mallet heads move farther than is necessary to accomplish the stroke. The following diagrams of the same three strokes (with their appropriate nicknames) have the unnecessary motions in brackets.

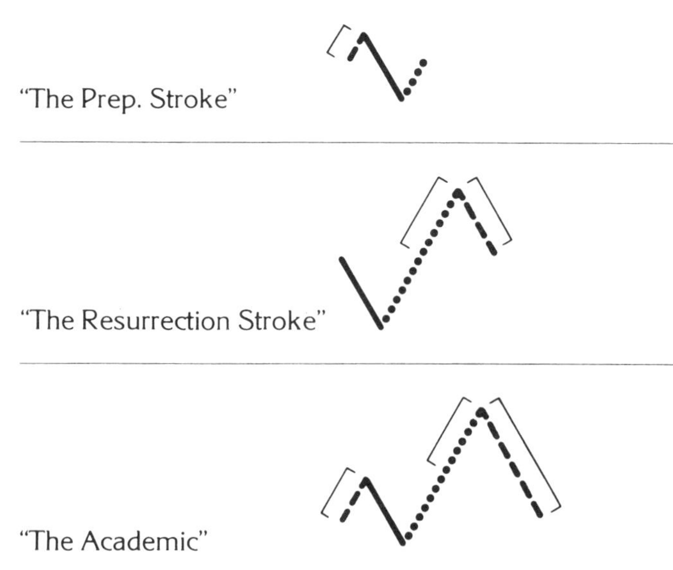

When the unnecessary motions are not drawn, all three strokes look very much like:

This piston or cyclic motion is the general stroking method recommended by the author.

There is nothing new or unusual about the piston stroke. Even players who advocate the use of preparation or lift routinely use a piston style stroke when playing fast passages. (There is no time between rapid stroke repetitions for preparation or lift.) Rather than have a "slow tempo stroke" and a "fast tempo stroke", this author strongly recommends that the marimbist use the same piston stroking method in practice and slow tempi as in performance and fast tempi. To do otherwise is to cultivate the common problem of "losing the feel" of a motion as speed increases.

The diagrams and discussion above demonstrate the superior distance efficiency of the piston stroke. The preceding paragraph demonstrates the superior **consistency** of the piston stroke. There are two additional reasons why the piston stroke is the best general stroking method: **accuracy** and **momentum** efficiency.

Any percussion stroke has a **minimum** of two parts in which mistakes can be made: The part(s) that go up, and the part(s) that go down. (The person who discovers a way to dispense with one — or both! — of these parts will deservedly become very famous.) Mistakes made in the **down** portion of the stroke are usually of the "Goodness me, I've gone and hit the wrong bloody note!" variety. The mistakes made in the **up** portion of the stroke fall into two basic categories: the "Foul invective! I seem to have strayed from the righteous path on the preparation. If I don't mend my ways forthwith, I'll soon tap the wrong slat." type, and the "Oh imminent impotence! I have pruned the recovery unripe. Now how shall I reap the fortissimo for which the audience verily drools?" brand.

The stroke with preparation precludes correcting the two types of errors found in the **up** portion of the stroke. Even at the slowest tempi, there is no time **between** preparation and stroke. If the preparation is horizontally miscalculated (ascends to a position above the wrong bar), there is no time to adjust, as the preparation and stroke are performed as a single gesture. The piston stroke **consolidates** the preparation into the recovery of the previous stroke. This pre-positioning does not **assure** that the preparation will be horizontally and vertically correct, but if it is wrong, one has a chance to rectify the error.

Not only is the piston stroke more accurate than any stroke that uses a separate preparatory motion, but it is also the **most efficient** stroke (at least until the invention of the perpetual down stroke). Every time the mallet head starts, stops, or changes directions, additional energy is used. The following diagrams compare all four previously mentioned strokes for energy usage. Every start is marked A, every stop is marked B, and every change of direction is marked C.

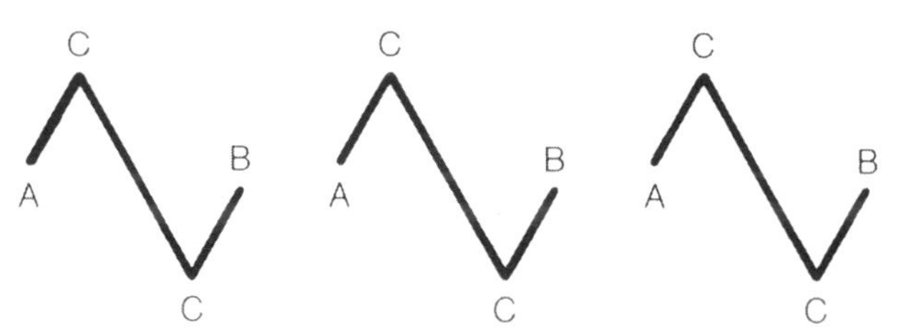

3 strokes with preparation   12 points

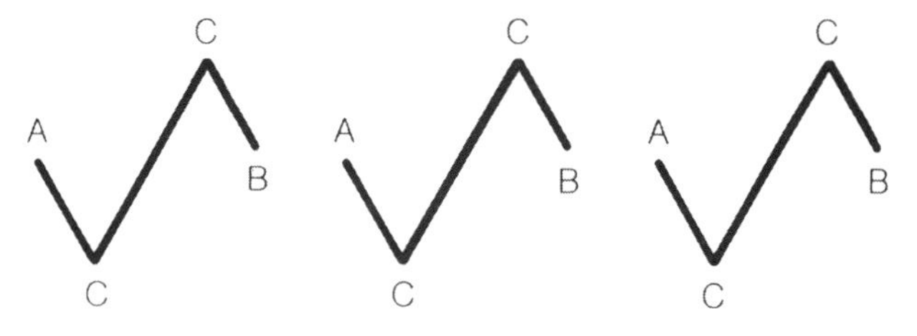

3 strokes with lift   12 points

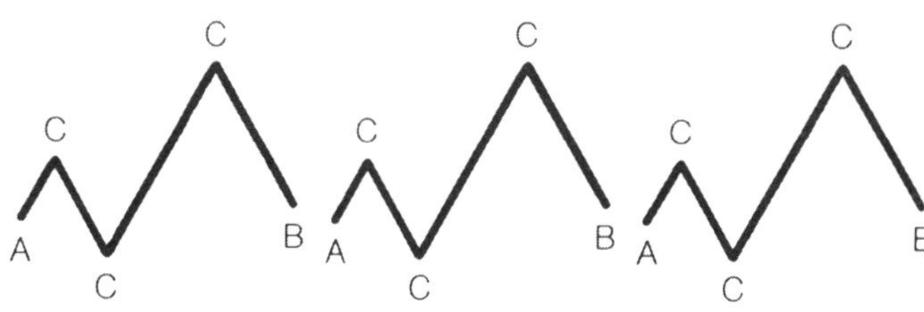

3 synthesis strokes (preparation and lift)   15 points

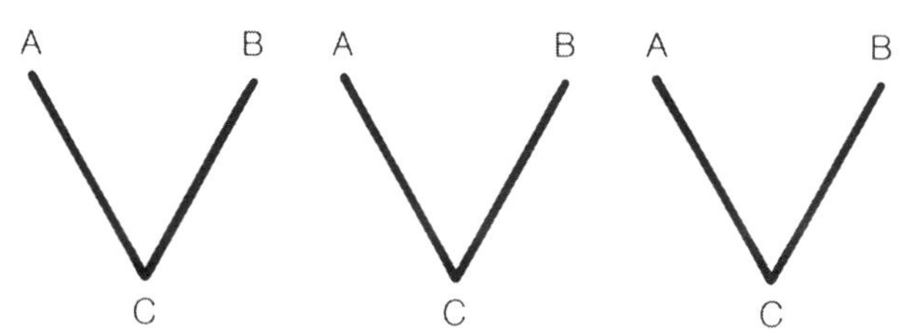

3 piston strokes   9 points

In this particular contest low score wins. The reason the piston stroke wins is because it does not waste **momentum:** there are no unnecessary stops or changes of direction. All motion after contact with the bar is in the service of the **next** stroke. The piston stroke **starts** at the correct height for the desired dynamic level and **recovers only as high** as is necessary for the **next** dynamic level.

Dynamic changes

Only when the **next** note to be struck with the **same hand changes** dynamic levels, is the mallet either (a) not allowed to return to the starting level of the previous stroke (down stroke); or (b) lifted higher than the starting level of the previous stroke (up stroke). The following is a simple passage with dynamic changes. The relative stroke height and recovery height is diagrammed below each pitch. P will stand for piston stroke at any dynamic level, U for up stroke at any dynamic level, and D for down stroke at any dynamic level. All P (piston) strokes recover to the **same** level as they started (to prepare for a stroke of **identical** volume); all U (up) strokes recover to a **higher** level than they started (to prepare for a stroke of **greater** volume); and all D (down) strokes do **not recover as high** as they started (to prepare for a stroke of **lesser** volume).

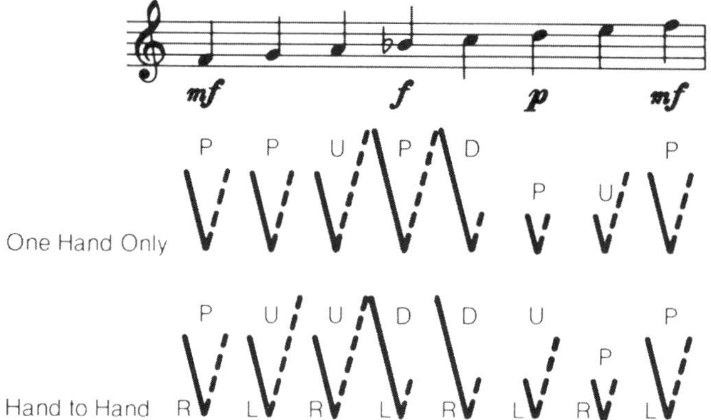

If the student has never had any problem with dynamic changes or accents, this author sees no reason to tamper with what the hands do naturally. But perhaps the above example is not sufficiently stark to point out the merits of "old fashioned" up and down strokes to facilitate dynamic changes. Sooner or later, the marimbist encounters a confounding pattern of dynamic changes:

A knowledge of up and down strokes can be of great advantage in practicing passages like the one above — even the "natural" player will profit. For those readers who are unfamiliar with this system, the above passage would be played:

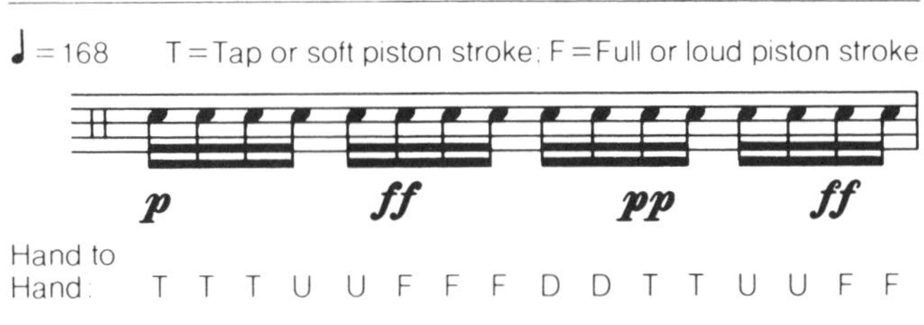

The student may ignore all this PUDFT business and follow three simple rules:

1. Start the mallet at the proper height for the desired dynamic level.
2. Do not stop the recovery of the mallet until it is at the proper height for **that hand's next stroke.**
3. Do not raise the mallet **past** the proper height for **that hand's next stroke.**

The above rules will insure that:

1. the mallets are always at the proper height for the desired dynamic level
2. a maximum amount of time is left for mistake correction
3. no distance or momentum energy is wasted.

Efficiency within the hand

Stroke efficiency is further complicated by the fact that significant amounts of energy can be wasted **within the hand itself.** Any pushing or pulling of the mallet shafts against the fingers or hand (during the stroke, recovery, or on the actual contact with the bar) wastes energy. When the wrist is used as the sole means of producing the stroke (no finger acceleration), the mallets should remain in the same exact alignment with the hand during all phases of the stroke. Any change of attitude of the mallets to the hand breaks the smooth acceleration or deceleration of the mallet heads.

This energy dissipation may be likened to the problems of driving a manual transmission automobile with a trailer attached. If the driver does not accelerate smoothly (at a rate that accommodates both car and trailer), the forward motion is accompanied by a series of backward jolts which are due to the uneven acceleration — the respective momentums of the car and trailer are not in phase. The driver would conserve fuel by accelerating in such a way as to keep the trailer in perfect alignment with the hitch.

The mass of the mallets, like the trailer, tends to lag behind the acceleration of the hand. The marimbist must endeavor to minimize the undesirable effects of this lag by smooth acceleration to the bars and smooth recovery. When the proper accelerative rate for a given dynamic is found (and therefore the proper starting height of the acceleration), the mallet shafts will not tug or pull in the hand — they will stay in perfect alignment. The marimbist should strive to create the feeling that the hand is flawlessly **following** the motion of the mallets.

In respect to energy consumption in the hand, the most critical point in the stroke is the moment of mallet and bar contact. It is here that both masses (mallet and hand) change direction. Not only is this point mechanically the most difficult to negotiate, it is the point at which the **potential** energy loss is greatest: at the moment of bar contact the mallets and hand have achieved maximum velocity and kinetic energy. **Any** opposition of the two forces will consume significant quantities of energy while uselessly dissipating the momentum of the mallets and the hand.

The principal symptom of out-of-phase hands and mallets during the change of direction is **contact shock.** Any jolt felt in the hands or fingers just before, during, or just after contact with the bars is a sign that the two masses (mallet and hand) are not negotiating the change of direction perfectly in phase. The marimbist **must minimize contact shock** just as he minimizes mallet shaft pull during the stroke and recovery.

When finger acceleration of individual mallets is added to the motion of the wrist, the mallets cannot remain in alignment with the hand. The marimbist, however, must still endeavor to accelerate the mallets smoothly to the bar, minimize contact shock, and smoothly recover. The mallets may be accelerated at different **rates,** but their momentums **must never oppose** one another.

Review

Accuracy and efficiency are reduced by mismanagement of distance and momentum. The mallets should not be moved anywhere that is not directly related to the task of striking the bars from the proper height and recovering to the proper height for the next note. The momentum of their movement **should not be interrupted** until the movement is complete. While the motion is in progress, care should be taken to **avoid any opposition** of momentums.

X Shift and Interval Change Efficiency

Shifting is the business of moving from one note to another. As with the rest of life, one has the option of doing it well or poorly. There are basically only two types of shifts: a shift that is connected to the stroke it precedes and a shift that is connected to the stroke that it follows.

If the above passage is played with **one** mallet at ♪=40 (this sticking is recommended for the sake of experiment, not efficiency), either of the above shifting procedures is capable of delivering the mallet to its intended target on time. If the passage is played with one mallet at ♩=120, the situation is quite different. Since there is barely enough time to traverse the two octave leaps in rhythm, the stroke and shift must merge into **one** gesture: the shift becomes an uninterrupted lateral extension of the recovery of the previous stroke. The first two eighth notes of the above passage played at ♩=120 would be diagrammed:

To a witness who could only see the mallet heads, it would appear that they were something on the order of superballs, bouncing back and forth between the bars. The student should strive to make the strokes and shifts **feel** this way as well.

The student may be wondering **when** the shift should be connected to the recovery of the previous stroke. Although it is sometimes unnecessary to connect the shift with the recovery of the previous stroke for the sake of **speed** (as in the above example at ♪=40), it is **always** highly advantageous for the sake of **accuracy.** If the two octave leaps are played with one mallet at ♪=40, the superior accuracy of the recovery-linked shift becomes apparent. The two possibilities are:

1. A shift that is connected to the note that is being moved to:

2. A shift that is connected to the note that has just been struck:

The main difference between these two methods is **where** one chooses to "wait" (X). In the first case the free time is wasted. What can one do hovering over a note that has just been struck? Contemplate its timbre? Study the grain of the wood? In the second case there are a variety of things one can do with the free time. Why not ask the question, "Is this really the bar I want to strike soon?" If the answer is **no,** there may still be a split second to correct the mistake. The first type of shift (connected to the note it is moving to), allows for no such correction. This is why, even in easy-to-negotiate passages, the shift is connected to the recovery of the previous stroke.

This recovery-linked shift also uses less energy. In the following diagrams, energy consumption points are marked in the same way as in section IX. Both examples diagram three piston strokes and two shifts.

1. Shift attached to following note

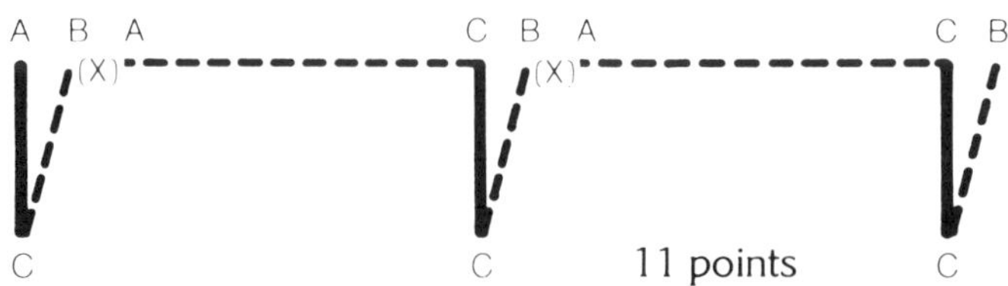

2. Shift attached to previous note (recovery-linked)

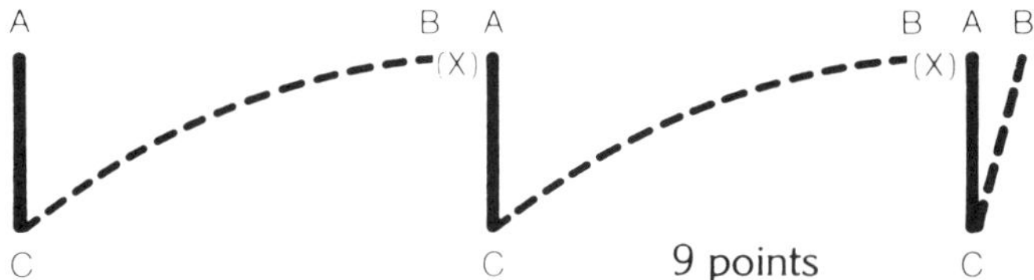

The reader may be curious why the first diagram uses straight lines and the second diagram uses curved lines. The two possible curved versions of diagram 1 have exactly the same number of energy consumption points.

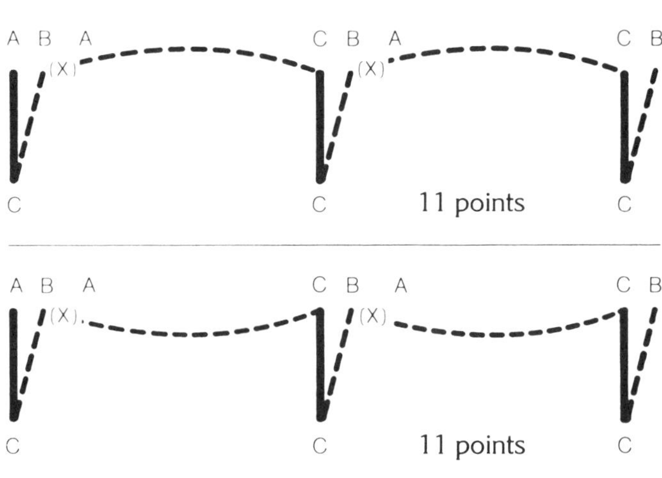

If, however, these diagrams could measure **distance/energy usage**, the curved diagrams above would prove to be even **less** efficient than the original straight line version. That is the point! **Curved gestures** conserve energy **only** when they are **properly timed.**

The options for timing interval changes are parallel to those of shifts. It is similarly advantageous for accuracy and conservation of energy to connect the interval changes to the recovery of the previous stroke. Since this method places any "Rest and Relaxation" at the disposal of the next stroke, the marimbist may have time to check position, stroke height, and interval spread. Any other method wastes these valuable moments.

If the student has read carefully this far in the book, he has noticed that **all** motions necessary to the next stroke are unbroken, fluid continuations of the previous stroke. The general rule for accurate, efficient movement around the instrument is

**Never interrupt the momentum
generated by a stroke
until the mallets are in position
for the next stroke.**

When all these tasks (shifting, interval changing, and stroke height preparation) are properly attached to the previous recovery, the resulting gesture **looks** graceful.

If the interval change and shift is dutifully being connected to the previous recovery but the gesture still looks awkward, the problem is the **relative speeds** of the three motions. If any one of the three tasks (interval change, stroke recovery, or shift) is accomplished too quickly or slowly relative to the other motions, the gesture will waste energy and appear inelegant.

Suppose the marimbist plays a small double vertical stroke (see the section on fundamental strokes) that prepares a larger double vertical stroke in the same general area of the keyboard:

If the interval change is **late** relative to the recovery, the mallet head motion will look like:

(The student may check these motions in a mirror or have a marimba-playing friend make the diagnosis from the audience side of the instrument.)

If the stroke recovery is held down or is late relative to the interval change, the mallet head motion will look like

If both recovery and interval change are timed smoothly, the mallet head motion will look like

The next example is complicated by a shift — a large double vertical that prepares a small double vertical in a somewhat distant area of the keyboard:

If the shift is late relative to the recovery, the mallet head motion will look like

If the recovery is too slow or held back momentarily, the mallet head motion will look like

If the shift and recovery are timed properly relative to each other, but the **interval** change is **late,** the mallet head motion will look like

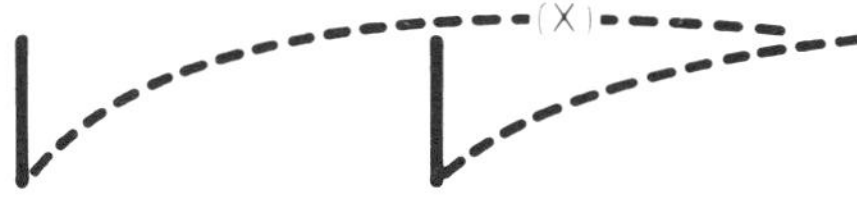

When shift, recovery, and interval change are **all** timed smoothly, the mallet head motion will look like

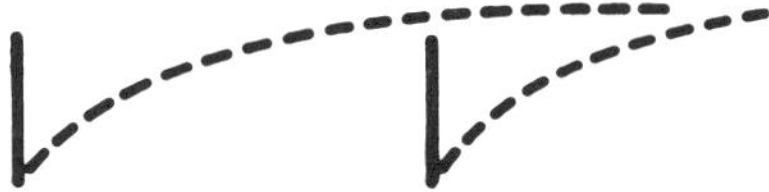

Elbow-Led shifts

Shifts which include significant adjustments in wrist curvature (angle formed between back of hand and arm — see figure 32) should derive some of their motive force from the whip generated by the necessary elbow motion.

The double vertical strokes above cannot be played with a stationary elbow. When performed with the right hand, the double notes D—E flat are most comfortable when the elbow is away from the torso. The double notes C sharp—D are most comfortable when the elbow is lightly touching the torso. Since the elbow (and the arm to which it is attached) is a larger, slower mass than the hand and mallets, it needs to **lead** the shift in order that it not arrive late.

The elbow is "tossed away" from and to the body by muscles in the area of the shoulders. This leading flip of the elbow automatically produces much of the necessary change in wrist curvature. The student is encouraged to perform the following demonstration:

Hold the elbow up, away from the body. Allow the wrist to hang freely. Reach across the body and place the other hand on top of the arm at the elbow joint. Briskly push the elbow and arm down and into the torso. The wrist will flip to the outside. See figure 19.

In a less dramatic way, the same motion should take place in shifts between any double notes that have accidentals on opposite sides. This elbow-led shift will significantly increase the potential speed of execution of passages that contain these alternations of wrist curvature and elbow position (e.g., chromatic one-handed harmonic thirds).

Figure 19 has never actually helped anyone to understand the concept of an "elbow-led shift". It continues to be included in the book because it was very expensive to produce, taking almost a full day with the photographer for this one shot (and it looks cool). Enjoy it for its esthetics, not its educational value.

Passive interval changes

Certain interval changes that are accompanied by shifts can be executed "passively". Instead of mechanically changing the interval, the inertia of one of the mallets is harnessed.

If the above passage is played with the right hand, the inside mallet (middle C) is left basically undisturbed while the outside mallet shifts to it. The fingers holding the inside mallet must be **passive** and merely adjust their position to the almost stationary mass as the hand and outside mallet moves. A perfect passive interval change is actually impossible no matter what the pitch configuration, but valuable quantities of energy can be saved by taking advantage of the inertia of a mallet.

The passive interval change is easier to employ when the shift is large.

In this case the marimbist should expend almost no energy on the interval change. The fingers holding the inside mallet remain passive until the shift has brought the outside mallet to a position a major third away from the inside mallet. This is not to say that the inside mallet is motionless during the first part of the shift but that its lateral speed is not as great as that of the outside. The passive shift is a **rare** example of beneficial opposing momentums.

19

XI Tone, Lift, Legato, Staccato

There are three popular misconceptions which obscure the issue of tone production on marimba:

1. "The second-best striking area for accidentals is between the node and the end of the bar". **False.**

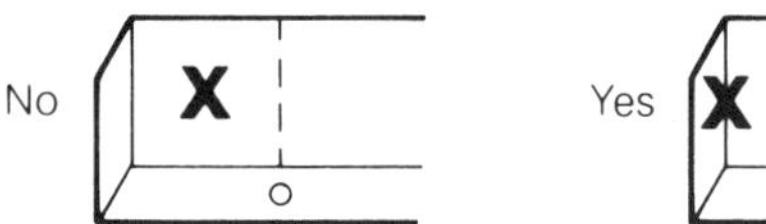

Significantly more solidity of tone is achieved by directing the stroke into **the upper edge** of the end of the bar.

2. "The resonators make the bars ring longer".

False. Actually the resonators amplify the sound through sympathetic resonance. This uses up the available energy faster than an unresonated bar, **shortening** the ring length.

3. "Lift strokes make the bars ring longer".

False. Lift strokes reduce the velocity of the mallet head before contact with the bar. Less energy means shorter ring length.

The "ring length" of a given object is determined by how much energy is applied to it. Although such factors as hardness of applicator and area of application are very important to timbre, the basic relevant equation for bar ring is $\frac{1}{2}M \times V^2$ (one half the mass of the mallet times the velocity squared – – unless the instrument happens to be rolling down a flight of stairs), and the mass of the mallet head is fixed (unless one changes mallets in mid-experiment). Therefore the control of bar ring is through **velocity** of the mallet head.

The difference in timbre which is heard when a lift stroke is demonstrated is due to a difference in velocity. The softer (slower) lift stroke lowers the audible ratio of overtones to fundamental. This produces a more "mellow" but **shorter** tone. Of course, the same exact tone can be achieved without the lift. If one craves long mellow struck tones, use a large, soft mallet to cancel the overtones, and strike the bar with great velocity. If this won't do, switch to cello ...

It is a much easier affair to shorten the bar ring, just drop or press a wrapped mallet head into the bar. These pressure strokes dampen the vibrations by absorbing energy. For those readers who are concerned that pressure strokes distort the tone of the bar, it should be pointed out that the marimba is no different in this regard from any other acoustic instrument. No acoustic instrument can produce a staccato note that sounds like a small portion of a sustained tone. This "distortion" of tone is intrinsic to the staccato effect. If one is attached to acoustical experiments, try this one: record several staccato bassoon notes (or any other instrument). Then splice out equally long sections from the middle of sustained tones of the same pitch. When the sounds are compared, it will be found that the "distorted" natural staccato is distinctly more charming than the "good tone" spliced version.

There is still disagreement among players of marimba as to the influence of tone of arm weight and pinching of the fingers. Several lines of thought present themselves. **If** any variation of the effective mass of the mallet can be achieved by dropping the arm or stiffening the wrist during the stroke, its effect, compared to a change in velocity, must be minuscule; any effect of a change of mass is halved, whereas any effect of a change of velocity is squared.

The question then arises whether the bar responds **differently** to changes of mass than to changes of velocity. Does the volume ratio of fundamental to harmonics differ in an audible way when arm weight or finger pressure is used from a wrist-produced, relaxed stroke of greater velocity? Another way of asking this same question is: Can the tone produced by an arm-weighted or pinched stroke be precisely duplicated by greater mallet velocity – without involvement of the arm or tension in the fingers? The author's experiments with both trained and untrained ears indicates that the answer to the last question is yes.

It is impossible to accurately describe this reality scientifically in a paragraph, so here is a hint of how to discover the principle on your own.

1. Review your old high school science textbook about how to test a hypothesis and how to design an experiment.

2. Design controlled experiments to test whether lift, arm weight, "pinch", fulcrum, mallet length or material, "legato-strokes" (see * top of **next** column) or "staccato strokes" actually change the sound of the marimba bar, when your experiment has controls on volume, playing spot and angle of the mallet.

3. Perform the experiment with blindfolds, or with the listeners turned away so as to not be influenced by the look of the stroke or the facial expression of the player.

Having performed this experiment approximately 241,627 times, I can assure you in advance that **when the volume, playing spot and angle of the stroke are identical**, it doesn't matter if the stick is tight or loose, or whether you use fingers, wrist, arm or foot: the sound heard by the ear of a conservatory-trained musician is identical. If a trained musician cannot hear the difference between pinch and relaxation, arm and wrist, front fulcrum/back fulcrum, etc., what will be heard in the concert hall by the general public, or on a recording?

To fully appreciate the relationship between volume and articulation, it is important to distinguish clearly between the terms **legato** and **tone**. First of all, there is no such thing as a legato tone or a legato stroke.* Legato refers to the **connection** of tones. Struck note legato style on marimba is a product of dynamics and rhythm. This quasi-legato connection between two struck notes is achieved by **matching the attack** of the second note to the **ring** of the previous note. The longer one waits to strike the second note, the softer it has to be.

The three main factors affecting tone (other than mallet choice and instrument) are dynamics, striking area, and angle of the mallet to the bar. It is a relatively easy task to imitate another player's tone with the same mallet on a single struck pitch. All one has to do is duplicate the velocity, exact area of contact, and angle of the mallet upon contact. Duplication of another player's tone on a four-note chord is quite another matter. Not only are there now **twelve** factors, but each of these factors is infinitely variable. Of course, the impression of tone received by a listener is not based on a single chord or a single pitch but on a series of chords or pitches. In a musical context, therefore, the relationships of the velocity, placement, and angle of each voice are heard not only relative to other members of the same chord but also in relationship to all of the individual members of neighboring chords. A visual representation of just one of these factors in a three chord passage might look like this:

Thus the "tone" produced by a player in an eight measure phrase is as individual as his speaking voice or handwriting.

Six timbre combinations ranging from "dark" (strong fundamentals and emphasis on lower pitches) to "bright" (strong harmonics and emphasis on higher pitches) are notated below.

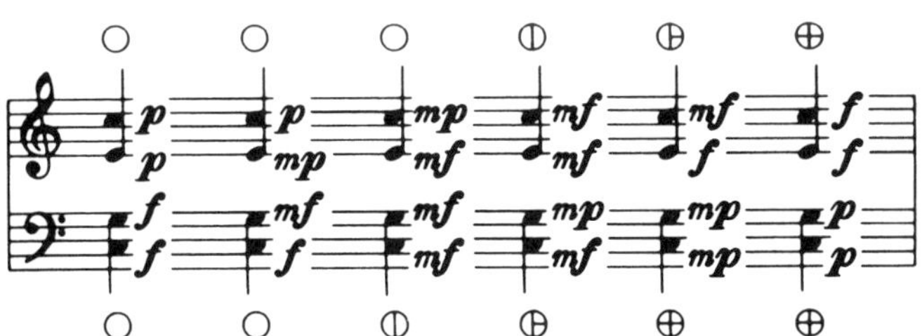

○ = On or near center or on end
① = Halfway between center and node
⊕ = Three-quarters of the way to node
⊕ = On or very near node

Each of these chords has a definite, easily heard character. None are of the lifeless, evenly balanced variety most often heard from musically inexperienced players. The musical artist considers an evenly balanced chord to be a special effect in much the same way a student considers the colorful examples above to be special effects. It is safe to say that chords voiced with equal dynamics and timbre are a rarity in expressive performance.

"Tone" then is the overall result of the interaction of a tangle of complex factors: the dynamic connection of every melodic note to its neighbor, the dynamic "voicing" of harmonic structures, mallet choice, angle of the mallets to the bars, and placement of the strokes on the bars. The goal of simultaneous conscious control of **all** the relationships among these factors is unattainable. By the time the marimbist has sufficient technical control to manipulate a few of these elements of tone, the musical imagination (if it is vivid) has already usurped many of the responsibilities of consciousness.

When the musical imagination begins to command the muscles directly, the responses will be those which have been consciously and individually trained in previous years. If the above mentioned factors that influence tone have been ignored in the technical and musical training of the marimbist, the imagination will have no musical reflexes to call upon. Such a player is left with perhaps a good **general** technique but a frustrating inability to produce the sounds he hears in his mind. Sadder still is the player who strives to control elements of tone only to find out years later that there is no substantial musical imagination to trigger those hard-earned reflexes.

Conscious and unconscious control of timbre is obviously for the purpose of musical expression. Technique without musical expression is a possibility to be guarded against, but artistic musical expression without a substantial technique is an impossibility, for musical expression can never be more than commensurate with technique: finer shades of musical meaning require finer shades of physical control. The marimbist is therefore encouraged to practice the manipulation of tone color.

*Instead of saying "legato Strokes" (which implies that a single note can be played legato, which it can't), we should pass a regulation that the next word after legato has to be either dynamics, style, bowing or connection. Violators will be punished with ridicule.

XII   The Fundamental Strokes of Four-Mallet Marimba Technique

All of the struck (non-rolled) notes in the four-mallet marimba literature can be broken down into six elemental one and two-note patterns.

1. Single notes to be played by an inside mallet (2 or 3)
2. Single notes to be played by an outside mallet (1 or 4)
3. Single note patterns to be played by the same hand, alternating the inside and outside mallets (1 2 / 2 1, etc., or 3 4 / 4 3, etc.)
4. Double notes to be played simultaneously by the same hand (1 and 2, or 3 and 4)
5. Fast, rhythmically adjacent notes to be played by the same hand — inside mallet **to** outside mallet (2 − 1, or 3 − 4)
6. Fast, rhythmically adjacent notes to be played by the same hand — outside mallet **to** inside mallet (1 − 2, or 4 − 3)

Even the most complicated struck note passages can be divided into these elements.

The six corresponding strokes which serve as the foundation for all non-rolled (and most rolled!) technique are:

    a) Single independent inside

    b) Single independent outside

    c) Single alternating

    d) Double vertical

    e) Double lateral inside

    f) Double lateral outside

A short example will suffice to demonstrate that these six strokes are the "rudiments" of four-mallet stroke technique:

Sticking	2 3 2 3	2 4 4 4	1 4 2 3	1 4 2 3	1 2 3 4	1 2 3 4	2/1 4/3	4 3 2 1
Stroke Type	A A A A	A B B B	C C C C	C C C C	C C C C	C C C C	D D	F E
Fast Tempo					F E	F E		

Note:

1. The author does not recommend the notated sticking in the first two beats of the first measure — they were chosen solely for a variety of stroke types in this hypothetical example.

2. The third and fourth beats of the first measure would be performed in most cases as notated — with single alternating strokes. Since the single strokes of each hand are separated by an eighth note, the tempo would have to be taken at a devilishly fast pace for the strokes to operate as double laterals.

3. The separate motions of each single alternating stroke in the first two beats of measure two **should merge** into single-motion double lateral strokes as the tempo approaches ♩ = 96.

4. The sixteenth note triplet at the end of the second measure would not operate as notated (double laterals) if the tempo slowed to the range of ♩ = 60. At that tempo the performer would find separate, single alternating strokes more comfortable.

Although there are six stroke types used in the exercise portion of this book, there are really only four **categories** of motion (single independents and double laterals are subdivided into inside and outside varieties). The remaining four sections of this text are devoted to the detailed study of these four motions:

1. Single Independent
2. Single Alternating
3. Double Vertical
4. Double Lateral

There are several other hand motions that are requisites of a comprehensive marimba technique but are beyond the scope of this study:

1. Independent roll motion - This motion should not be confused with fast single alternating strokes - see Chapter XIV. The independent roll will be covered in a future book about rolls.

2. Multi-lateral strokes. The technique used to play fast 3 and 4-note alternating figures in one hand, such as would be found in a one-handed baroque trill, or in certain arpeggiated figures, is neither "fast single alternating strokes", nor a short one-handed roll. The feel and motion of the hand and use of the fingers is entirely different.

In the above examples, the mallets perform the equivalent of a snare drummer's 3 or 4-stroke ruff. This technique will also be covered in a future book.

Unlike the auxiliary motions listed below, the independent roll and multi-lateral strokes mentioned above are fundamental to a complete technique. They are also different enough in execution from other stroke types to justify separate categories.

Adding these two categories of motion gives us a "final" list of six motion categories. If we include both 3 and 4-stroke versions of multi-laterals, and include the inside and outside versions of each, we have just added another four strokes to the list. This would give us a "grand total" of eleven distinct stroke types. At least there aren't 26 of them.

Then there are some variations on basic strokes that alter the sound, contact area, or are only very rarely used:

3. The raised inside mallet variation of the double vertical stroke used by many players for "Musser roll" – not to be confused with the author's version of Musser roll, which is produced with outside double lateral strokes.

4. The motions used for the three levels of staccato: drop, pressure and dead strokes.

5. "Stick clicks" produced by striking the handles on the edges of the bars

6. The special "col legno" techniques introduced in the mid 1980's in Rhythmic Caprice ("marimshots" and "splash clusters").

Technical mastery of a passage in music literature is achieved through repetition of the precise **set** of motions that will be used in performance. The student is reminded that these motions do not consist exclusively of strokes. Such physical factors as shift and stroke efficiency, holding the mallets, interval changes, dynamic voicing of chords – in short, the entire preceding text bears critically on the proper and consistent execution of a single stroke!

The same approach holds for the practice of the exercises in the second half of this book. The student should practice, not a series of strokes, but a method, a habit of movement around the marimba keyboard. Similarly, the remaining text should not be viewed as a study of strokes but as an integration of strokes into a larger system of motion. The marimbist is therefore encouraged to assiduously study all of the foregoing text before commencing the next four sections.

XIII   Single Independent Strokes

One of the most crucial steps in the quest for mallet independence is the development of an independent single stroke—the ability to strike single (or repeated single) strokes without moving the unused mallet held in that hand.

To appreciate the advantages of an **independent** single stroke, let us imagine the opposite extreme: when playing passagework with the inside mallets, traditional crossed-stick grip players often use **twice** the energy they would use playing the same passage holding two mallets. Because the shafts are held as a unit, the unused mallet often flails wildly—even during mezzo-forte playing. This excess motion in the unused mallet not only siphons off energy which could be channeled into the stroke but also adversely affects accuracy by pushing and pulling the striking mallet from its intended targets.

If the proper kind of stroke is employed, passage-work with the inside mallets should not significantly differ in difficulty from two mallet playing. The stroke outlined below will allow the marimbist to play single or repeated notes with little or no motion in the unused mallet.

Single Independent Strokes

The first important step for the student marimbist interested in learning an independent single stroke is to realize that the palm-down stroke (similar to waving), which forms the foundation of stroking technique for most percussionists, has no application to an independent single stroke on marimba. The author's single stroke is produced with **torque** of the wrist and forearm. The motion is like that used to quickly screw in a light-bulb. Imagine the socket to be in a wall (so that the bulb is parallel to the floor). The right hand **outside** (4) single stroke is much the same as screwing **in** the bulb (clock-wise), and the right **inside** (3) single stroke is like **un**screwing the bulb (counterclockwise). Naturally, the left hand single strokes have reversed directions: inside (2)—clockwise and outside (1)—counterclockwise.

In the very center of the manufacturer's label on the bulb there is a point which does not move but just spins in place. The analogous point in a single independent stroke is the point at which the **unused** mallet shaft touches the hand. If the unused mallet were perfectly aligned, there would be no vertical or horizontal motion produced by the stroke of the other mallet. The unused mallet would just spin in place. This is what one strives for in an independent single stroke.

It is here that the amateur electrician analogy breaks down. The dot is not **placed** in the center of the bulb, but the bulb is **built around** the dot. In other words, the position of the unused mallet is not changed to fit the stroke, but the stroke pivots around the unused shaft wherever it lies. In this way one can pre-position the unused mallet to the next interval that is needed:

Start with the mallets spread about a fifth. Screw the lightbulb **in** five turns and **out** one.

To examine some of the details of the outside single stroke, assume the basic hand position described in section VI, except spread the interval to about a sixth. Since the outside mallet is going to strike, it should be poised in readiness at the proper distance from the bars—perhaps mezzo-forte, six inches. The unused inside mallet should be hanging close to the keyboard. The thumb, first, and second fingers should be relaxed. This relaxation of the fingers holding the unused mallet is **essential** to keeping it still. If the fingers are tense, any miscalculation in the pivot point will make the unused mallet twitch vertically and/or horizontally. **Relaxed** fingers act as shock absorbers—any misguided energy of the stroke will be absorbed by the fingers and produce an innocent, smooth pulsation in the unused mallet head.

When the stroke is properly powered by torque, the edge of the wrist (which faces up in a resting hand position) will turn as if it is a point on the surface of a rotating cylinder:

This rotary motion dissipates as it is progressively examined up the forearm toward the elbow. If the bone on the edge of the wrist is moving about an inch, the flesh half-way to the elbow will move about half that much. As the interval grows smaller, more wrist torque will be necessary to produce a given volume. Likewise, the arc inscribed by a point on the wrist joint or forearm will be greater.

Those readers who are confused by the relationships among interval size, torque, and lightbulbs should try to visualize a drawing compass. The needle that leaves the nasty little holes in the paper is the unused mallet. It **spins in place** as the drawing end inscribes its arc. As the distance between the needle end and the drawing end is adjusted for a larger circle (interval), the drawing end travels farther (stroke height or distance) per degree of arc (per amount of rotary wrist motion):

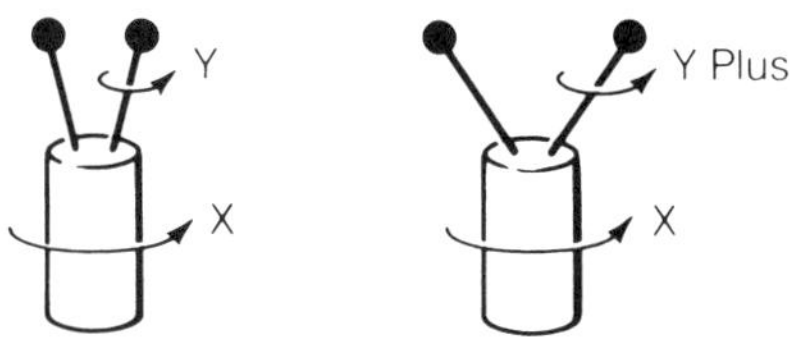

Y = Distance mallet head travels (stroke height/dynamic level)
X = Degree of wrist turn (rotary energy)

Simply stated, it takes less energy to play single independent strokes when the interval is close to 90 degrees than when the mallet shafts are almost parallel. Because of this (and the corresponding problems of finding the correct pivot point around the unused mallet), it is advisable to begin practicing the single strokes with an interval spread something on the order of a sixth.

The following points may be helpful when practicing single independent strokes.

1. Although the inside and outside single independent strokes are theoretically mirror images of one another, wrist curvature (see figure 32) will be slightly more exaggerated in the outside single stroke than in the inside single stroke.

2. Many students find it easier to execute the single independent strokes softly and a bit faster than would ordinarily be wise for working on a new technique. Those students should work at gradually slowing down and achieving more volume while retaining the same "feel".

3. In the initial stages of studying the single independent strokes, the student should lightly rest the unused mallet head in the free hand (to hold the outside mallet reach **over** the inside). This practice method allows one to feel as well as see any dysfunctional motion in the unused mallet. See figure 20.

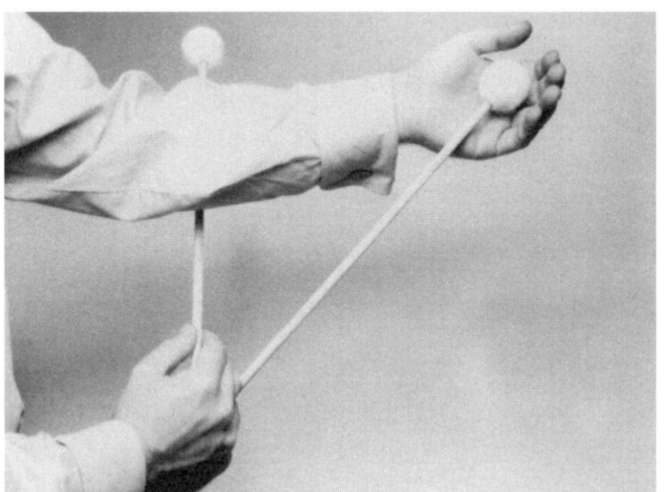
20

4. When playing scalar passages with one mallet, the unused mallet should lag slightly behind (slinky toy fashion) when direction changes are made.

5. As the author does not recommend the use of finger acceleration or accents until the basic wrist stroke is well developed, the following information is for the use of intermediate and advanced students.

(a) Finger acceleration is **added** to the basic wrist stroke for accents in single independent strokes and dynamic voicing in double vertical and double lateral strokes. Finger "strokes" are rarely used by themselves — except for small amounts of practice devoted to the development of strength. The wrist supplies the basic motive power of the stroke.

(b) Finger acceleration takes place **after** the wrist stroke begins. The stronger wrist overcomes inertia, and then the fingers boost the acceleration.

(c) The finger motion used for the outside mallet is almost opposite the motion used in the exercise for the development of interval changing strength (p. 14). Instead of the third and fourth fingers pulling up toward their first joint, they push down into the palm. It is helpful to imagine the tips of fingers three and four "jabbing" the flesh of the palm. The first section of the second finger will follow the mallet and assist slightly in the acceleration.

(d) The finger motion controlling the inside mallet is more natural and easier to learn. The thumb merely bends slightly at the second joint. This little "twitch" of the thumb (which rarely moves more than a half inch) is enough to add considerable velocity to the mallet head.

Review

1. The two most important aspects of the single independent stroke are the pivot around the unused mallet shaft and the shock absorbing relaxation of the fingers holding the unused mallet.

2. If the unused mallet is properly functioning as the axle of the stroke and if it is being supported by relaxed fingers, it will hang low — close to the keyboard — and merely turn or pulse smoothly without any influence over the striking mallet.

3. Each stroke should be completed at the same height as the stroke started. The student should not experiment with up and down strokes until the piston stroke is an acquired habit.

4. One should not lose sight of the fact that the ultimate objective is **even sounding, effortless strokes.** A well-behaved, unused mallet is poor compensation for strain or uneven volume production.

5. Study figures 21 – 28.

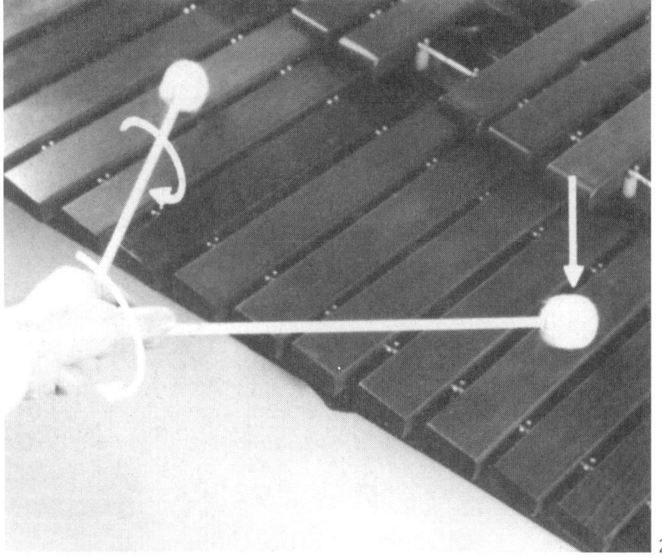

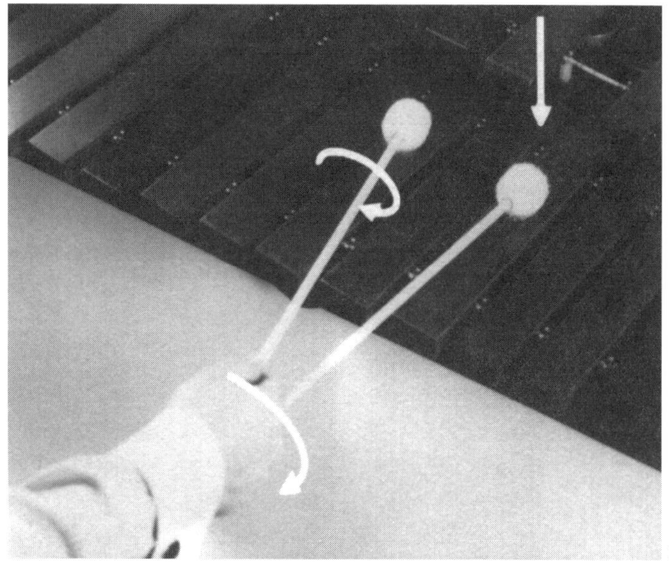

Single independent inside strokes at an octave, fifth, and third. Note that the rotary motion is equally pronounced at all intervals. The unused mallet spins in place.

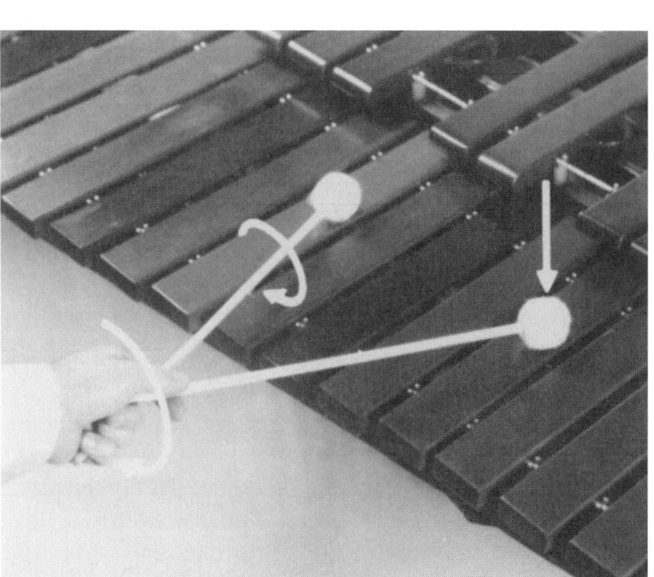

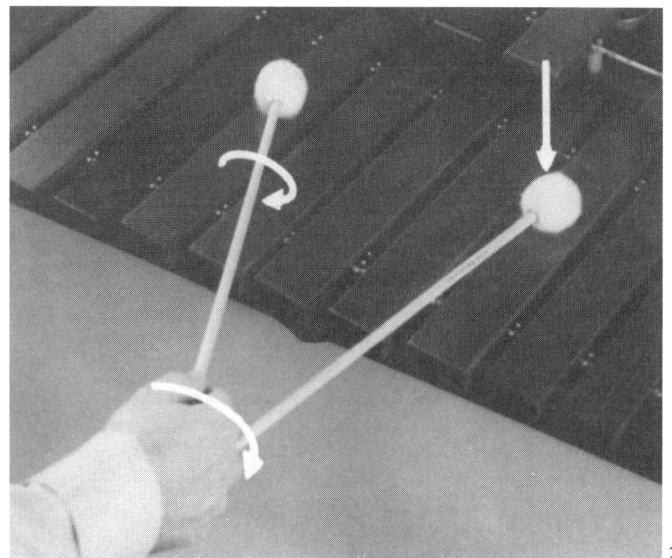

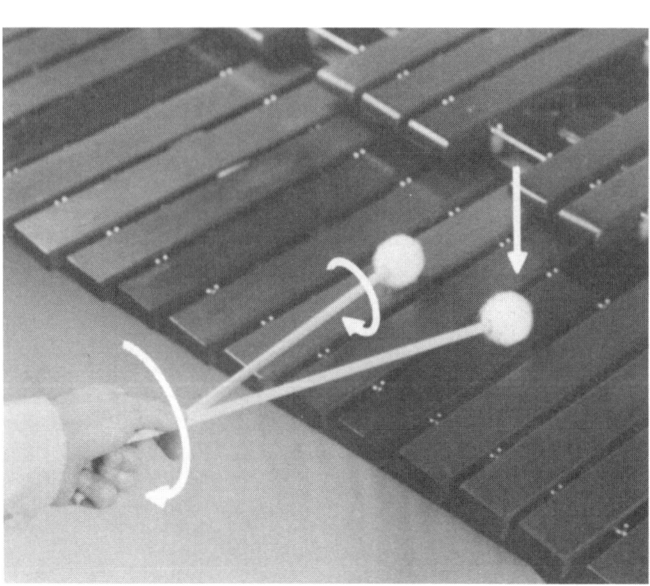

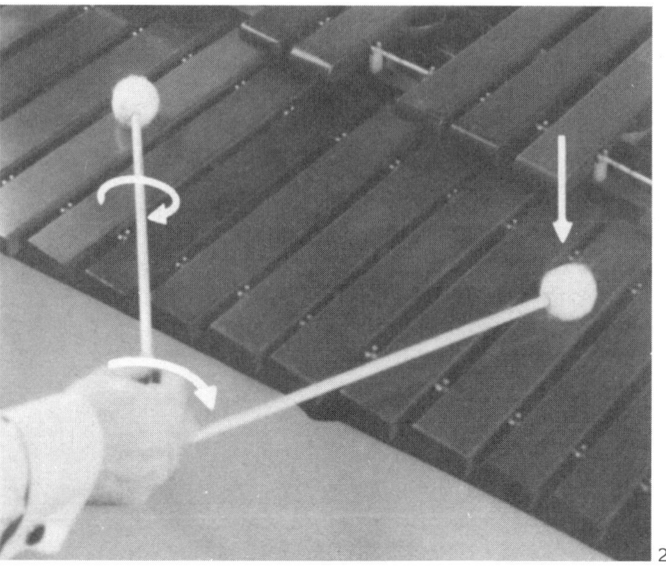

Single independent outside strokes at a third, fifth, and octave. Notice that the rotary motion becomes more pronounced as the interval closes. The unused mallet spins in place.

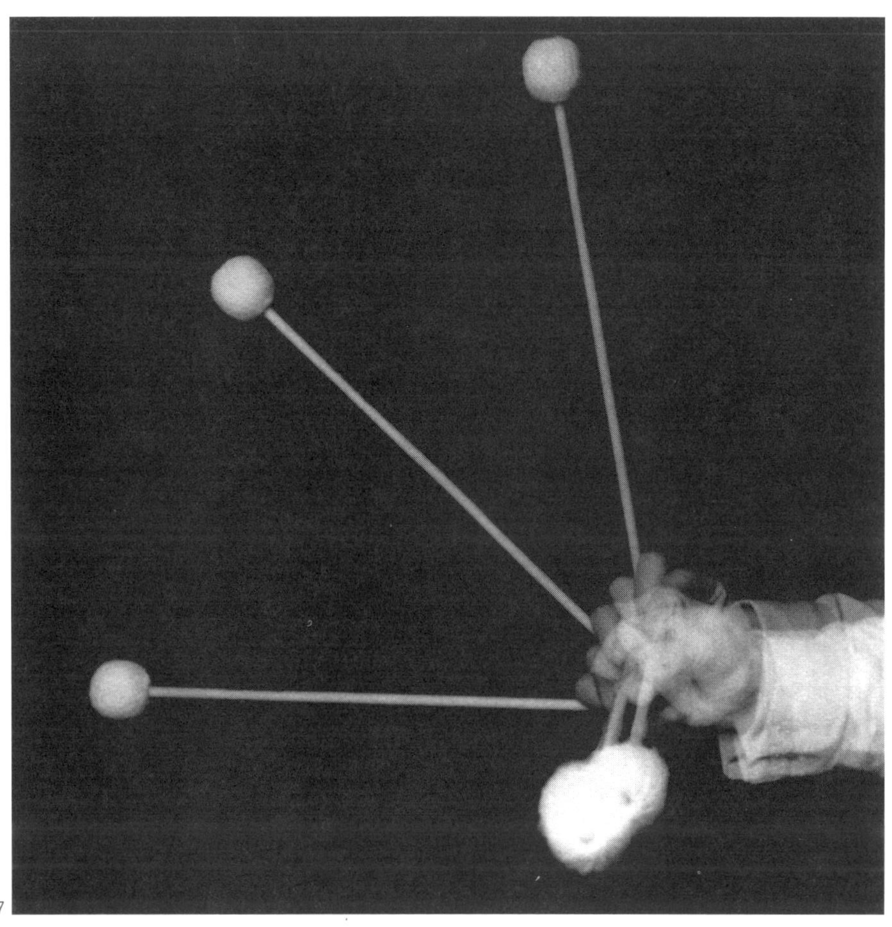

Greatly exaggerated single independent strokes. Note the large arc that the striking mallet travels while the unused mallet stays in place.

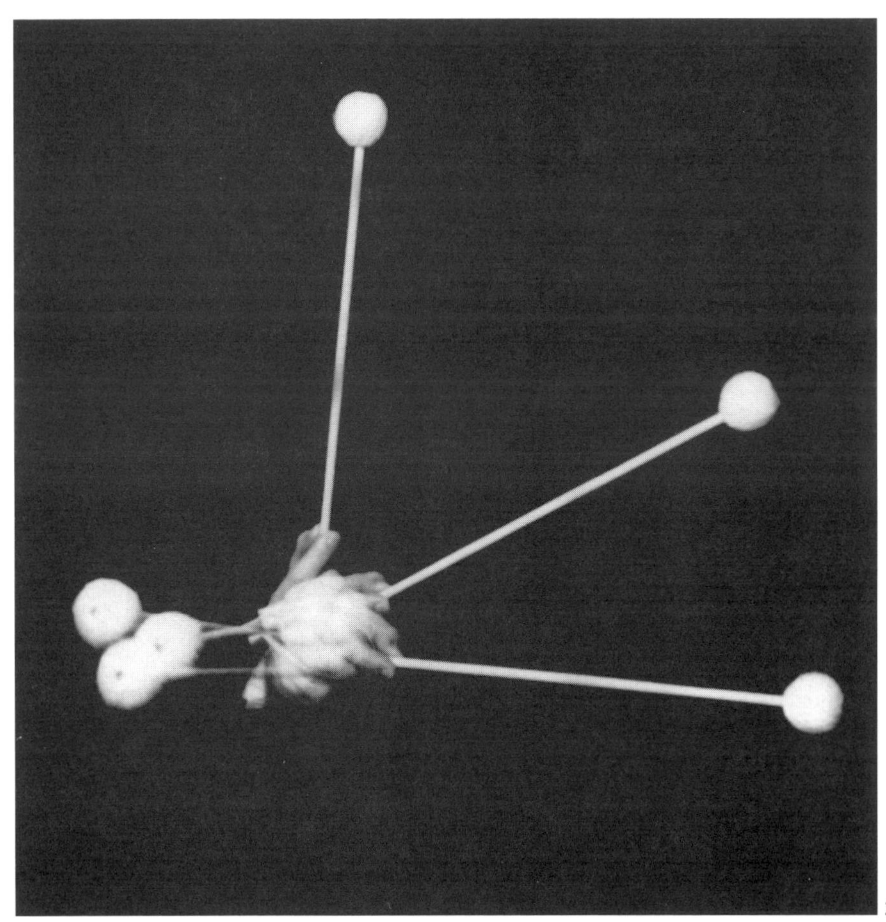

As we have learned in the last chapter, independence of motion is critical when playing melodic scale material or rolling with the inner mallets, hand-to-hand. However, in a passage like

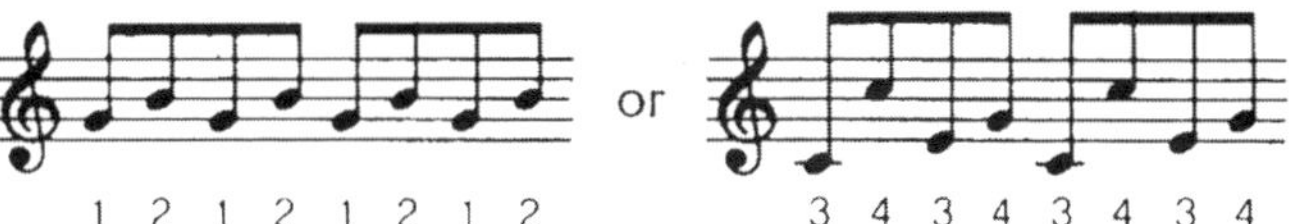

the situation is quite different. Here it would be pointless to attempt to play each pitch with an independent stroke.

Passages like this are executed with strokes that are closely related to single independent strokes, but without concern for motion in the other mallet, and without fine-tuning of the axle of the pivot point. As a result, relaxed single alternating strokes are not 100% pure rotary motions like Single Independents. While each stroke is **mostly** produced with a turn of the wrist, there is also a bit of **vertical**/forward motion of the hand. It's almost as if you are blending the motions used in double vertical and single independent strokes into a new stroke that is approximately 20% vertical and 80% rotary. As a result, single alternating strokes look like imperfect single independents.

This "imperfection" is a result of the pivot point rocking back and forth as the mallets alternate. As the outside mallet produces a stroke, the pivot point moves toward the inner mallet. Then the inner mallet produces its stroke and the pivot point swings back toward the outer mallet. See figure 29. As the pivot point swings back and forth off center, the hand should automatically blend the rotary and vertical motions in the correct proportions.

No physical or mental effort need be made to isolate the movements of the individual mallets as you would with single independent strokes. The fact that the pivot point is not perfectly aligned with the other mallet means that there will be some reaction in the mallet that is not currently striking. Do not attempt to keep it motionless, but do not stiffly lock them into a unit either. If they operate as a unit, the strokes will not be able to "bounce" off the bars and smoothly recover - one mallet will be down and the other up - like a windup toy snare drummer.

The proper end result of this "loosely-linked" operation is that the mallet not currently striking will have a tendency to pop up a centimeter or so as the other mallet descends to the bar. When performed in a

relaxed fashion, the hand will look like it is producing a type of "hopping motion", back and forth, as the pivot swings left and right.

Adjusting Dynamics

The pivot point of single alternating strokes will change as the relative dynamics of the inside and outside mallets change. The student will remember from the section dealing with single independent strokes (section XIII), that maximum efficiency in the outer mallet is achieved when the axle of the stroke is in line with the inner mallet handle. Maximum efficiency in the inner mallet is achieved when the axle is in line with the outer mallet handle. This principle holds for single alternating strokes as well: the axle of the stroke is always **closer** to the handle of the mallet having the **lower** dynamic level.

If the outside mallet increases in volume, the stroke will pivot around a point closer to the inside mallet handle. If this imbalance of dynamics is accentuated to the degree that only the outside mallet is audible, the pivot point of the stroke is then identical to that found in outside single independent strokes; that is, the inside mallet handle then functions as the axle of the motion. See figure 30.

Relationship to Independent Roll

Although independent roll is not a motion covered in detail by this book, it is necessary to bring this technique into the discussion because of its relationship to single alternating strokes. The author wishes to make clear that they are not the same: the "look" and "feel" of the hand are **entirely different**. Single alternating strokes consist of discrete, side-to-side rotations of the hand with the pivot point swinging in contrary motion to the mallet that is currently striking. The independent roll is a continuous rotary shaking of hand and forearm with no discernible parts and a pivot point that stays right down the middle between the mallets.

Minimum and Maximum Tempi

Both independent roll and double lateral strokes (covered in section XVI) have **minimum tempi**, below which they do not operate. At this minimum tempo these two stroke types **become** single alternating strokes. Conversely, single alternating strokes, when sped up, become either double lateral strokes (if the notes are rhythmically grouped in twos) or independent roll (if the rhythm is a continuous, evenly-spaced pattern).

The **maximum** tempo at which single alternating strokes operate (before being transformed into independent roll or double lateral strokes) depends on the interval spread. Small interval single alternating strokes may be played faster than large interval single alternating strokes. As the interval widens, the continuous motion characteristic of independent roll takes over earlier, obscuring the feeling of distinct strokes. In addition, less force is necessary with large intervals because of the greater leverage afforded by the angle of the mallets to the pivot point between the handles.

The following points may be of help in practicing single alternating strokes:

1. The student will notice that it feels and looks awkward to attempt to recover fully each mallet to its original height when playing slow single alternating strokes. The rule set forth in section IX concerning full recovery of every stroke applies in single alternating strokes to both mallets considered as a unit – not each mallet individually. The descent of the outside mallet will produce the recovery of the inside mallet, and subsequently, the descent of the inside mallet will complete the recovery of the outside mallet.

2. Hand position angles vary according to intervalic configuration in almost the same manner as in double vertical strokes (see figure 31).
   (a) Single alternating strokes composed of two accidentals or two naturals use a hand position a few degrees short of vertical.
   (b) Accidentals on the outside mallet produce a more flat-palmed hand position.
   (c) Accidentals on the inside mallet produce a more vertical hand position.

3. For stationary intervals, the use of fingers in single alternating strokes is extremely limited. The student will produce better results by working with the pivot point of the stroke as discussed earlier in this section.

4. Fingers do become a factor in dynamic control of single alternating strokes when the interval between the alternating pitches is changing. When alternating between melodic octaves and thirds, for example, (as in the example on page 30), some of the horizontal velocity generated by the fingers to achieve the interval change will unavoidably be channeled into the stroke. The faster the strokes alternate and the more radical the interval changes involved, the greater the proportion of energy produced by the fingers.

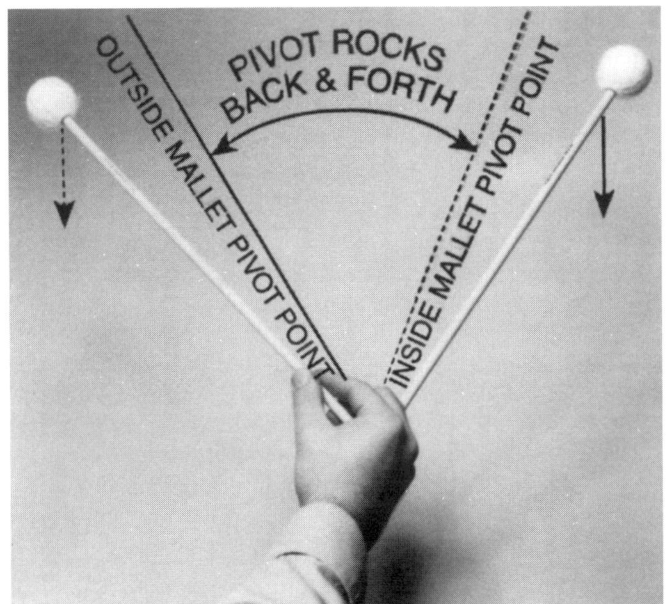

29. Pivot point is slightly to the left of center when the outside right mallet strikes, slightly to the right of center when the inside mallet strikes; this example is with even volume single alternating strokes.

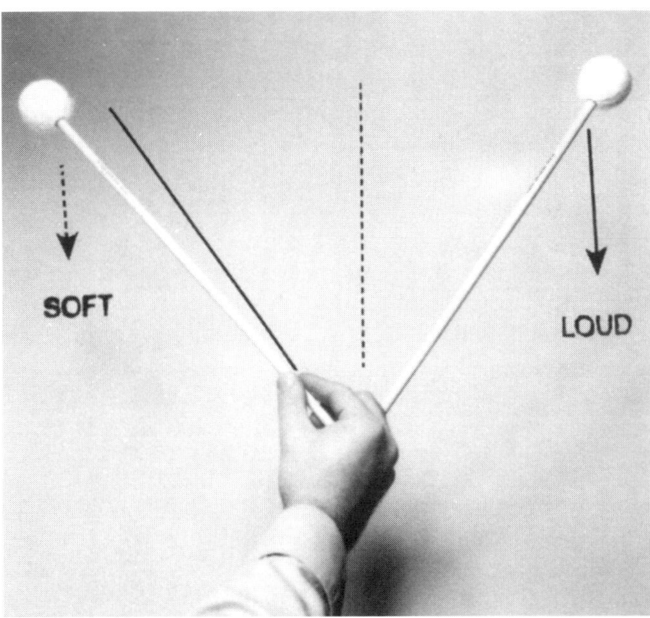

30. Pivot point moves closer to other mallet (more like perfect rotation of a single independent stroke) when volume of one of the mallets increases. In this example, outside mallet is louder, so pivot is closer to inside mallet.

XV Double Vertical Strokes

It is suggested that the student review the sections on stroke, shift, and interval change efficiency (pp. 16–21) before commencing study of double vertical strokes. The apparent simplicity and familiarity of this stroke type tempts the student to plunge ahead with abandon, more deeply embedding any previously learned dysfunctional habits.

A double vertical stroke is one that produces two pitches simultaneously. This author urges that two pitches played together on marimba not be referred to as "double stops". This is an anachronous term from the days when xylophone terminology and literature was borrowed from the violin, and marimba technique was borrowed from the xylophone. It is becoming increasingly evident that the xylophone and marimba are distinctly different instruments with dissimilar literature, function, and technique. Double notes on xylophone are usually played with **two** hands (simultaneous single strokes). Double notes in the solo marimba literature are more often played by **one** hand. Whatever names are ultimately accepted for the strokes and other motions used in solo marimba playing, they should be derived from phenomena intrinsic to **marimba** technique not from the technique of an instrument so distantly related as the violin.

Double vertical strokes

The first problem usually encountered with the double vertical stroke is getting the mallets to strike absolutely together. Initially there is also a tendency to contract finger muscles during the stroke, thereby slightly closing the interval before contact with the bars. The student should keep in mind that interval and angle of the hand are not maintained through tension. The mallets will not change intervals of their own volition — if the fingers are relaxed during the stroke, the mass of the mallet heads will assure a straight, true, and smooth trajectory to the bars. If any adjustment needs to be made during the stroke, relaxed fingers will accomplish the task faster and more accurately than fingers whose suppleness rival those of a manikin. Until these minute adjustments are made unconsciously, the student must strive to disconnect mentally the principal muscle sets which control the interval (fingers) and stroke (wrist).

The problems that arise in the initial study of double vertical strokes are usually related to incorrect hand posture, wrist curvature, or improper stroking method (not using a piston stroke). In the following list of hand and wrist configurations (which social-climbing marimbists will memorize) all degree measurements of hand position are the **inside angle** formed by the back of the hand and the horizontal (see figure 31). One should not confuse these angles with wrist curvature — the angle formed at the wrist between hand and arm — measured on the **outside** (see figure 32).

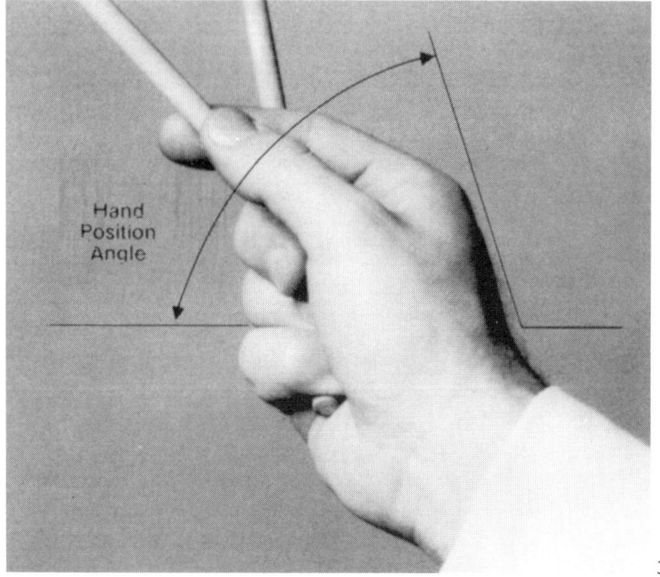

31

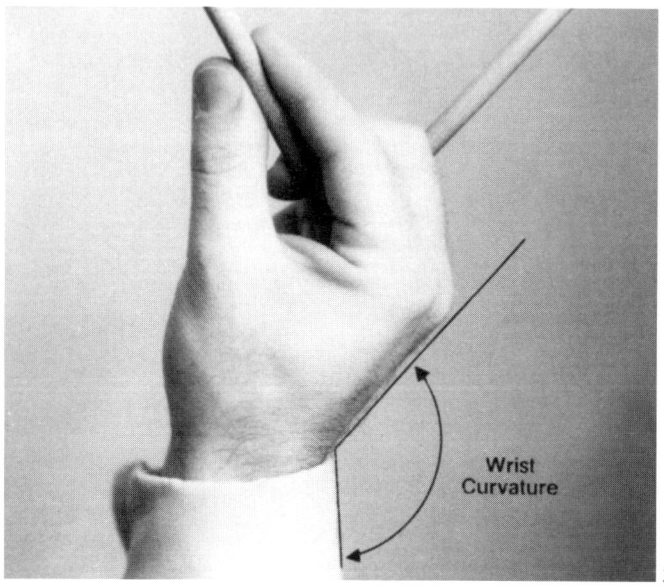

32

Small interval double vertical strokes

1. Whenever possible, strike small interval double vertical strokes with a hand position a few degrees short of perpendicular. The edge of the wrist should face slightly to the inside. A completely perpendicular hand position (when used on double notes directly in front of the torso) necessitates the use of small, stiff wrist arc described in the section dealing with the different grips (page 9).

2. Use a more vertical hand position for double notes with an accidental on the **inside** mallet (80° – 100°).

3. Use a slightly more flat-palmed hand position for double notes with an accidental on the **outside** mallet (45° – 80°).

4. Wrist curvature **decreases** for double notes with an accidental on the outside mallet.

5. Wrist curvature **increases** for double notes with an accidental on the inside mallet.

6. Wrist curvature increases proportionally to hand position angle.

7. As wrist curvature and hand position angles approach 90° (increase for an accidental on the inside mallet), the stroke becomes a rotary twist to the outside - clockwise for the right hand and counterclockwise for the left hand. (See section on single independent strokes, page 26.)

8. As wrist and hand position angle decrease, the stroke becomes more like a traditional snare drum or xylophone stroke.

Large interval double vertical strokes

1. Large intervals use an 80° to 90° hand position regardless of accidental configuration.

2. Wrist curvature will increase or decrease slightly on large intervals according to the configuration of accidentals (items 4 and 5, above), but the **rotary powered** double vertical stroke (item 7, above) becomes unworkable as the mallet spread approaches 90 degrees.

The following points will be of help in practicing the development of strong, efficient double vertical strokes.

1. Use complete strokes – no unconscious preparation or lift. Make sure the mallet heads return directly to the position at which they started.

2. Although there is almost no rebound to harness, the stroke should **feel** like it is bouncing off the bars. This concept will help keep the speed of the descent and recovery smooth and natural.

3. If the speed of recovery is correct, the hand will feel like it is merely following the mallets back into their original position. If this is not the case, adjust the stroke height and speed of stroke and recovery.

4. **Beware of involving the arm** in the stroke! Take special care with large intervals to make sure that the stroke is produced solely by the wrist. The arm should not drop during the stroke. When a large interval double vertical stroke is played, the wrist joint will appear to move in **contrary** motion to the mallets. As the mallets heads descend, the wrist will "pop up" slightly.

5. The basic motions effecting finger acceleration are the same for double vertical strokes as they are for single independent strokes. (See page 27.) It is recommended that the student not use finger acceleration until the wrist motion is strong and well coordinated.

6. The double vertical stroke varies in difficulty according to interval: small intervals are plums; large ones can be as treacherous as poison kumquats. Spend proportionally more time cultivating the latter fruit.

7. Study figures 33–37

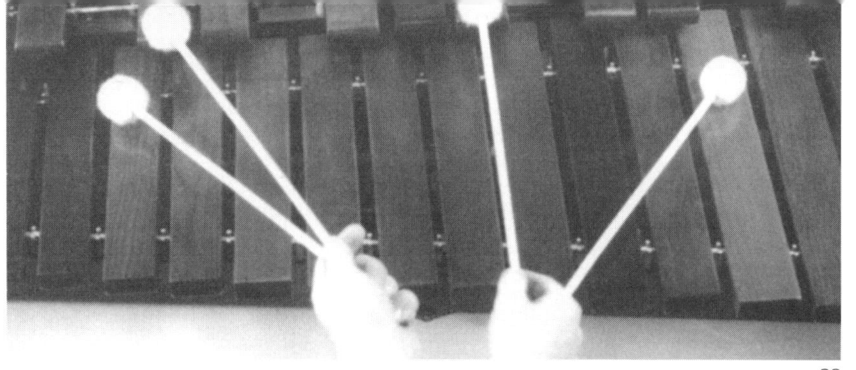

Palm turns up and wrist curvature increases for double verticals with an accidental on the inside mallet.

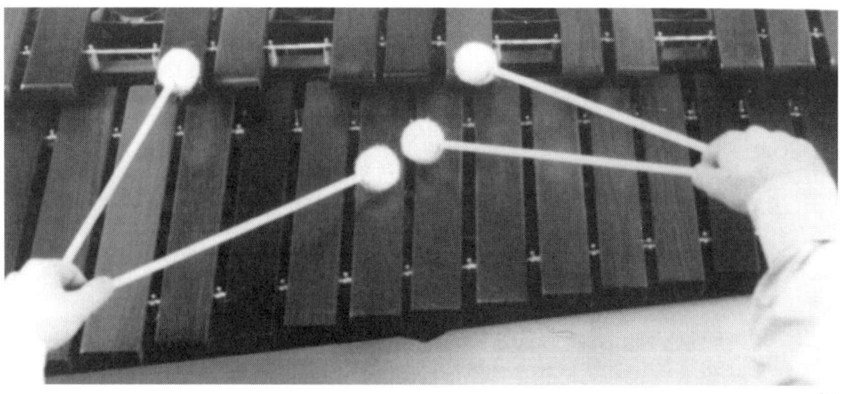

Palm turns down and wrist curvature decreases for double verticals with an accidental on the outside mallet.

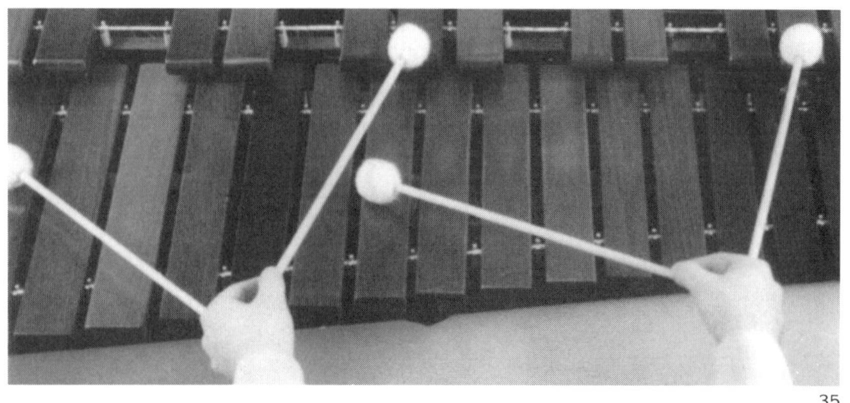

Palm is perpendicular to the keyboard for all large interval double vertical strokes.

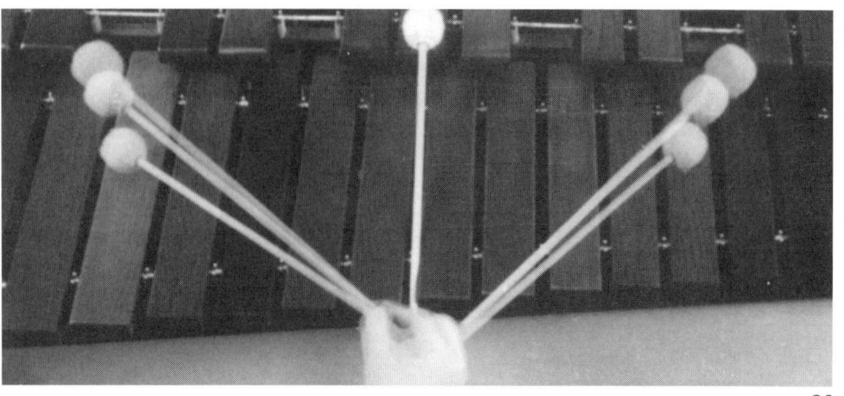

For evenly balanced large interval double vertical strokes, the student should imagine himself to be powering a third mallet that bisects the two real shafts.

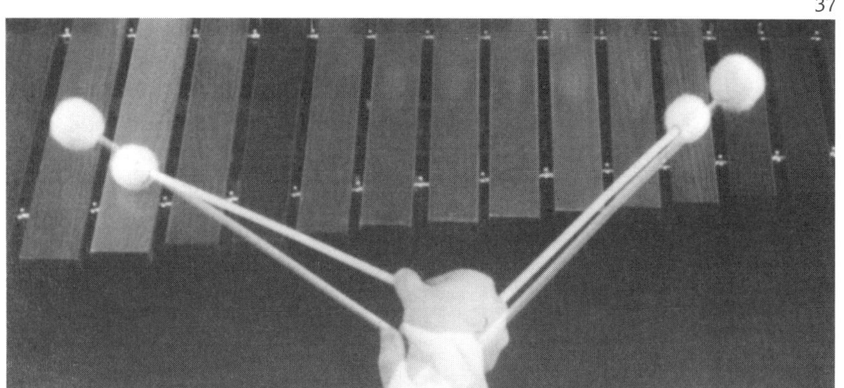

An exaggerated large interval double vertical stroke. The edge of the wrist moves up slightly as the mallet heads descend.

XVI Double Lateral Strokes

The double lateral strokes (double inside 2−1, 3−4; and double outside 1−2, 4−3) are **single motions** that produce two successive pitches. The use of double lateral strokes reduces the number of strokes and shifts by half (compared to two-mallet playing). Unlike double vertical strokes, large interval double lateral strokes (sixths to octaves) are easier to execute than small ones.

The double lateral stroke should not look, feel, or operate like a single independent inside stroke followed by a single independent outside stroke (or visa versa). If this were the case, only very limited speed could be produced, as two strokes and a change of pivot point would be necessary for every two pitches.

The double lateral stroke should not operate like single alternating strokes either. The student should resist the temptation to use single alternating strokes when practicing double lateral passages at slow tempi. The author suggests that the rhythm of the passage be altered to maintain the consistency of stroke from practice to performance. Practice this passage

like this:

Now that it has been determined how the double lateral strokes should **not** be played, attention will be given to the more productive positive point of view.

Double lateral strokes

In general terms, the double outside stroke starts as a double vertical stroke but goes through a split second metamorphosis just as the outside mallet strikes the bar. At this point the motion changes into a single independent inside stroke. Since the double lateral inside stroke is basically a mirror image of the double outside, it too starts as a double vertical but ends like a single independent outside. The key to the double vertical portion of the stroke is that as the stroke begins the descent, the mallet heads are not exactly at the same distance from the bars. The mallet which is to strike second is

held slightly higher than the mallet to strike first. This difference in height is enough to assure that the second mallet does not strike at the same time as the first. If one were to continue this vertical motion without the rotary twist at the end, it would resemble the raised inside mallet version of the double vertical stroke used in the original Musser roll.

The rotary twist at the end of the stroke is needed to generate power in the second mallet. In other words, the relative dynamics of the two notes are **controlled** by the **ratio** of vertical to rotary motion. If on the double outside stroke one wishes to accentuate the outer mallet, then the vertical descent is strong and the rotary twist is weak. If one wishes to have the inside mallet stronger, the velocity produced by the wrist twist at the end of the stroke should be quite strong compared with the velocity produced in the outside mallet by the vertical descent.

In the simplest terms the outside double lateral stroke is a **down** and **out** scoop, and the double inside stroke is a **down** and **in** scoop. However, these descriptions do not convey the importance of **unity of gesture —** one curvaceous motion.

The following points may be helpful in practicing the double lateral strokes:

1. Since the rotary power (of a single stroke) is highly efficient when the mallets are spread about 90°, the student will find that the second half or torque portion of the double lateral stroke is **less pronounced** with large intervals.

2. A great amount of torque needs to be generated when the interval is small; otherwise, the second pitch will not speak with volume equal to the first pitch.

3. Wrist curvature changes slightly during the double lateral stroke. Concentrating on this may help smooth out the motion and generate more power. In general, wrist curvature will be at a **minimum** (almost a straight line from the back of the hand to the forearm) when the **outside** mallet **contacts** the bar. This will be the case in both inside and outside double lateral strokes. However, when the double **outside** stroke **starts** with a hand position that is bent to the inside (wrist curvature greater than 180°), wrist curvature will be closest to a straight line when the **inside** mallet strikes the bar. The double **inside** stroke is almost unusable when the wrist curvature is greater than 180°

4. If one has difficulty generating power in the second mallet of a double lateral stroke, try a sip of the following tonic: hold the free hand open, palm down, a few inches above the leading mallet head (for outside strokes, hold the hand above the outside mallet head) Snap the mallet away from the bar into the waiting, trembling palm. The harder one manages to hit the palm, the louder the second note will speak. See figure 40.

5. Double lateral strokes **do not function slowly.** For two pitches which are convenient to play with one hand but are not rhythmically close enough to strike them with **one motion** (and still produce enough velocity for the required dynamic level), opt for single alternating strokes.

6. When double lateral strokes are repeated in one hand (as in the author's version of the Musser roll), the motion described resembles two tilted ellipses. If the reader has a vivid imagination (but insipid double lateral strokes), he should picture himself to be holding two paint brushes (Musser grip), drawing a series of double curlicues on a canvas. The imaginary artwork should look something like:

Right double outside or left double inside

7. Until the basic wrist motion is acquired, one should not attempt to achieve additional power or control through the fingers. Most students find that the double lateral strokes naturally begin to harness finger control and power after a few months of practice using the wrist to produce the basic gesture.

8. When finger acceleration is added to a double lateral stroke, the finger motions are identical to those used for single strokes. The problem lies in the timing of the muscular contraction. If only one mallet is being accentuated, the timing complications are minimal. If both mallets are using finger acceleration, the contraction for the second mallet must be started slightly later than the contraction for the first mallet. Incorrect rhythmic distance between the two pitches of a double lateral stroke indicates incorrect timing of the two finger contractions. If the two pitches sound too close together, the **second** finger contraction should be delayed.

9. Study figures 38 — 44.

Double lateral outside stroke.
The student should use this
practice method to increase the
volume of the second mallet
in double lateral strokes.

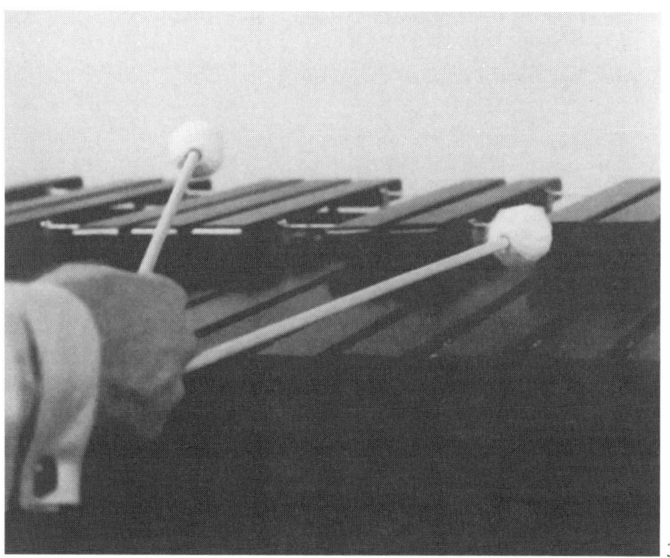

38

Starting position for outside double lateral stroke. Note that the outside mallet is **slightly** closer to the keyboard than the inside mallet.

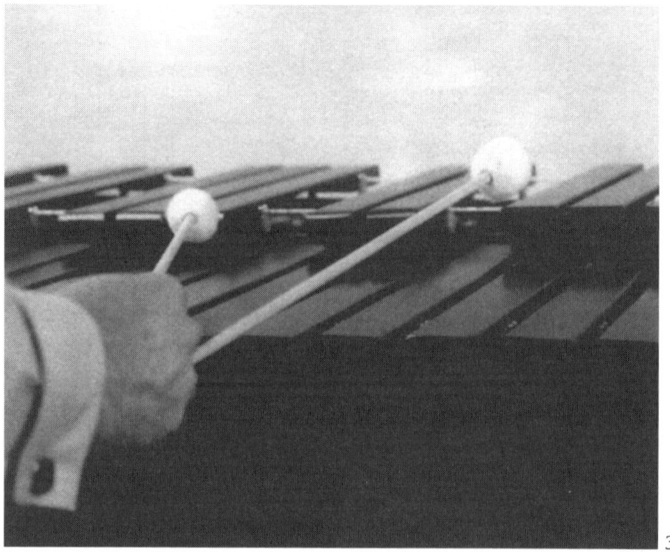

39

Starting position for inside double lateral stroke. Note that the inside mallet is **slightly** closer to the keyboard than the outside mallet.

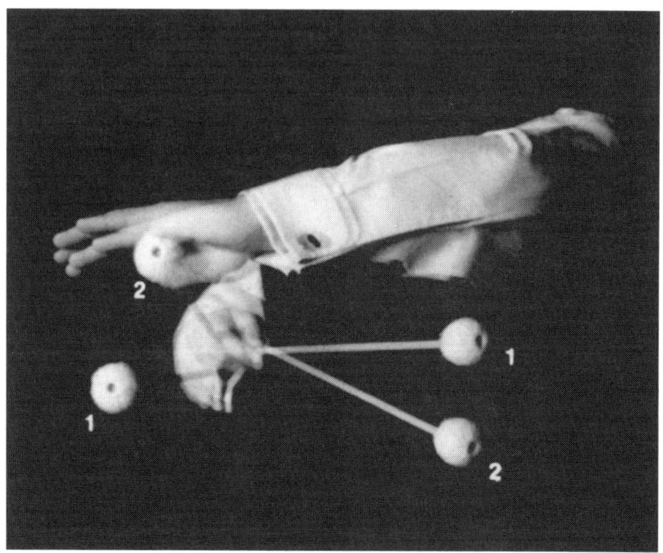

40

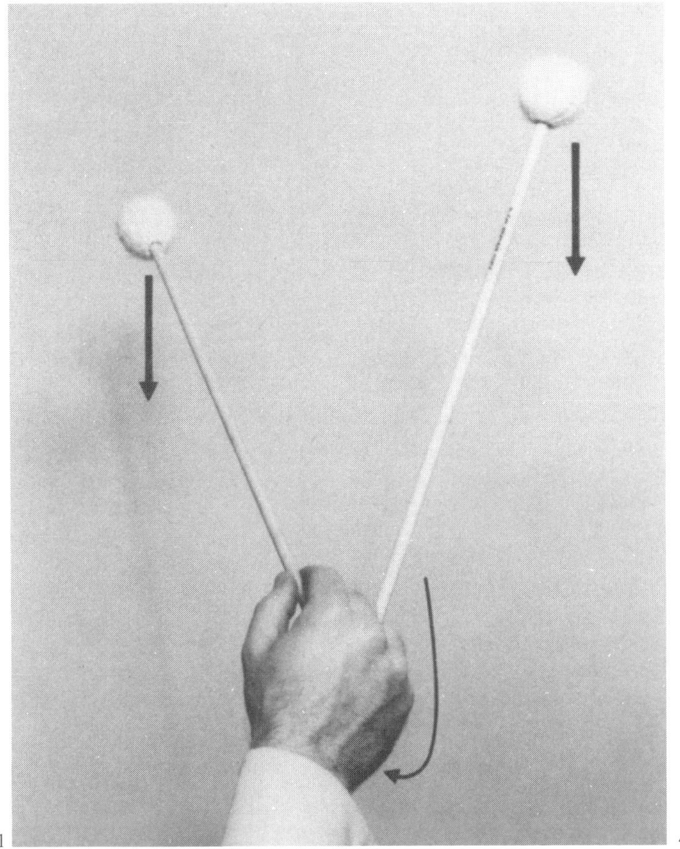 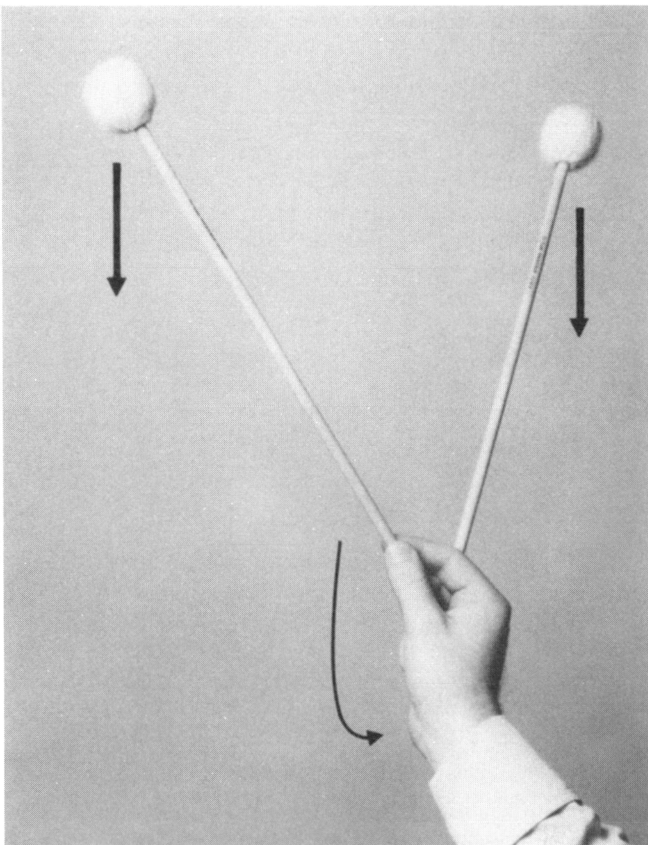

Think of the wrist turning in a clockwise ellipse for a right hand inside double lateral stroke.

Think of the wrist turning in a counterclockwise ellipse for a right hand outside double lateral stroke.

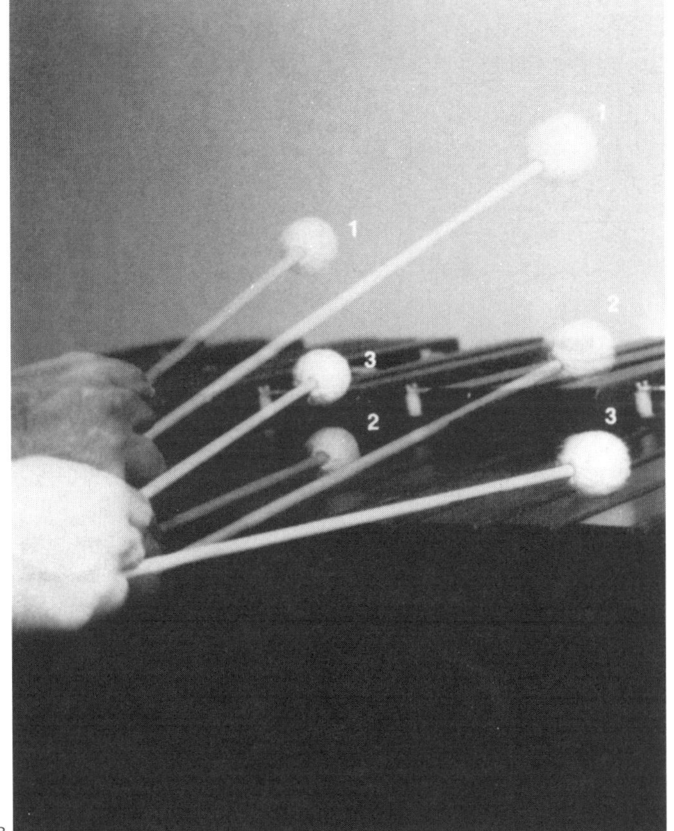 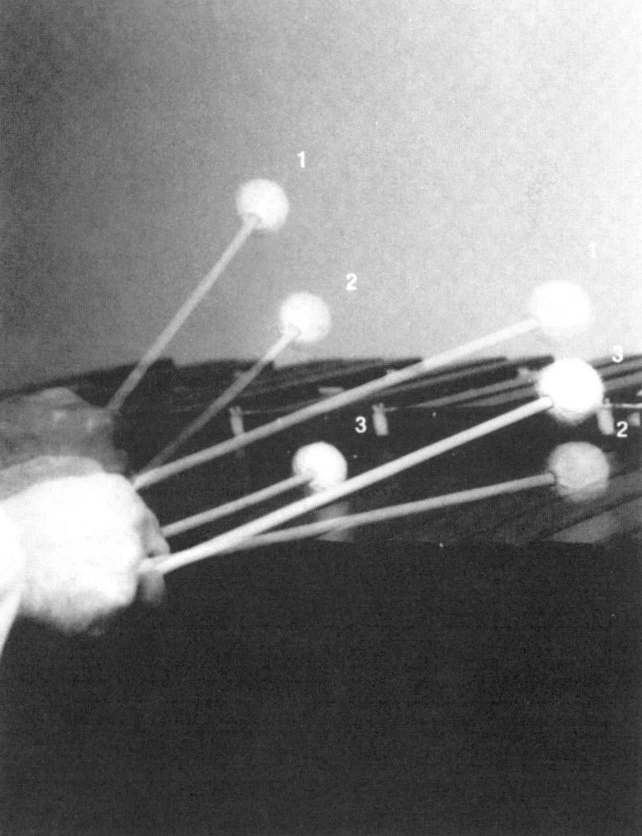

Double lateral inside and outside strokes. Note that the strokes are incomplete: these multiple exposure photographs illustrate the motion to the point of contact between the 2nd mallet and the bar.

XVII Summary

The marimbist should strive

to **combine individual physical tasks into gestures**. The three most basic tasks of interval change, shift, and stroke recovery should merge into a single motion.

to **time the components of gestures to produce curved motions.**

to **conserve distance**, but not at the expense of curved gestures or smooth acceleration.

to **separate muscular duties**. The fingers should remain poised and ready to change intervals even when the neighboring wrist muscles are producing fortissimo strokes. Under the same conditions the arm should remain relaxed, ready to perform shifts.

to **use efficiently both momentum and inertia.** The former should be sustained until the completion of a particular gesture; the latter may be used to execute passive interval changes.

to **employ all technique in the service of musical expression.**

XVIII Leigh's Laws

The following "laws" are excerpted from a larger collection of LHS aphorisms about music, life, and the development of musicianship and technique. Since this book is focused primarily on the development of technique, only those that relate to subjects mentioned in MOM are included.

About Practice
You perform the way you practice: practice sloppily, perform sloppily.

"Practice makes perfect . . . if you practice perfectly". We've all heard that, but only some of us have tried to do it on a regular basis.

A few days before your next performance you may say to yourself "If I only had another week! I could really polish things up and do a great job." Do that week of practice this week and next week.

About stroke preparation
What goes up must come down, but it doesn't necessarily come down in the same place.

About shifting
A slow shift is like using a grayscale to determine position - if you shift slowly, positions will not be perceived as exact and repeatable.

About tension
Having to use 90% of your strength will always produce tension - develop enough strength so that you are only using 50% of your power at *ff*.

About Strength
Of course, developing strength requires repeated contraction of the muscles to the point of tiring. You won't get stronger without working your muscles.

About Articulation
Most instruments produce a variety of articulations without even trying, just because of the nature of bowing or blowing. The same applies to the release of the note at the end of the sound.

Marimbists just have to try harder or all of our attacks and releases will sound the same.

Corollary: If we're not careful, we will produce perfect articulation. (Not a good thing: it's boring!)

Tone
Performing with "single tone mallets" on the marimba is something like a classical guitarist playing with a guitar pick - all the expressive timbral possibilities of using combinations of the flesh and nails are lost.

Second Part
Exercises

I Single Independent Strokes

Exercises 1 — 3 do not contain any interval changes. Pre-set the interval spread and **keep** each mallet over its assigned pitch even when it is not stroking. Watch out for angular motion in the unused mallet. There should be no vertical or horizontal motion in the arm except at points of transposition. Remember: repeat and transpose each exercise through all twelve keys.

Exercises 4 and 5 contain small interval changes. The mallet must be moved on the stroke recovery of the last 16th of beats 3 & 4. Do not stop the motion of the mallet until it is over the next pitch.

♪ =60 − ♩ =80

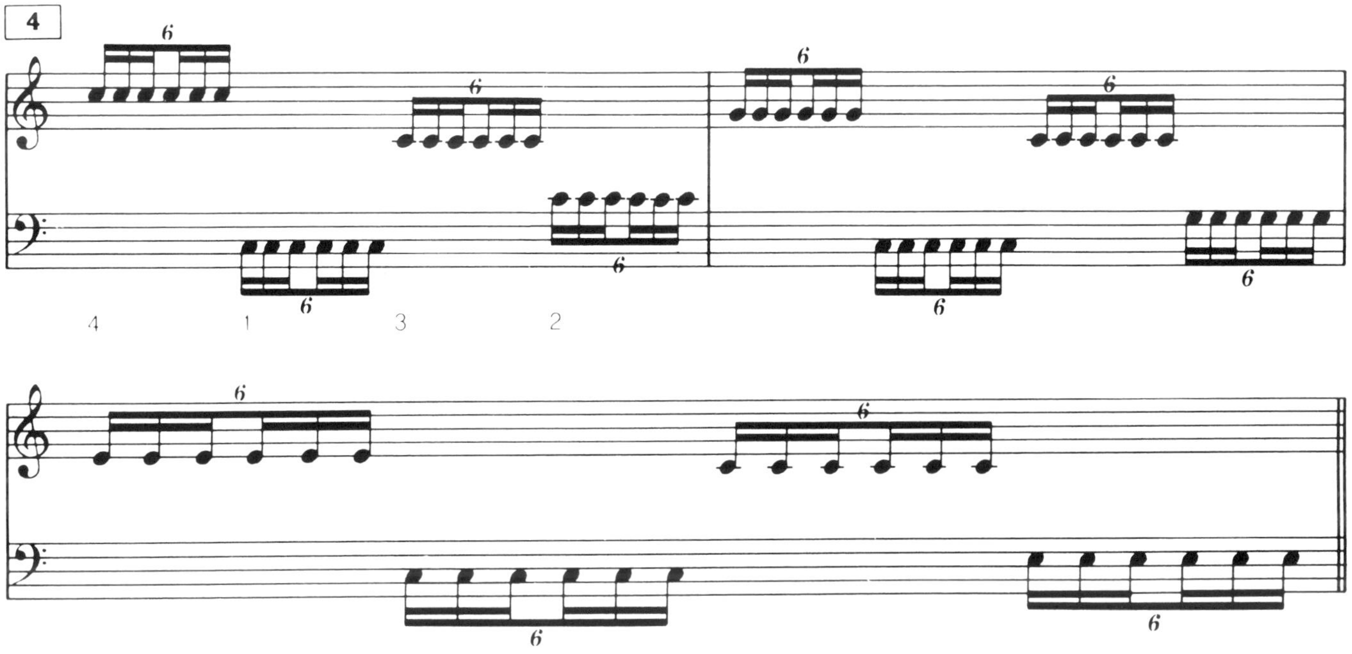

♪ =60 − ♩ =88

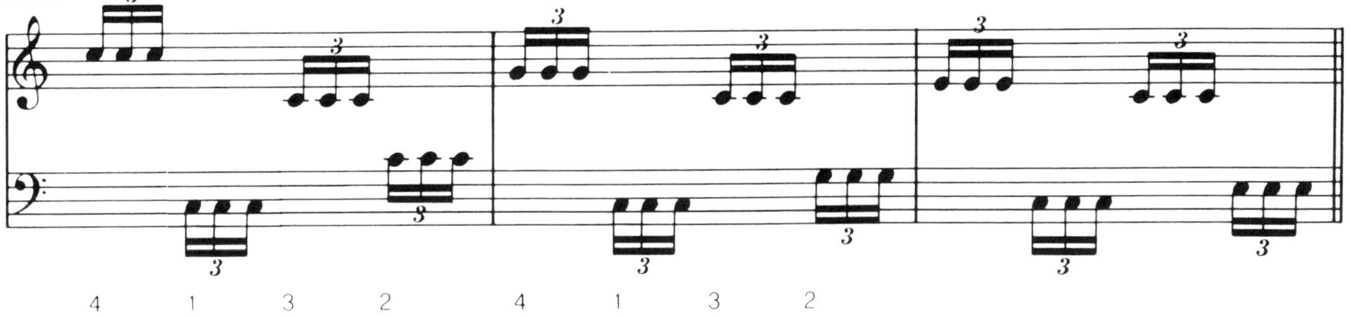

Exercises 6—18: Strive for evenness of dynamics and rhythm. Produce the stroke with the wrist only. When reviewing these exercises at some future date, attempt to play each group of 16ths partially with the fingers.

16

17

18

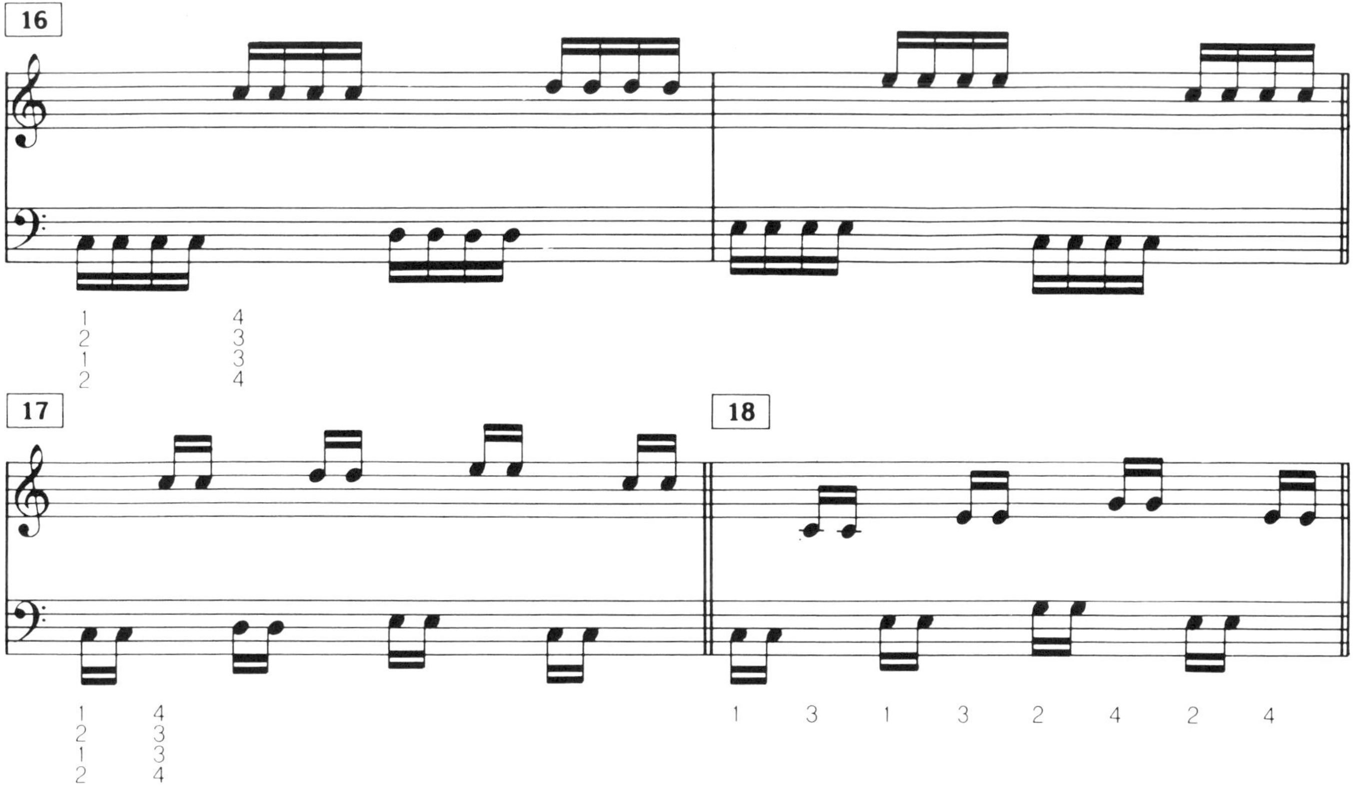

Exercises 19 – 22: Let the unused mallets hang loose and relaxed a few inches above the keyboard. When playing the exercises with mallets 1 and 4, close the interval to keep mallets 2 and 3 from interfering with one another.

19 ♪ = 116 – ♩ = 152

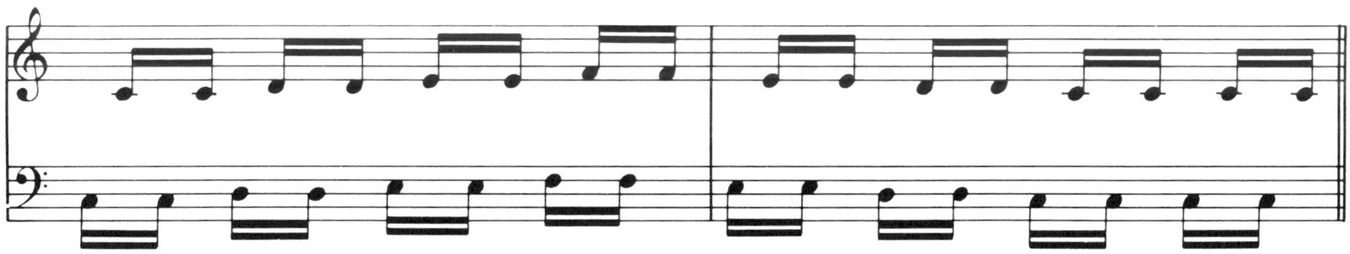

20

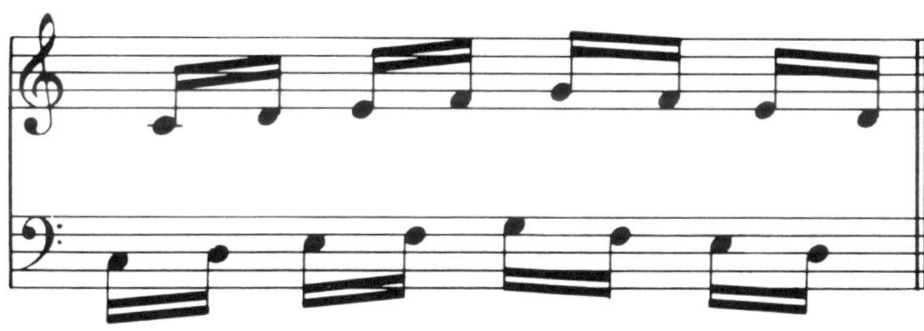

21

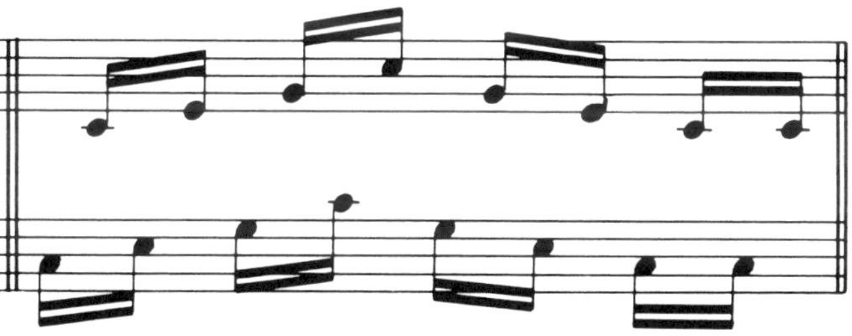

22

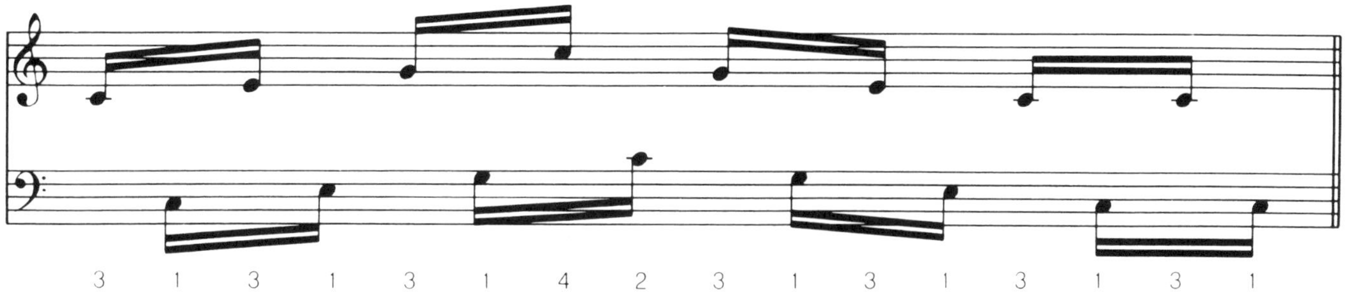

Exercises 23 – 26: Perform the independent strokes as smoothly as if the pitches were not changing. Let the arm and wrist glide the mallet heads over the second (Ex. 23, 24) and third (Ex. 25, 26).

23 ♪ = 88 – ♩ = 144

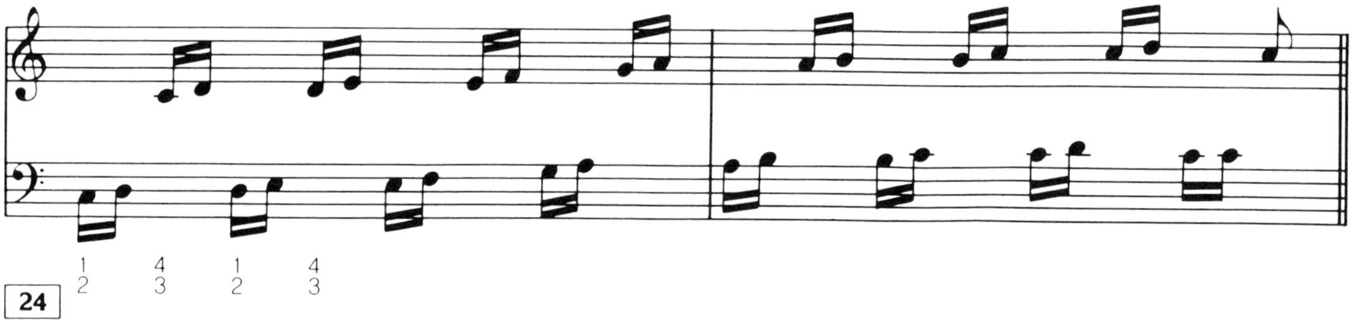

24

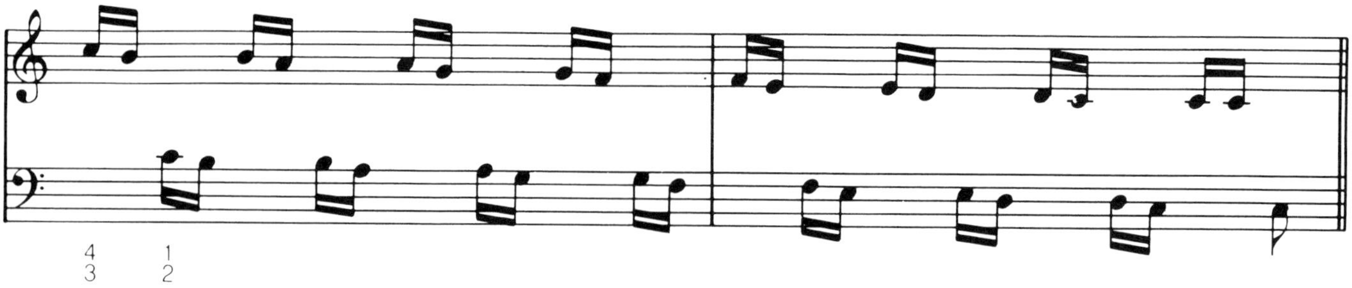

25 ♪ = 66 – ♪ = 160

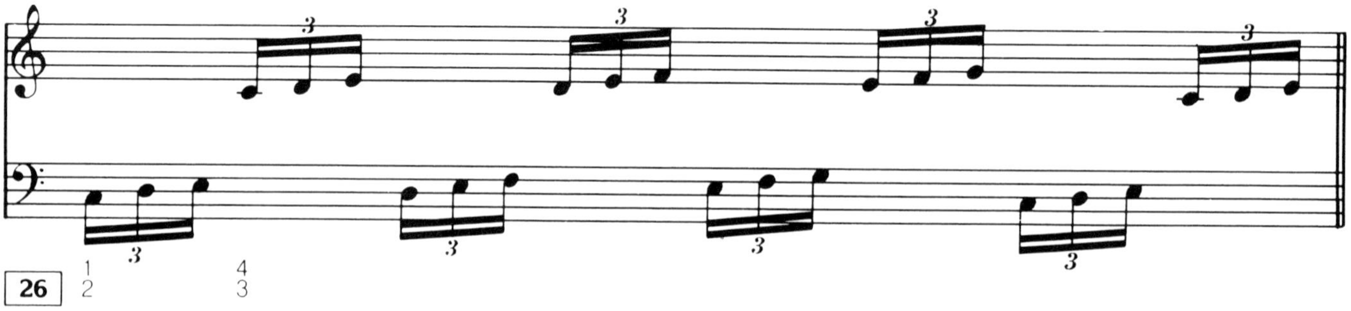

26

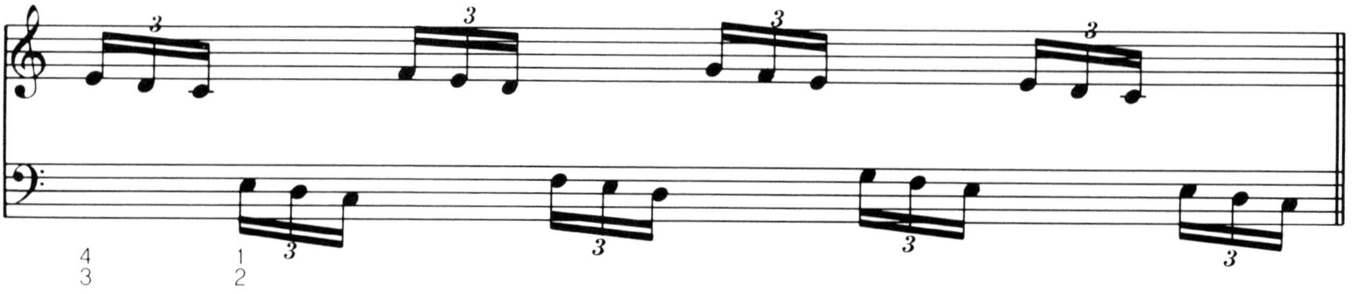

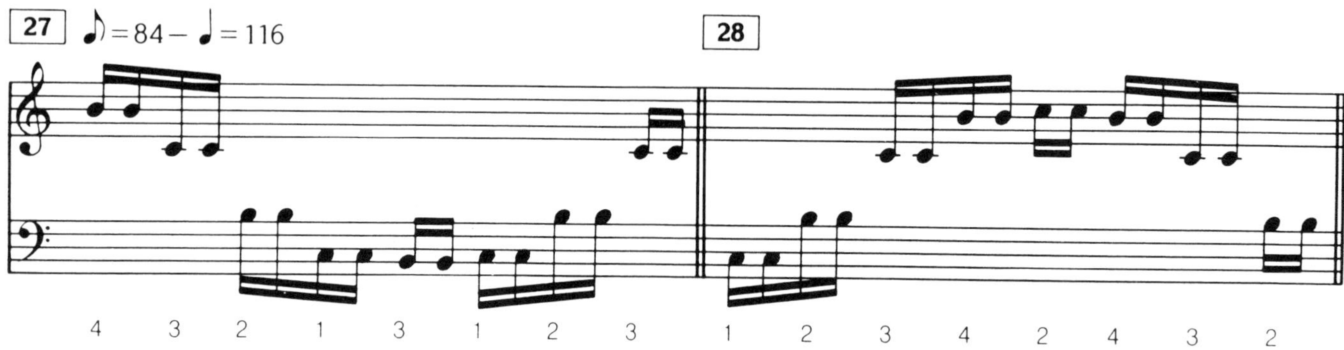

Exercises 27 – 28: These exercises require the crossing of hands. Ex.27 – cross right over left. Ex. 28 – cross left over right. In these exercises play in the center of the bars whenever possible. The author recommends these sticking patterns for the last movement of the Robert Kurka Marimba Concerto. Marimbists with four octave instruments should start ex. 27 on C.

27 ♪ = 84 – ♩ = 116 **28**

Exercises 29 – 31: Independent strokes are crucial to the relaxed execution of scalar passages. Make sure that the unused mallet(s) hang loosely and calmly near the keyboard. Do not hold them aloft! In ex. 30 keep the interval spread small so that the arm does not have to shift every time the sticking changes.

29 ♪ = 72 – ♩ = 104

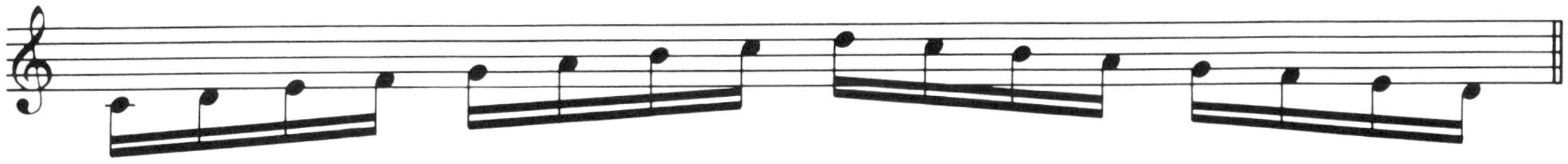

1 Sempre
2 Sempre
3 Sempre
4 Sempre
a) Loco b) 8 bassa c) 8 va

30

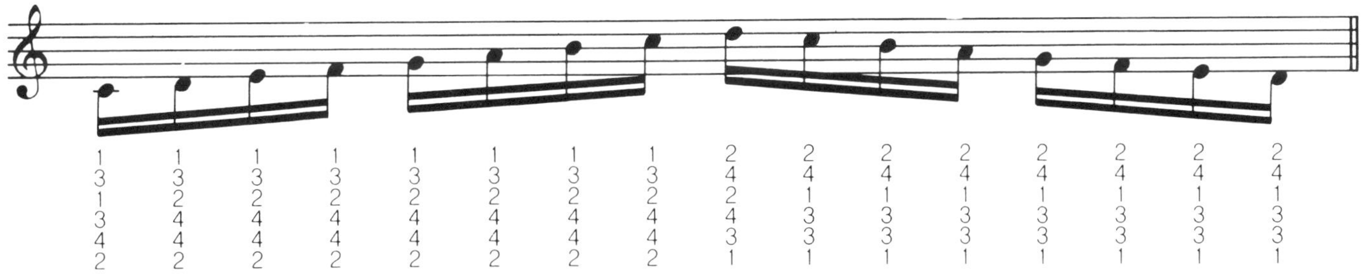

31 ♪ = 92 – ♩ = 168

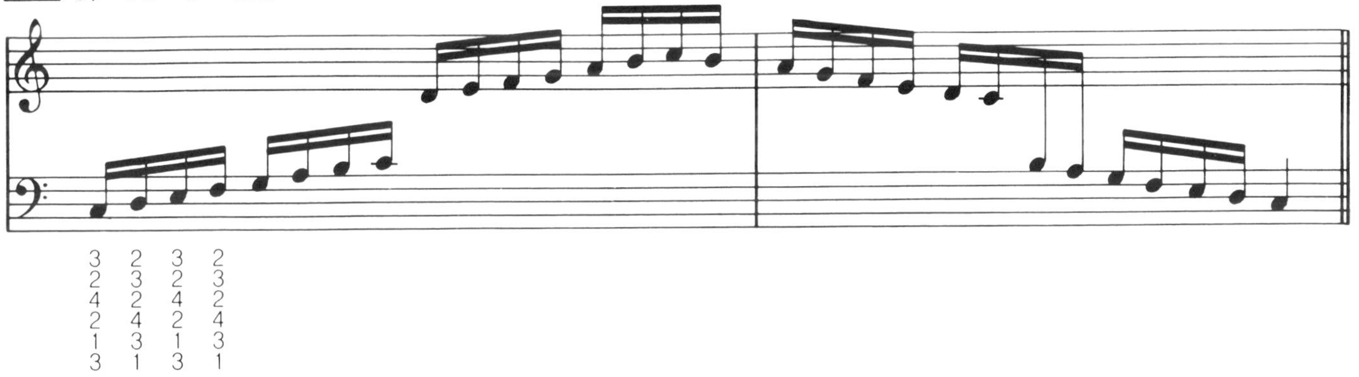

Exercises 32 – 49: Double sticking is slightly more problematic when holding four mallets than when holding two. The influence of the extra mass can be minimized by keeping the unused mallet completely relaxed when it is not actually involved in a stroke. Exercises 43 and 48 have direct application to Raymond Helble's Preludes No. 4 and No. 6.

32 ♩ = 40 – ♩ = 96 **33**

34 **35**

36 **37**

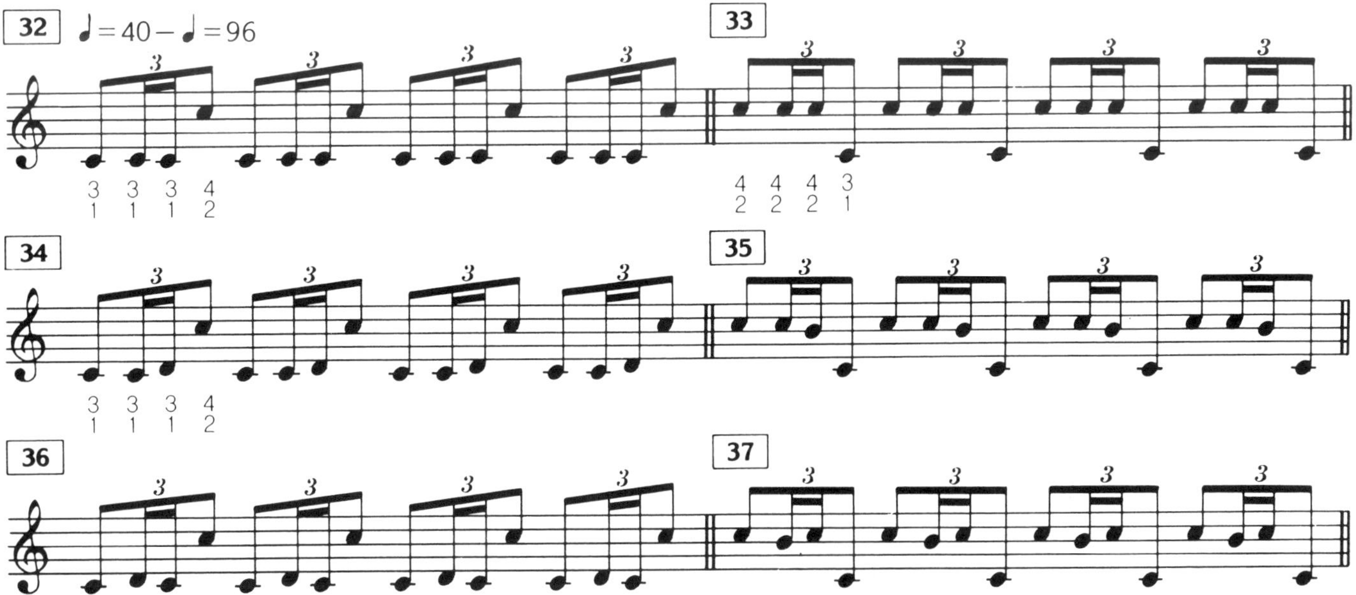

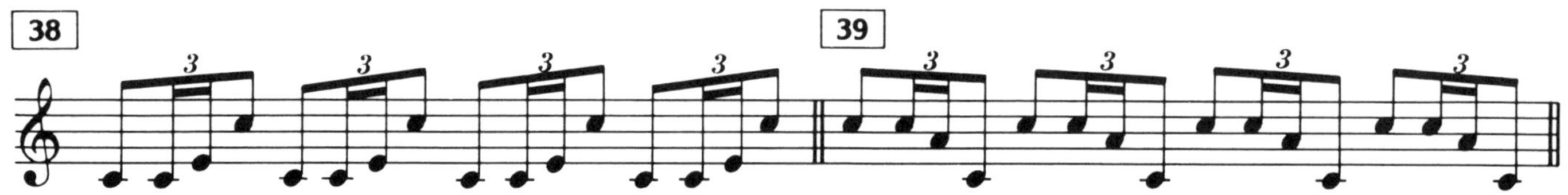

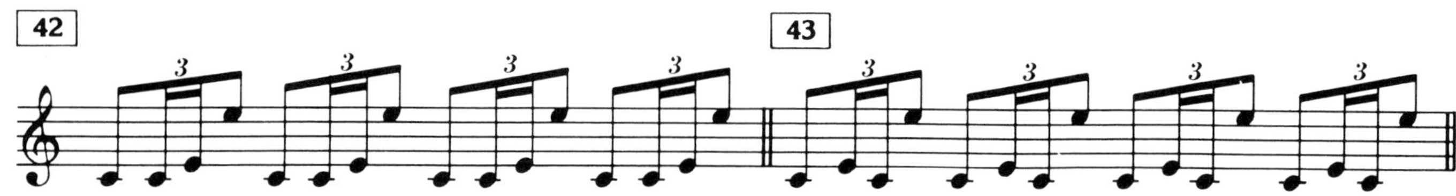

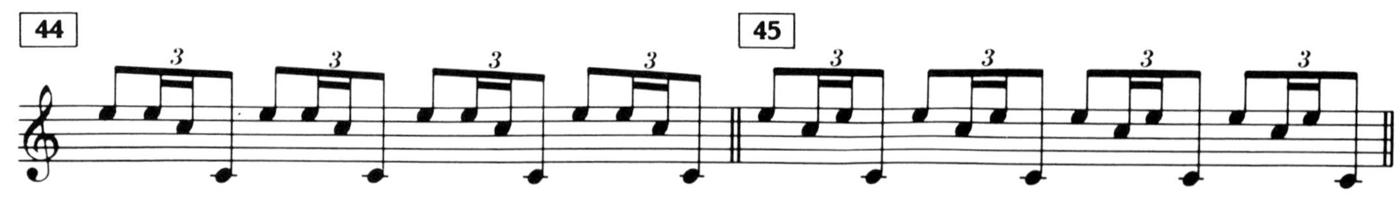

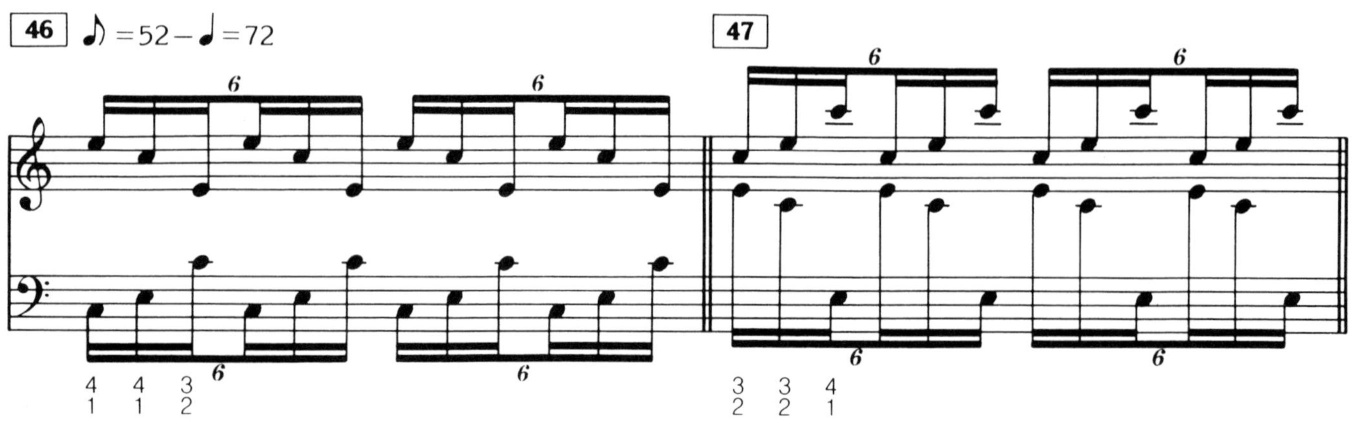

Exercises 48 & 49 cannot be transposed a full octave.

II Single Alternating Strokes

Exercises 50 – 69 are to be practiced one hand at a time. 50 – 59 start the left hand 8 bassa. 60 – 69 start the right hand 8 va. Pay close attention that the intervals open and close **all the way** to their next position. The arm should not have to compensate for lazy fingers. The small interval single strokes will require much more torque than the large interval single strokes. As the interval contracts, think crescendo. As the interval expands, think diminuendo. Transpose each exercise chromatically through the twelve keys.

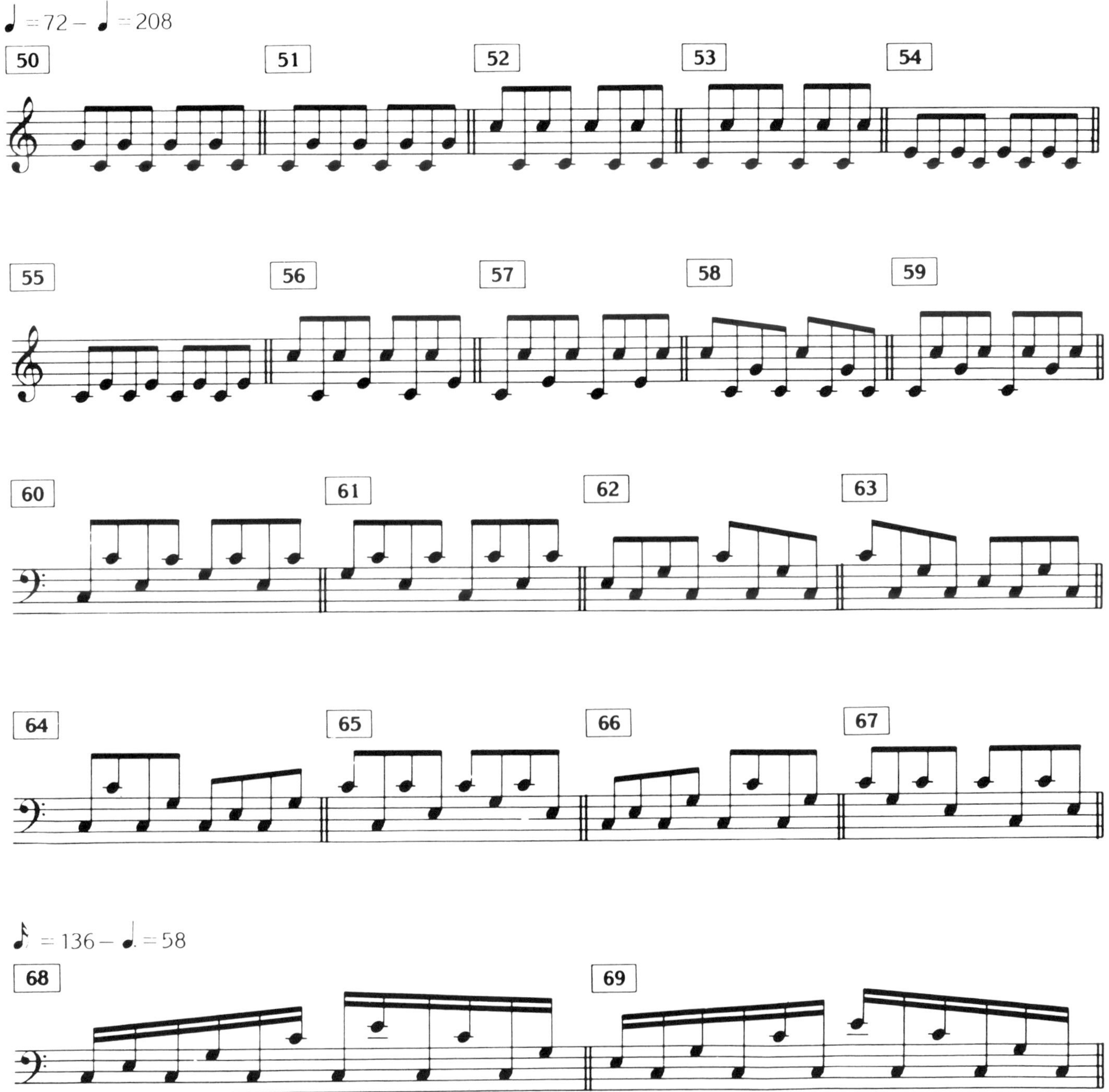

Exercises 70 – 125 are based on the eight single stroke permutations. When returning to these exercises for review, use the following practice method: Do each exercise four times. The first time accent mallet 1, the second time accent mallet 2, the third time accent mallet 3, and the fourth time accent mallet 4.·Transpose every example through all twelve keys.

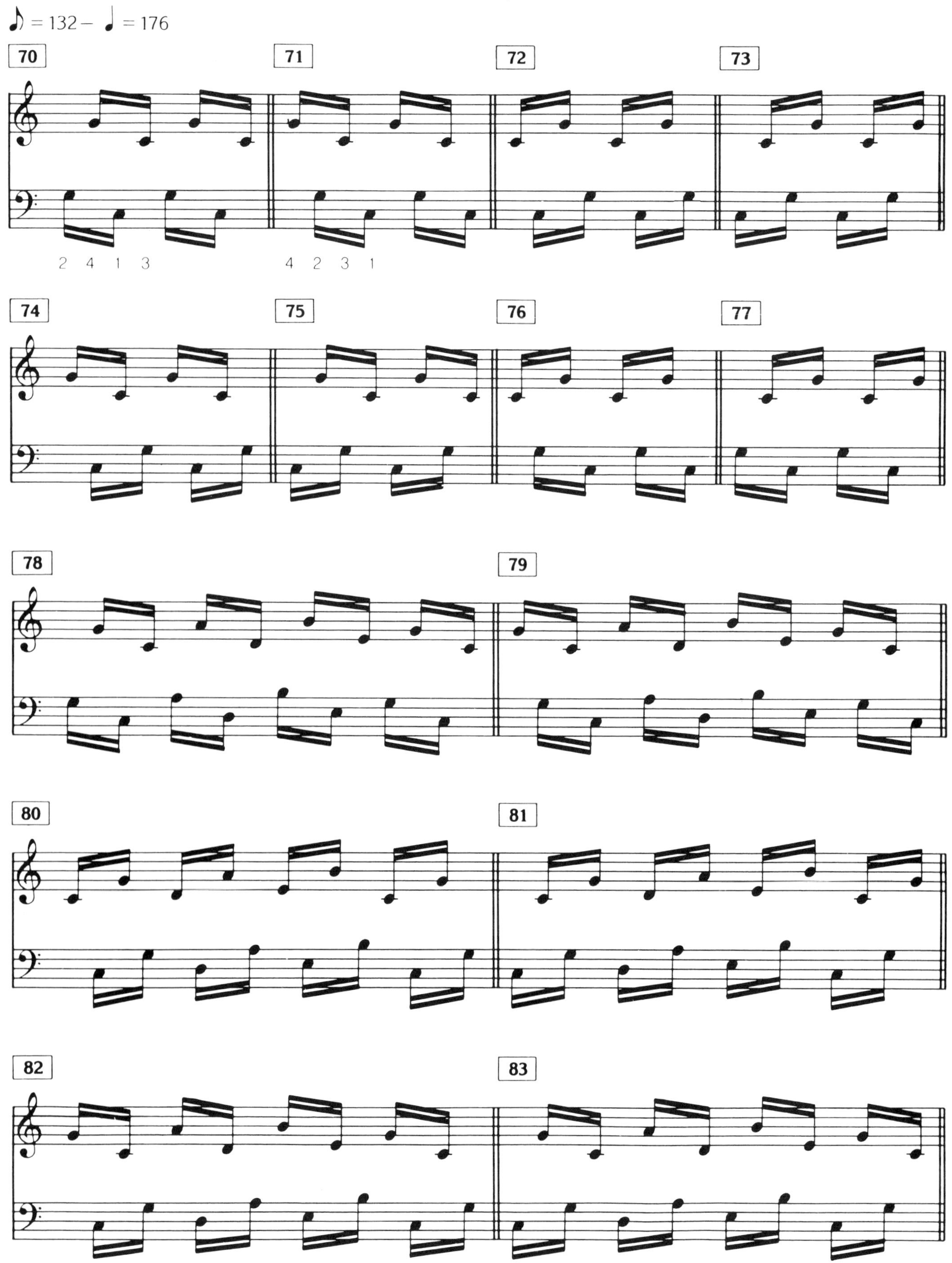

84 | 85

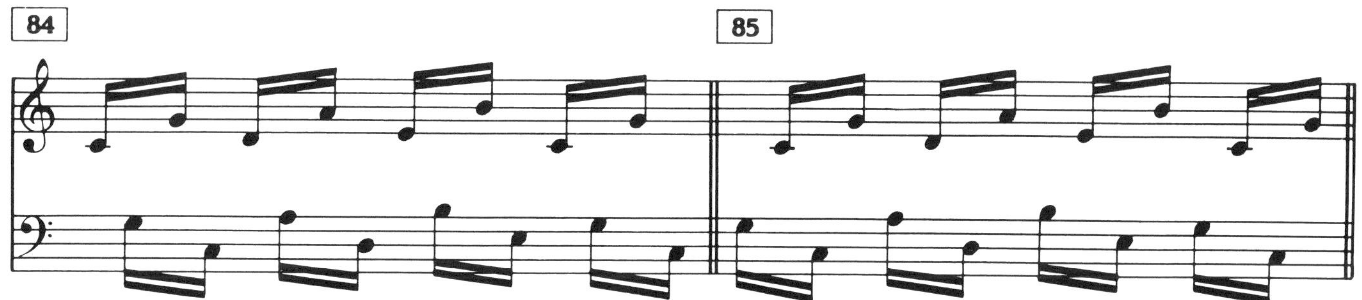

Exercises 86 — 101: Do not attempt these exercises until the eight basic patterns are under control. It may be necessary to flatten the hand position slightly when mallets 1 and 4 are playing accidentals. Shifts should be connected to the second 16th note of each beamed group of two. Exercises 86 — 93 cannot be transposed a full octave.

♪ = 60 – ♩ = 152

86 | 87 | 88 | 89

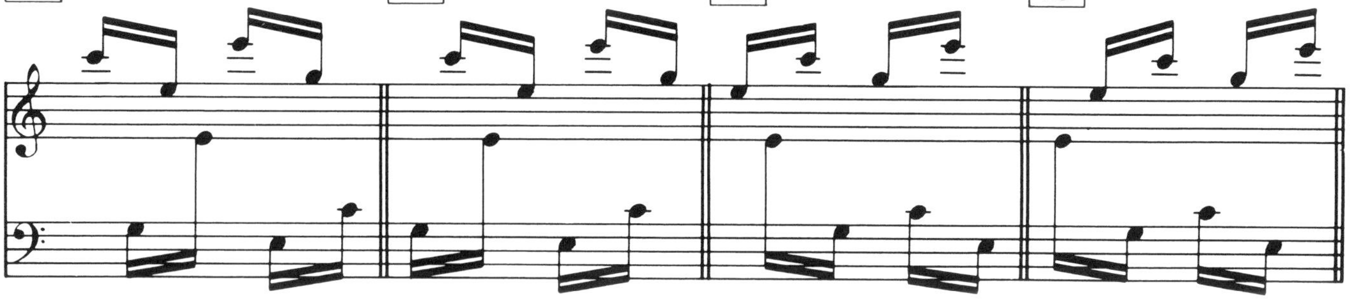

90 | 91 | 92 | 93

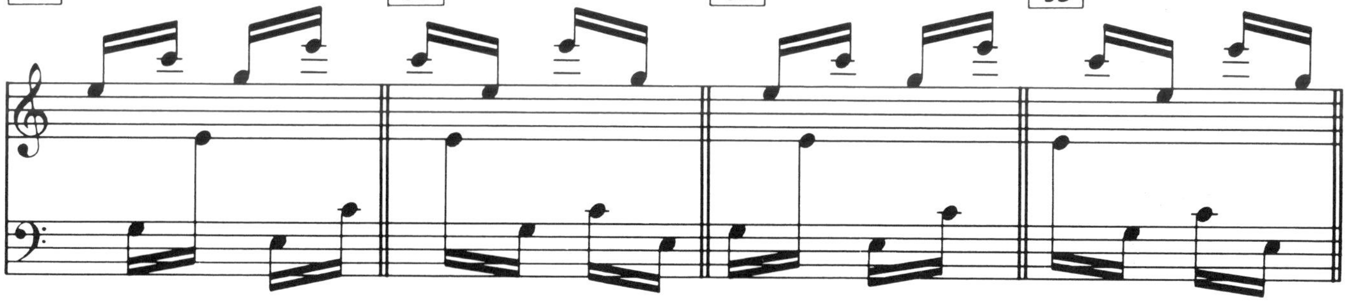

94 | 95

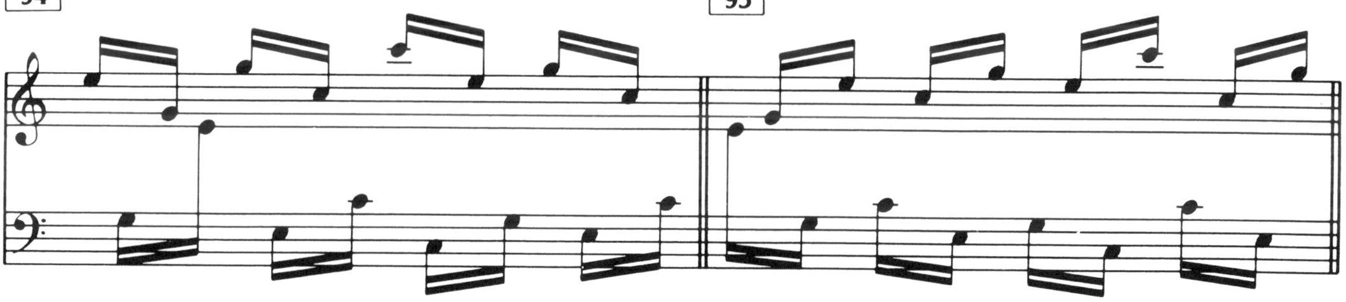

96 | 97

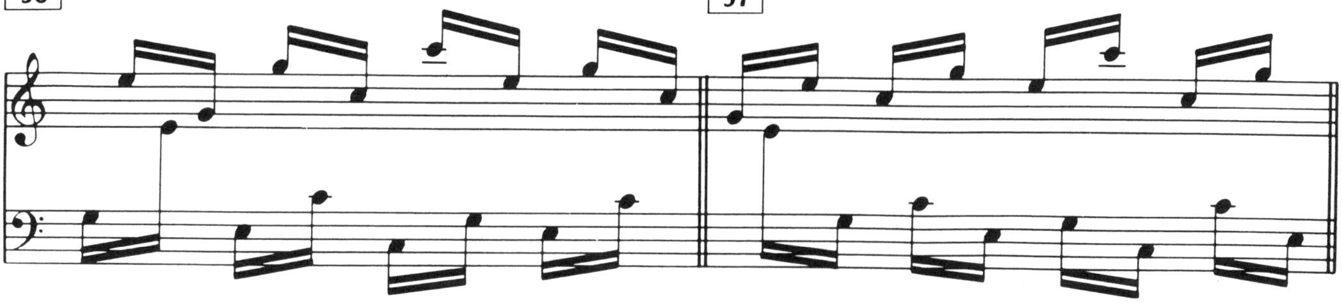

98 99

100 101

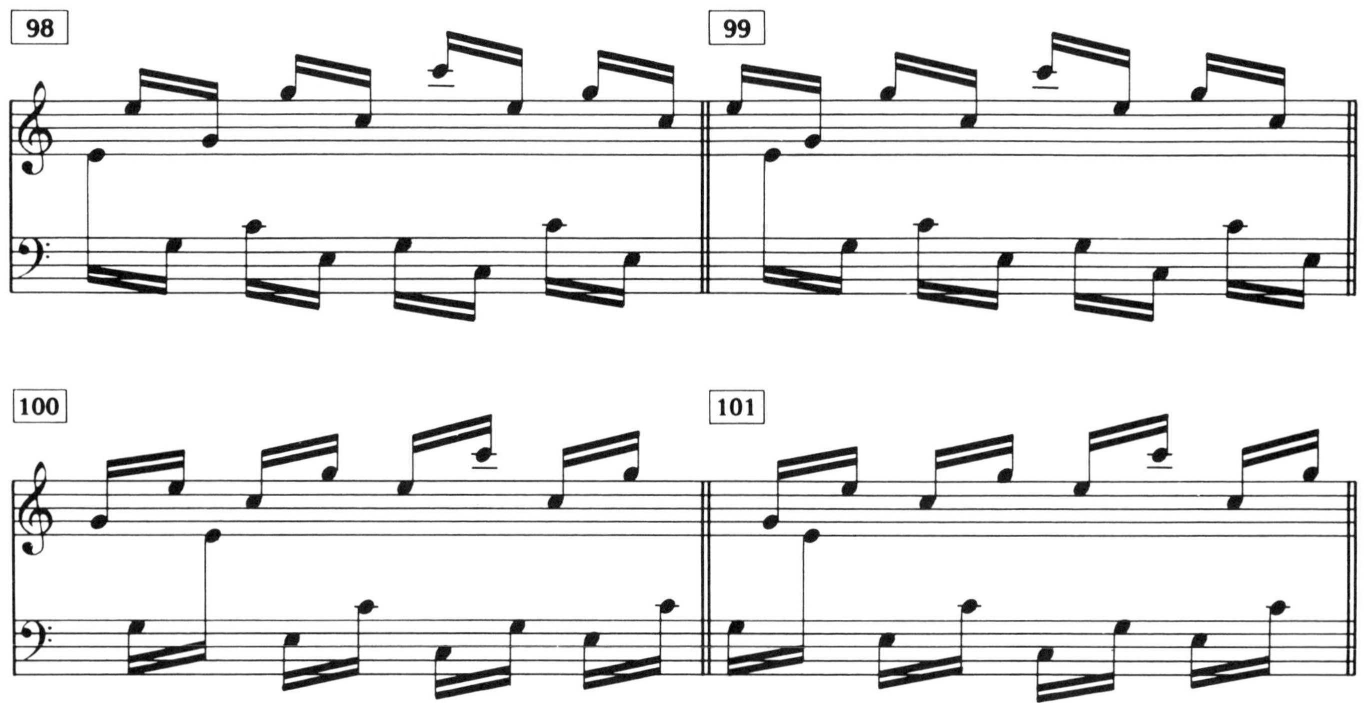

Exercises 102 – 125 are similar to 86 – 101. The same advice is even more applicable since these exercises are a bit more difficult due to the smaller intervals.

♪ = 72 – ♩ = 152

102 103 104 105

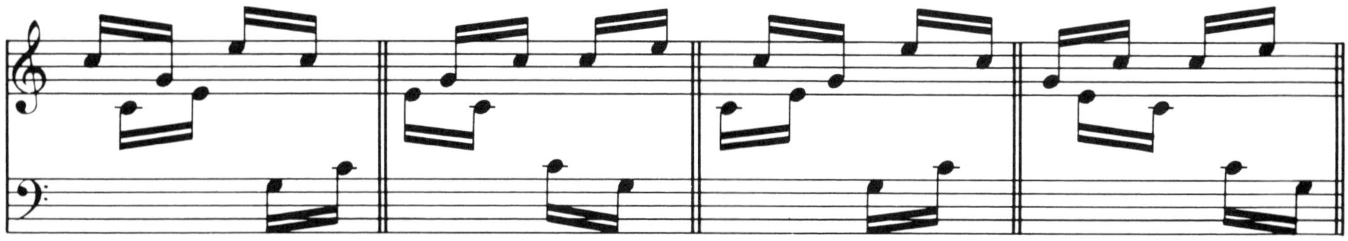

106 107 108 109

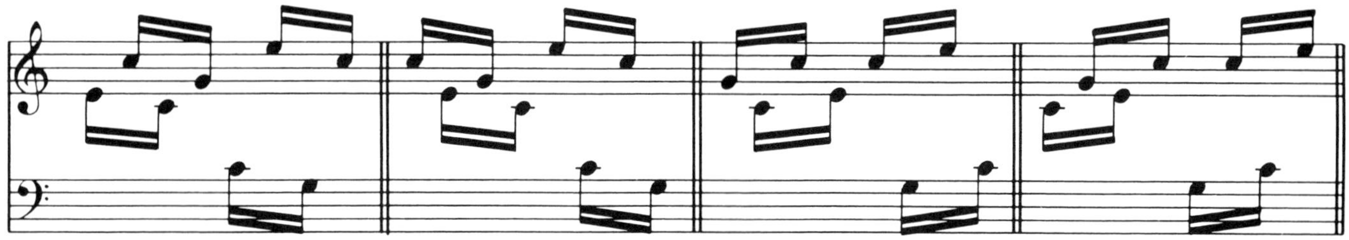

110 111

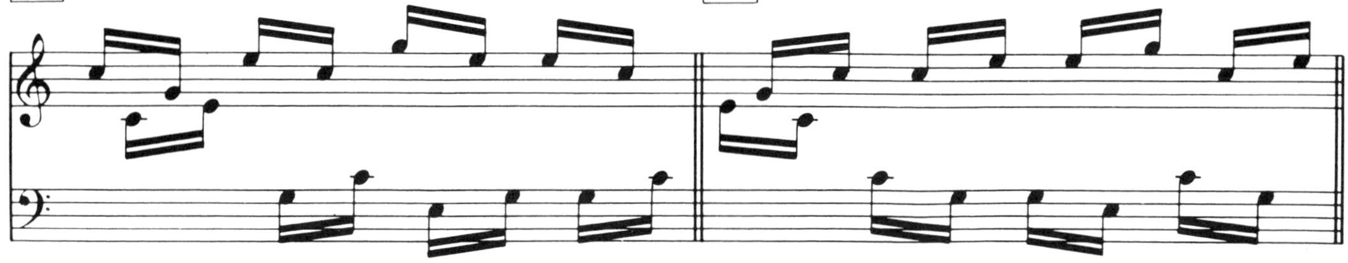

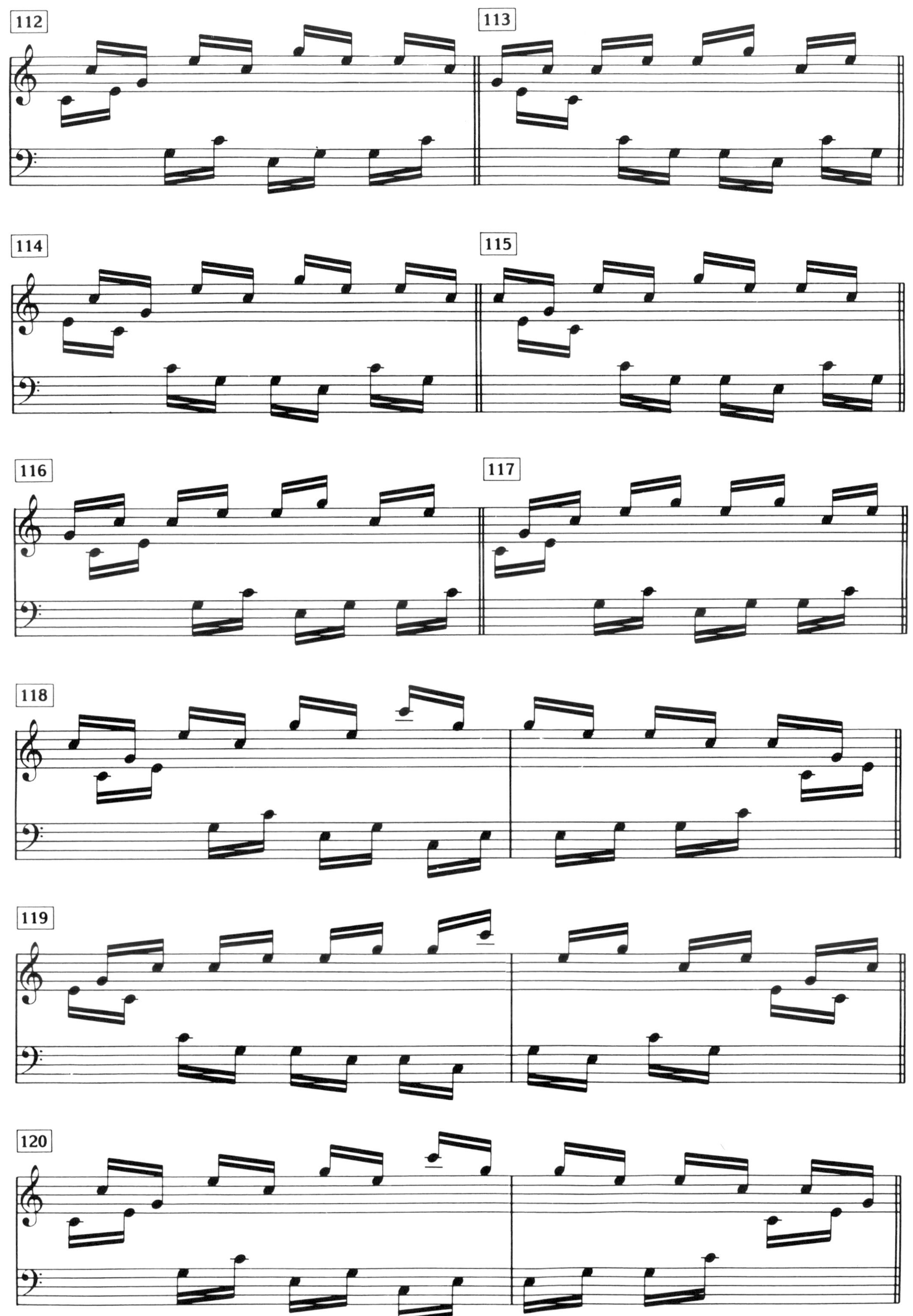

112
113
114
115
116
117
118
119
120

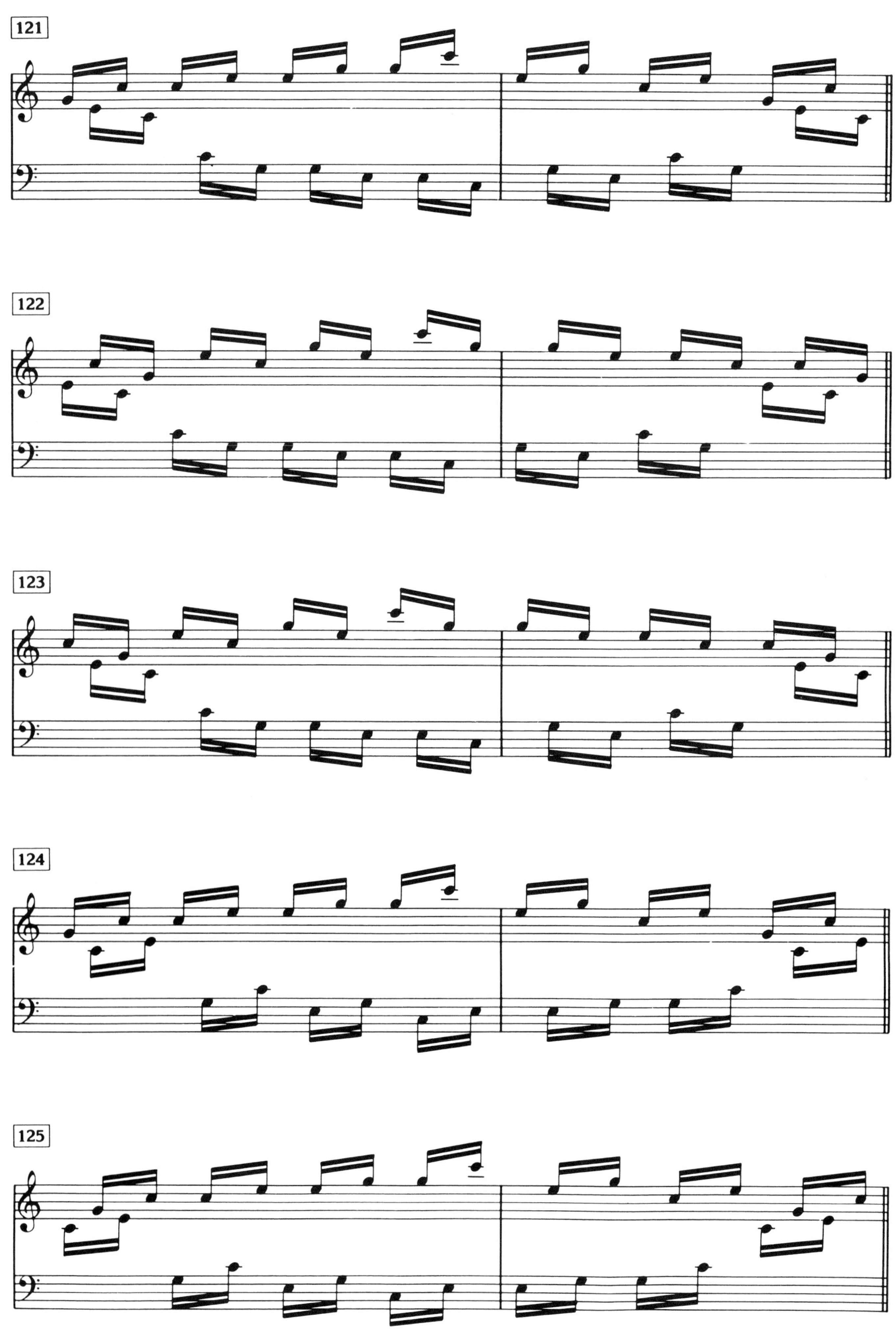

Exercises 126 – 133 have larger interval changes than the previous sets of permutations and for this reason it will be more difficult to maintain even dynamics. Try **not** to accent the outside notes.

♪ = 66 – ♩ = 144

126 127 128 129

1 3 2 4

130 131 132 133

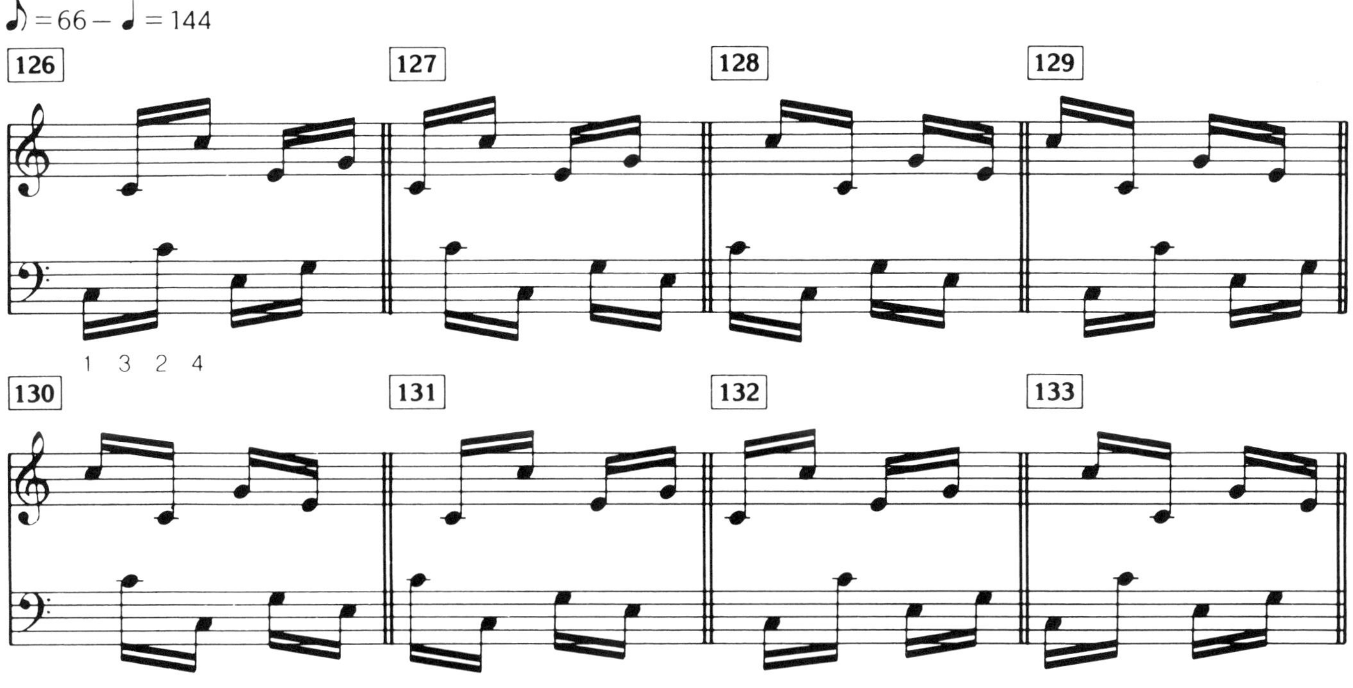

Exercises 134 – 161: Alternating single strokes – hands together. These exercises pose problems of co-ordination and timing. Tension throws timing off. Concentrate on striking both parts together.

♪ = 72 – 𝅗𝅥 = 108

134 135 136 137

4 3 4 3
1 2 1 2

3 4 3 4
2 1 2 1

138 139 140 141

142 143 144 145

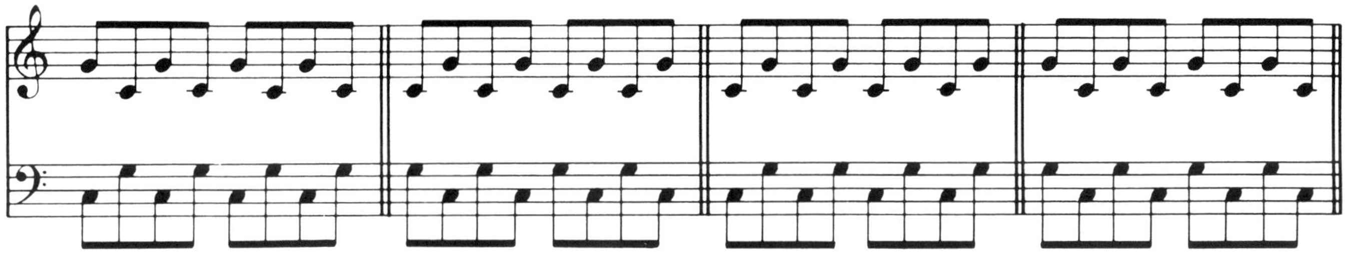

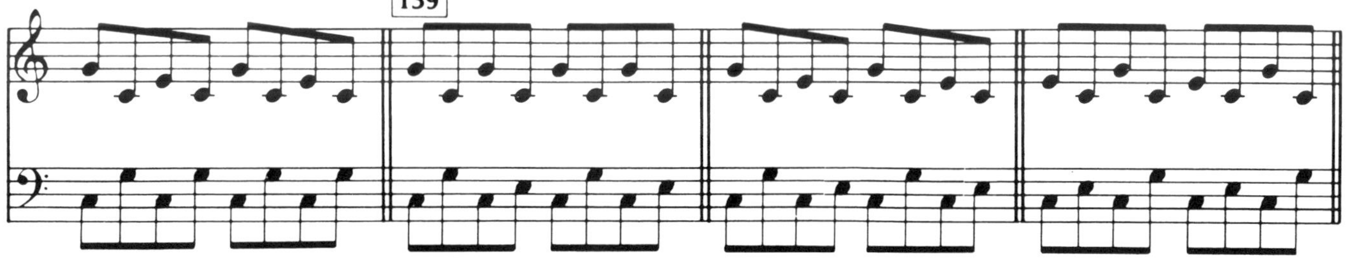

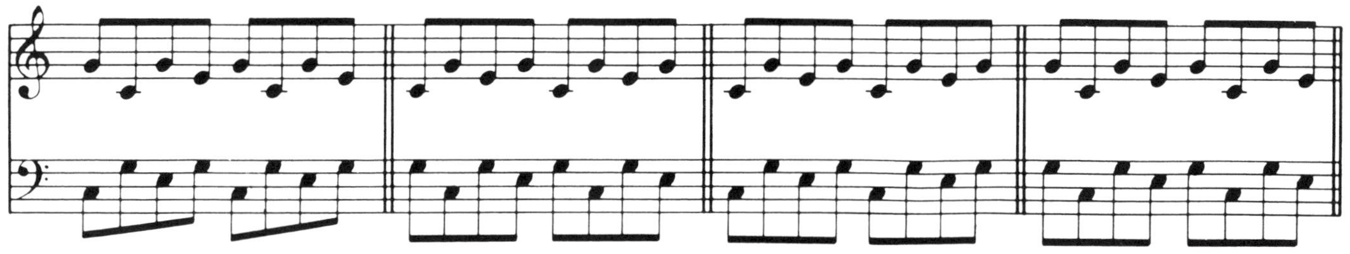

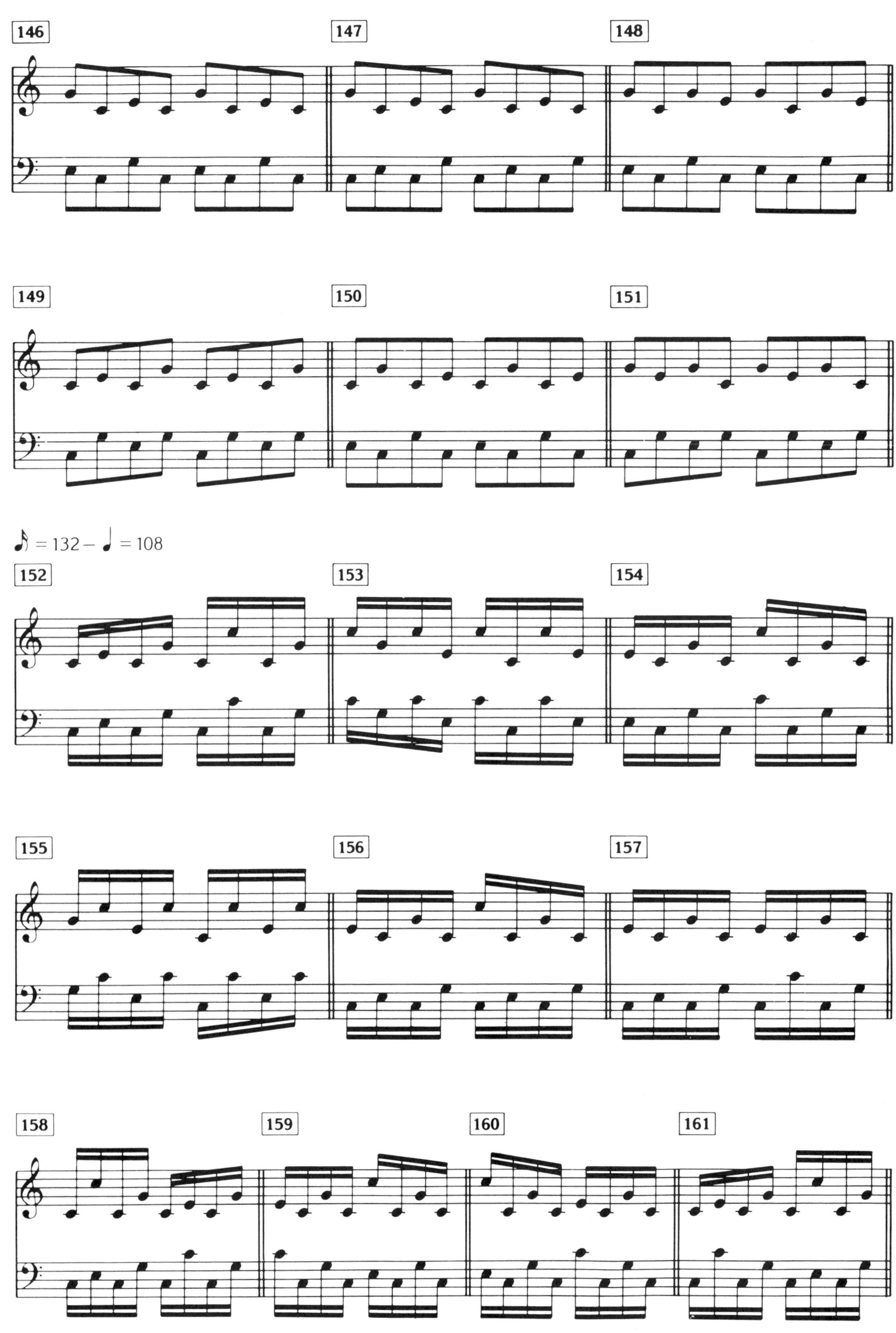

146
147
148
149
150
151
♪ = 132 — ♩ = 108
152
153
154
155
156
157
158
159
160
161

III Double Vertical Strokes

Exercises 162 – 170 look so simple one may be tempted to skip them. **Don't!** Their simplicity is ideal for getting the "kinks" out of double vertical strokes.

Adjust the stroke and recovery speed in order to eliminate most of the contact shock. Repeat each exercise and transpose through the twelve keys. Play the left hand an octave lower.

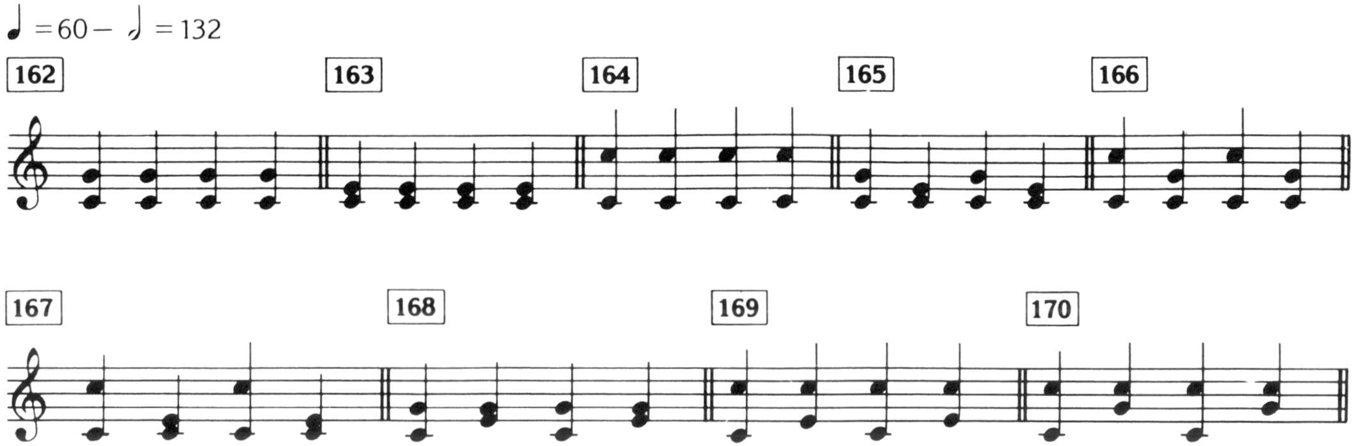

Exercises 171 – 193 are in rhythmic unison. Ex. 174 introduces small interval changes in parallel motion. Ex. 183 introduces parallel shifts. The interval changes

and shifts appear also in contrary and oblique motion. Think of the goal of the shift and the amount of interval change **before each stroke.** Ex. 190 cannot be transposed a full chromatic octave.

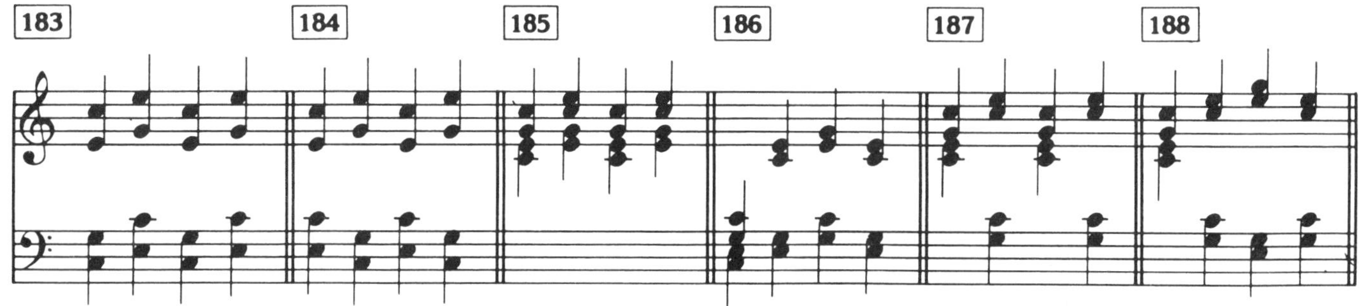

Exercises 194–201: As with most of the contrary motion exercises in this section, not all the pitches can be seen at once. Start very slowly so that the position of each hand can be checked. When reviewing this section at a later date, try watching only the inside mallets or watching one hand while "feeling" the position of the other hand. Exercises 196, 198, and 199 cannot be transposed a full chromatic octave.

Exercises 202—206: Before each stroke think of where the shift is going to end. Judge the lateral position without lowering the mallets to the bars: no pre-stroke "twitches".

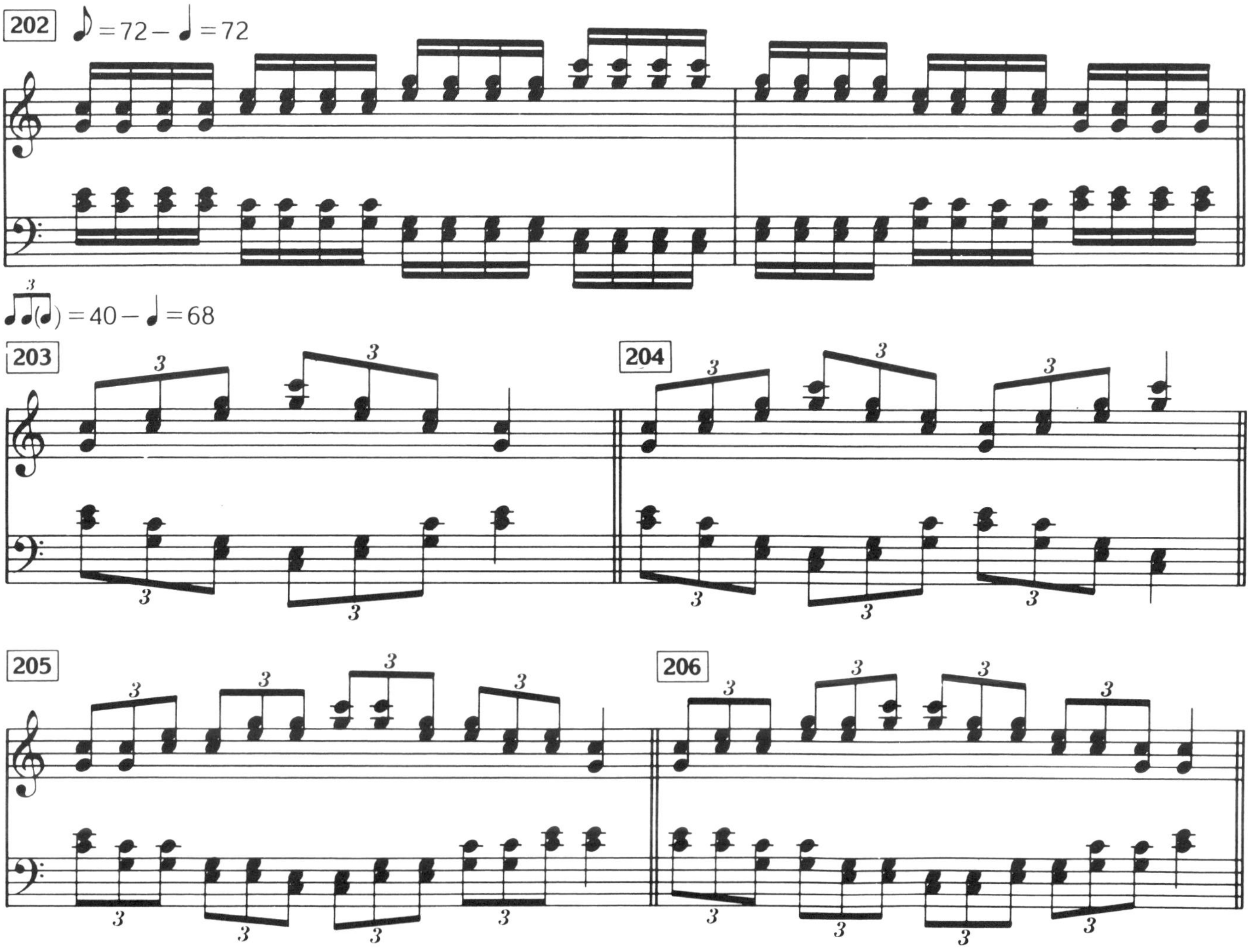

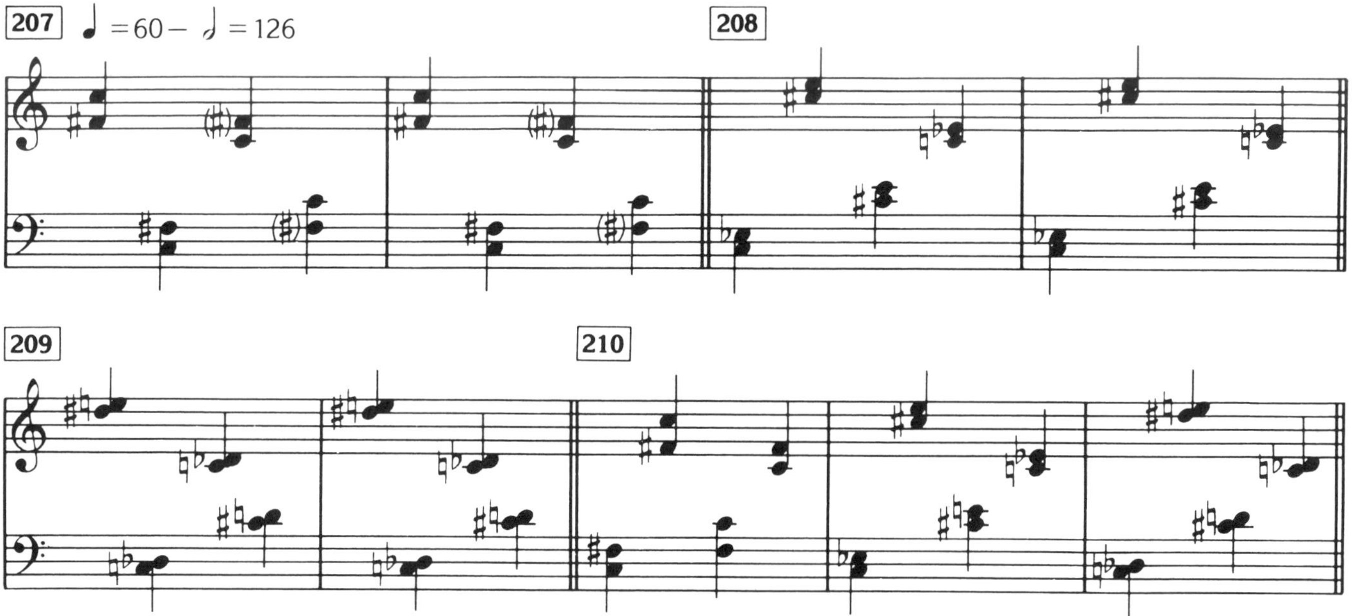

Exercises 207—210: These exercises deal with elbow motions. During the stroke recovery, flip the elbow into the next position. If the wrist is relaxed, the elbow will whip the mallet heads into the basic area of the next stroke. Make any minor corrections with the wrist. The smaller intervals require faster elbow motion.

Exercises 211—219: Pay strict attention to the position of the elbows. It is impossible to play the right notes if they are out of position. Since the arm is slow com-pared with the wrist, give it a head start by leading with the elbow. Practice exercises 211—217 one hand at a time. Ex. 211—215 left hand loco, right hand 8va. Ex. 216 & 217 right hand loco, left hand 8 bassa.

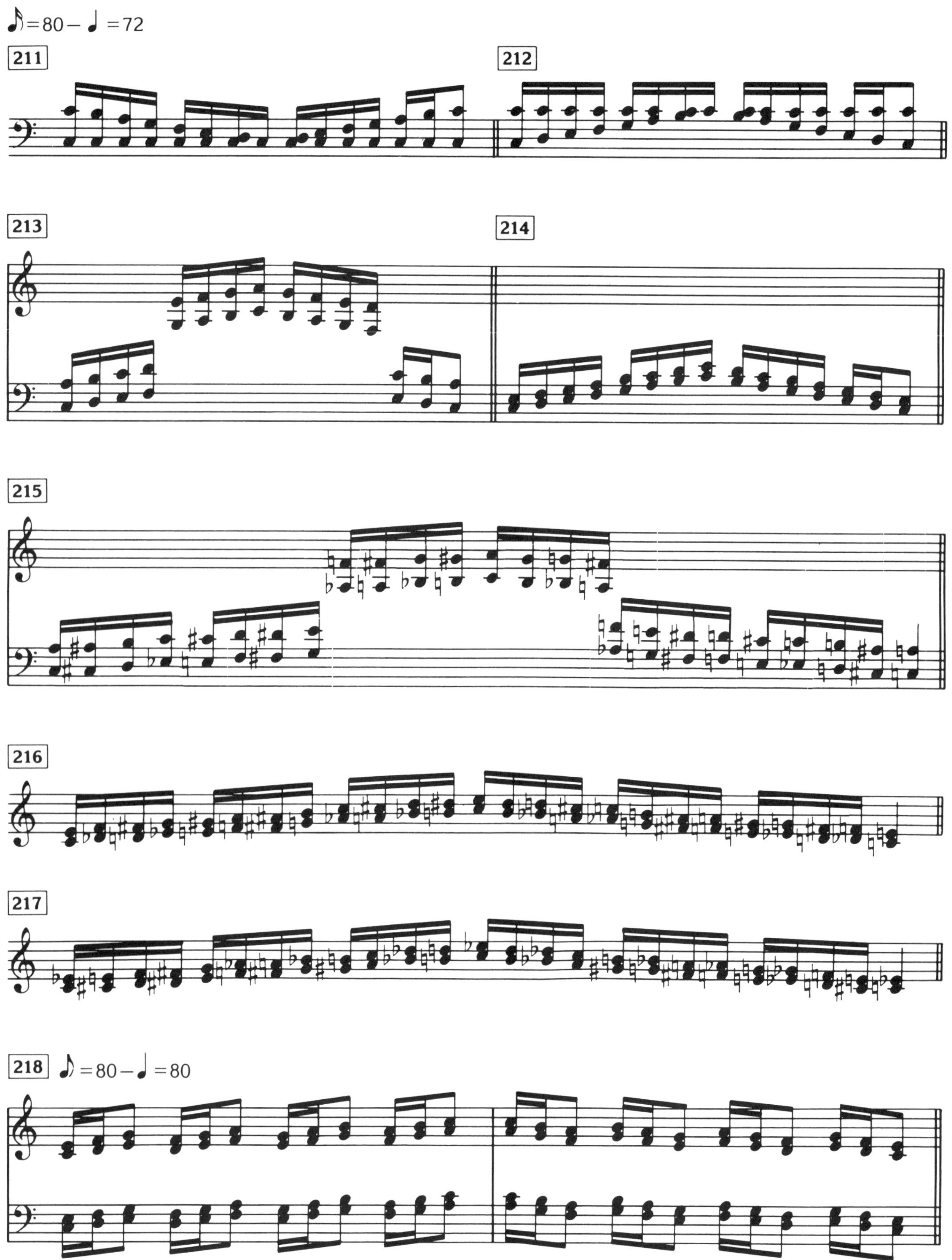

♪=80 — ♩=72
211
212
213
214
215
216
217
218   ♪=80 — ♩=80

219 ♪ = 40 – ♪ = 96

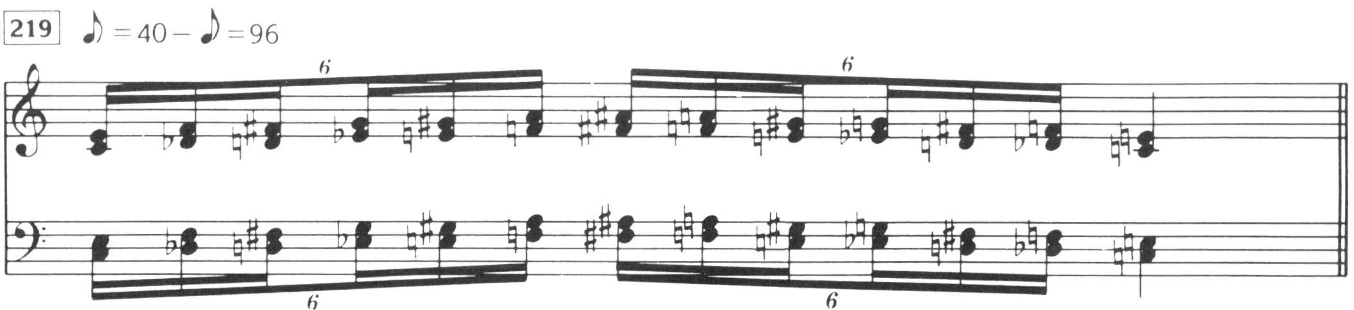

Exercises 220 – 224: The elbow motions are mixed: parallel, oblique, and contrary. Marimbists with four octave instruments should start exercises 220 – 222 on E flat.

♪ = 50 – ♪ = 178

220 **221**

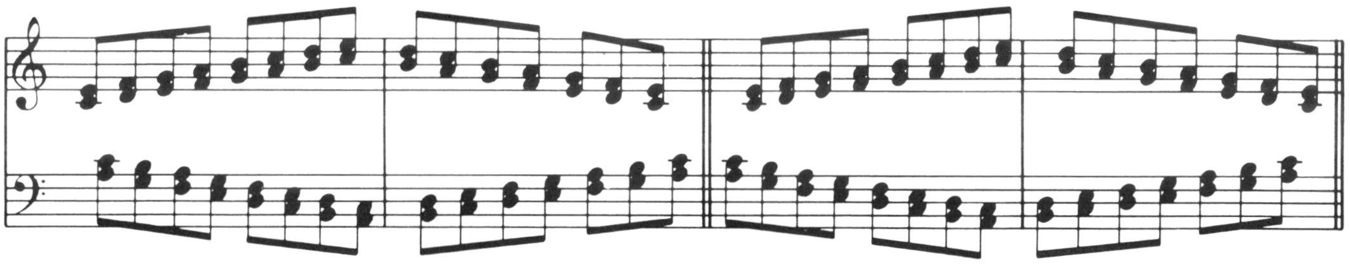

222 **223**

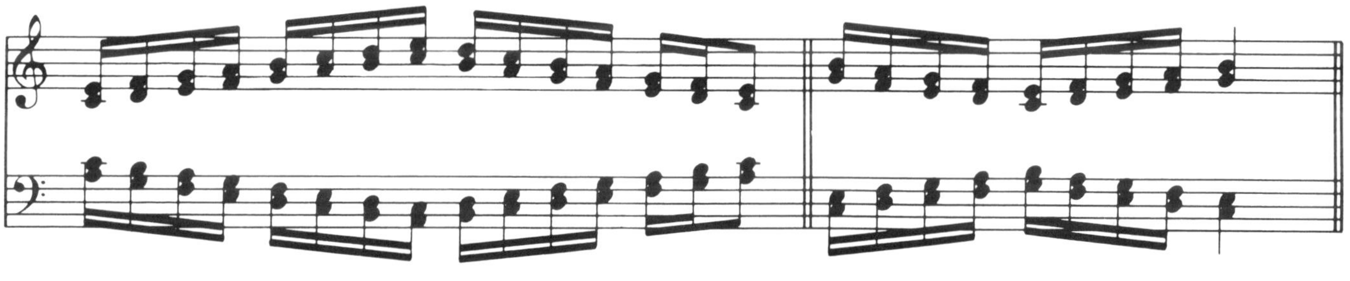

224

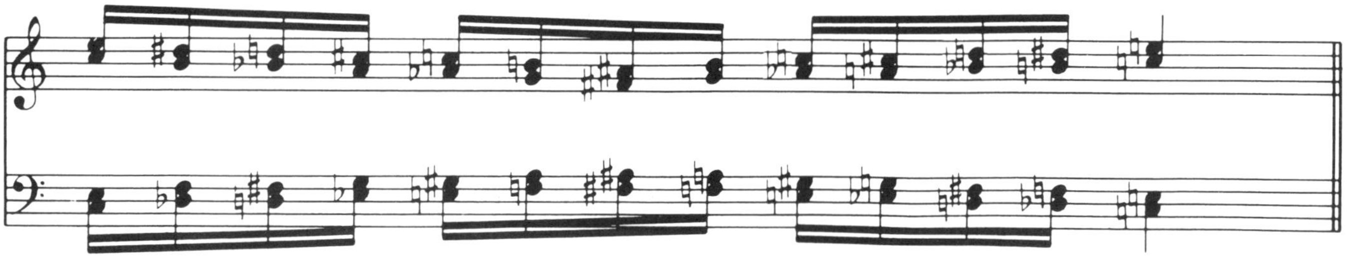

Exercises 225 – 256: These exercises are to be practiced one hand at a time. Start the left hand 8 bassa.

Remember that tension in the fingers reduces the
potential speed of interval changes.

Exercises 257—262: Begin these exercises one hand at a time. When putting both hands together, the feel of each part should not change.

Exercises 263—266 contain interlocking octaves similar to the type found in some of Gordon Stout's Etudes. The arm should not drop during the stroke: all of the power should come from the wrist.

264

265

266

Exercises 267 – 270: Chromatic octaves. The two handed versions are difficult because the hands remain crossed. The position will be less awkward if the shoulders are relaxed. Use double sticking for all E – F and B – C half steps. Similar passages can be found in the Helble Marimba Concerto. In addition to the indicated stickings, practice these exercises one hand at a time.

267 ♪ = 40 – ♩ = 104

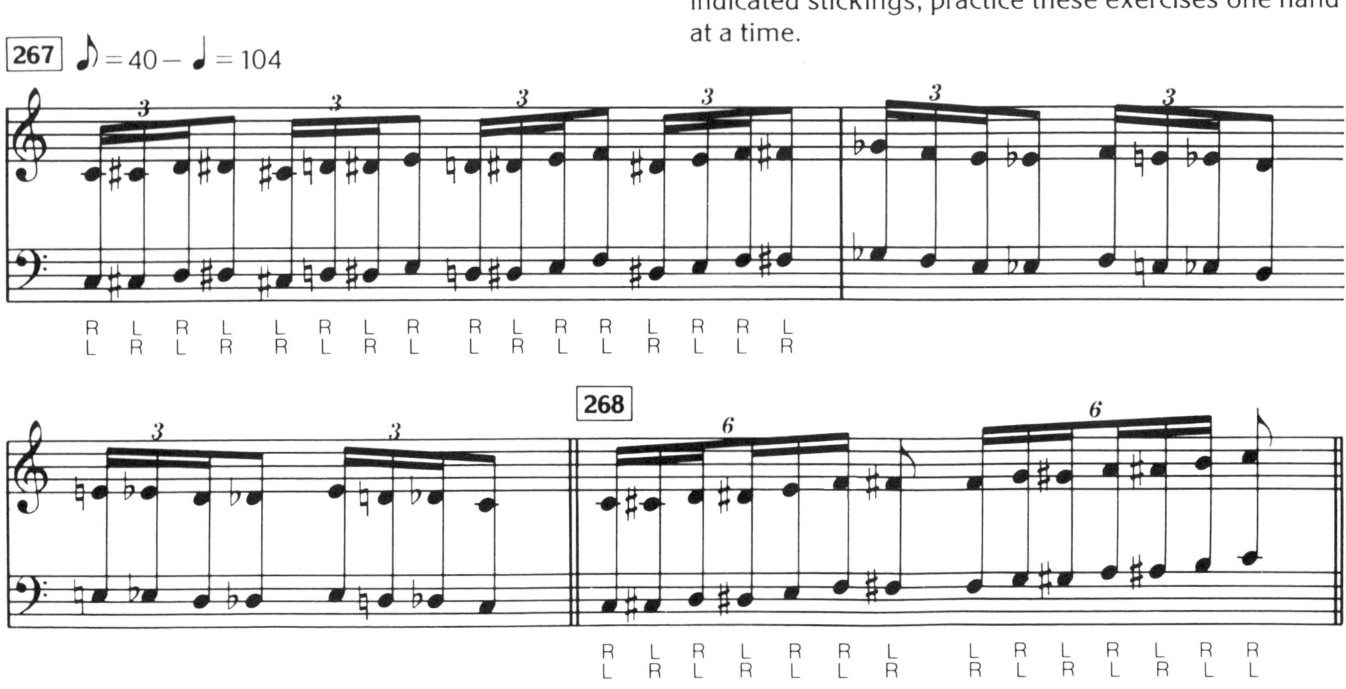

Exercise 271: One-handed octaves. This exercise is essential to the development of good octave technique.

Make sure that the hand position stays vertical and that the arm is not involved in the stroke. Start the right hand 8va.

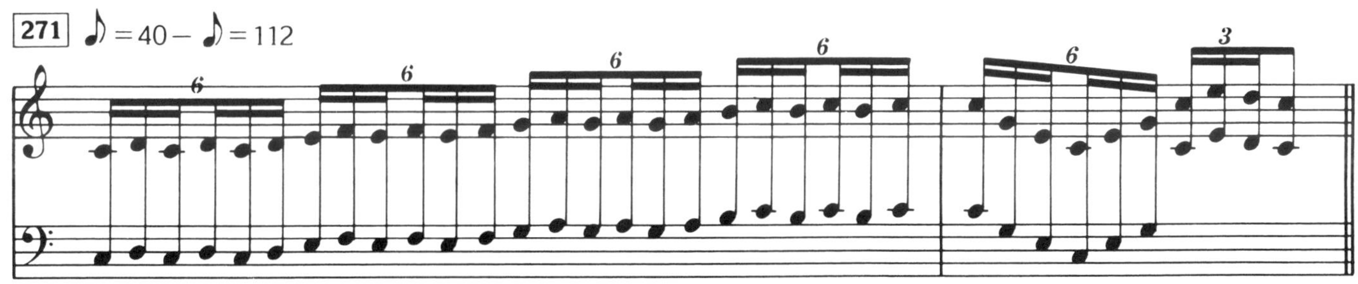

Exercise 272: Repeated interlocking octaves. Make sure that the second and fourth 16th notes speak as loudly as the first and third. Do not use the arm to produce power.

Exercises 273–278: Disjunct double vertical strokes. The problems here are footwork, sticking, and crossing hands. All six require giant-sized foot shifts. Ex. 275 and 276 also use reverse stickings — playing the higher pitch of a double vertical stroke with a lower numbered mallet or playing the lower pitch with a higher mallet. In some keys it is necessary to move a hand out of position to make room for the hand that is performing the cross. See the photographic examples of reverse stickings below.

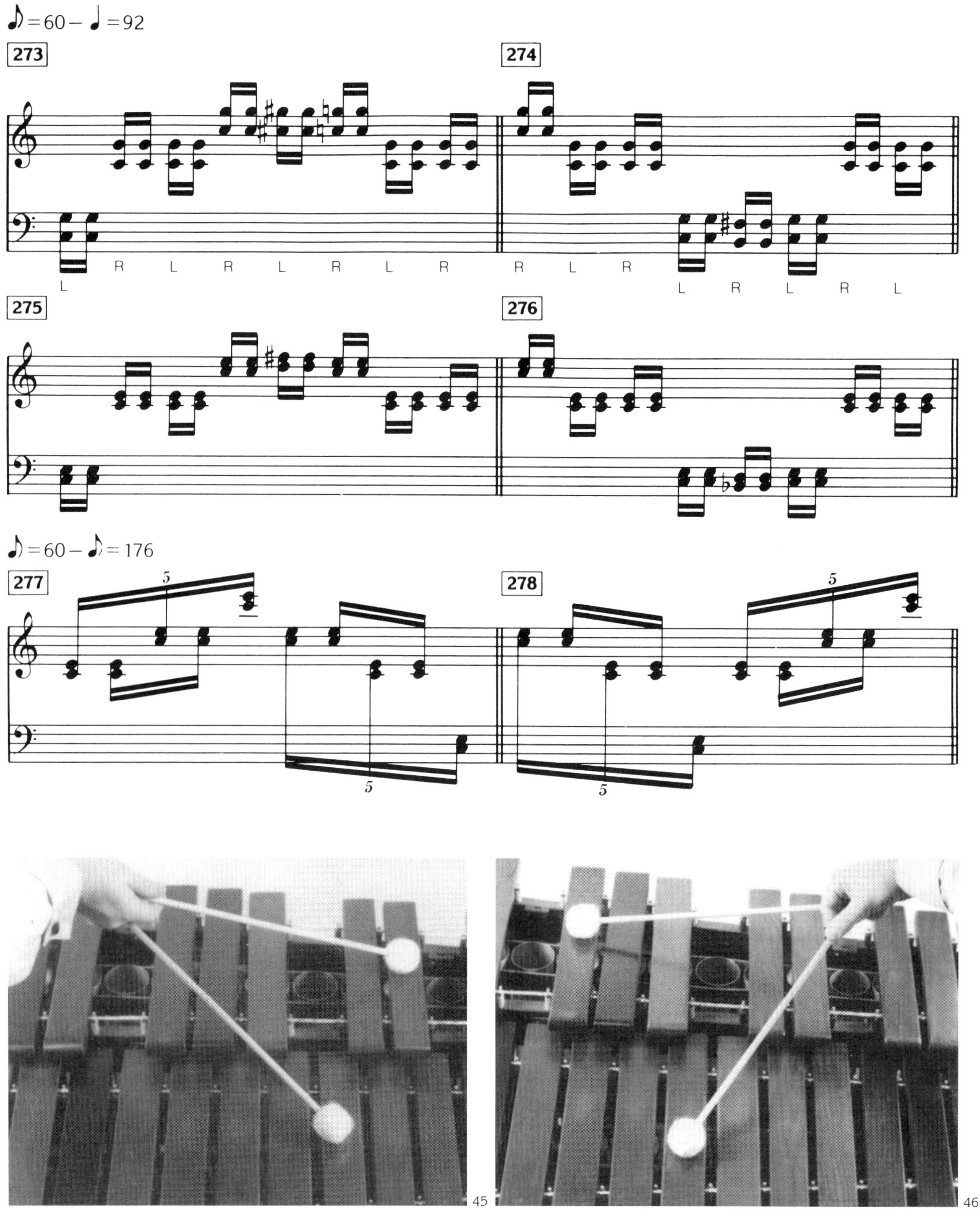

IV Double Lateral Strokes

Exercises 279—294 are preliminary studies to be practiced hands separately. Do not confuse the placement of the lateral stroke. The two pitches that are closest together **rhythmically** are played with one motion. Start the left hand 8 bassa. Transpose each exercise chromatically through the twelve keys.

Exercises 295 — 326 are double lateral strokes with shifts and interval changes. Exercise 317 introduces alternating double lateral strokes: inside to outside and outside to inside. All shifts should be part of the recovery of the second pitch of each double lateral:

X = Double lateral stroke   Y = Shift

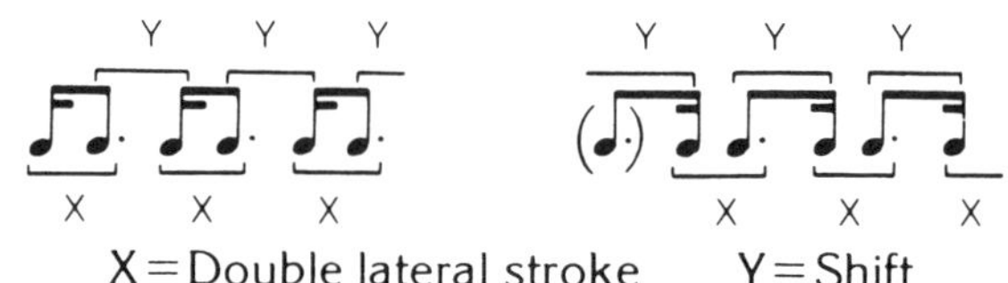

♩ = 96 – ♩ = 208

295   296

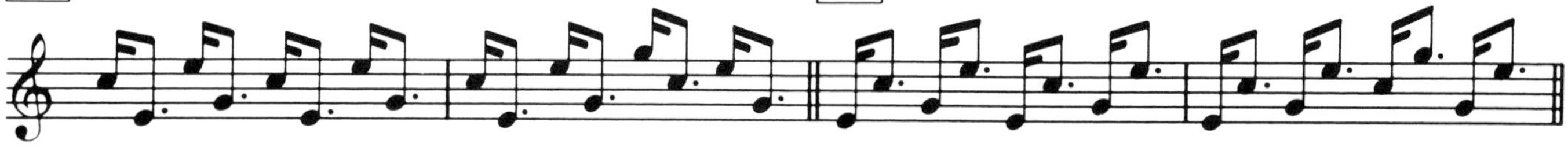

297   298

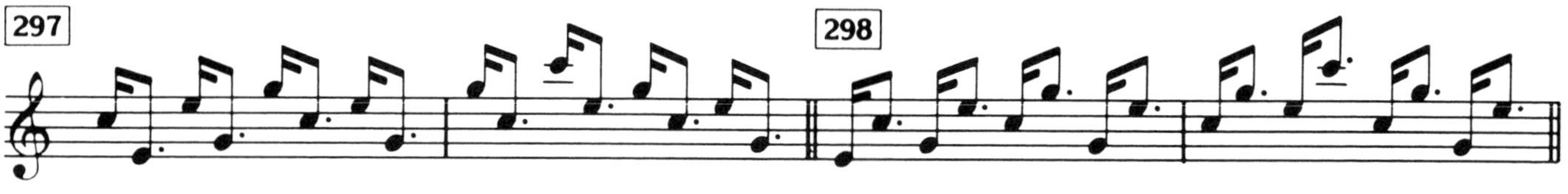

299   300

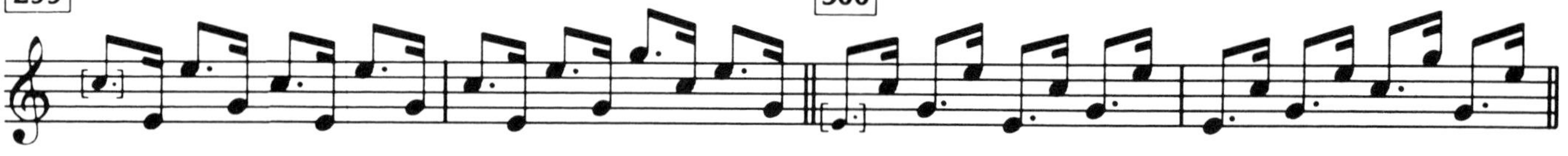

[ ] 2nd time only

301   302

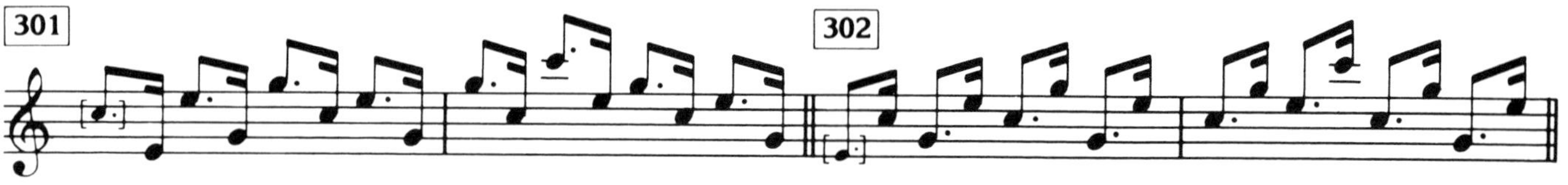

303   304

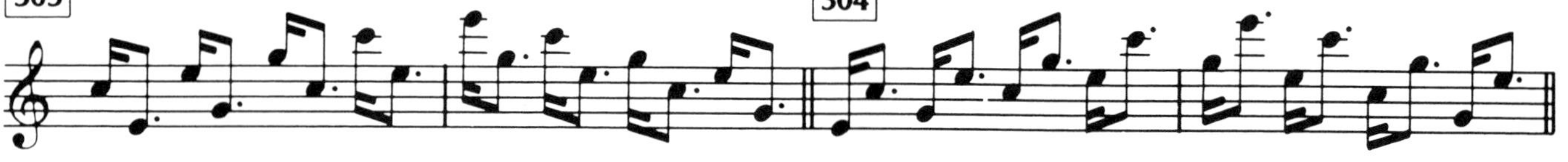

305   306

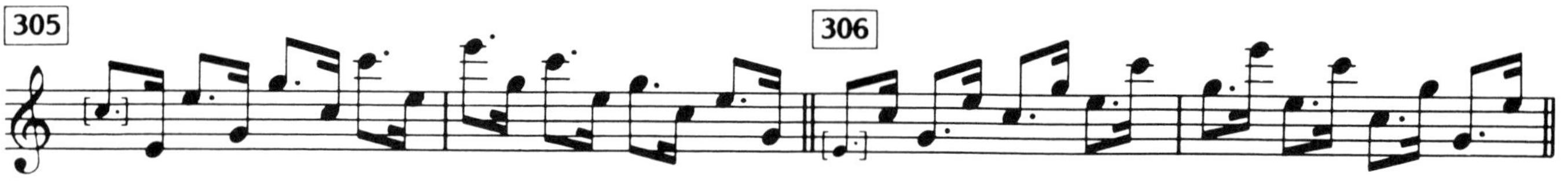

307   308

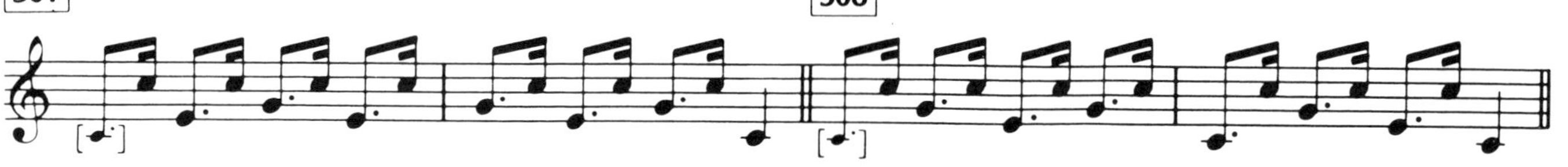

Exercises 327 – 382: These exercises are based on the eight sticking permutations of double lateral strokes.

♩ = 100 – ♩ = 168

327 328 329 330

331 332 333 334

Exercises 335 – 342: Shifts are introduced.

335 336

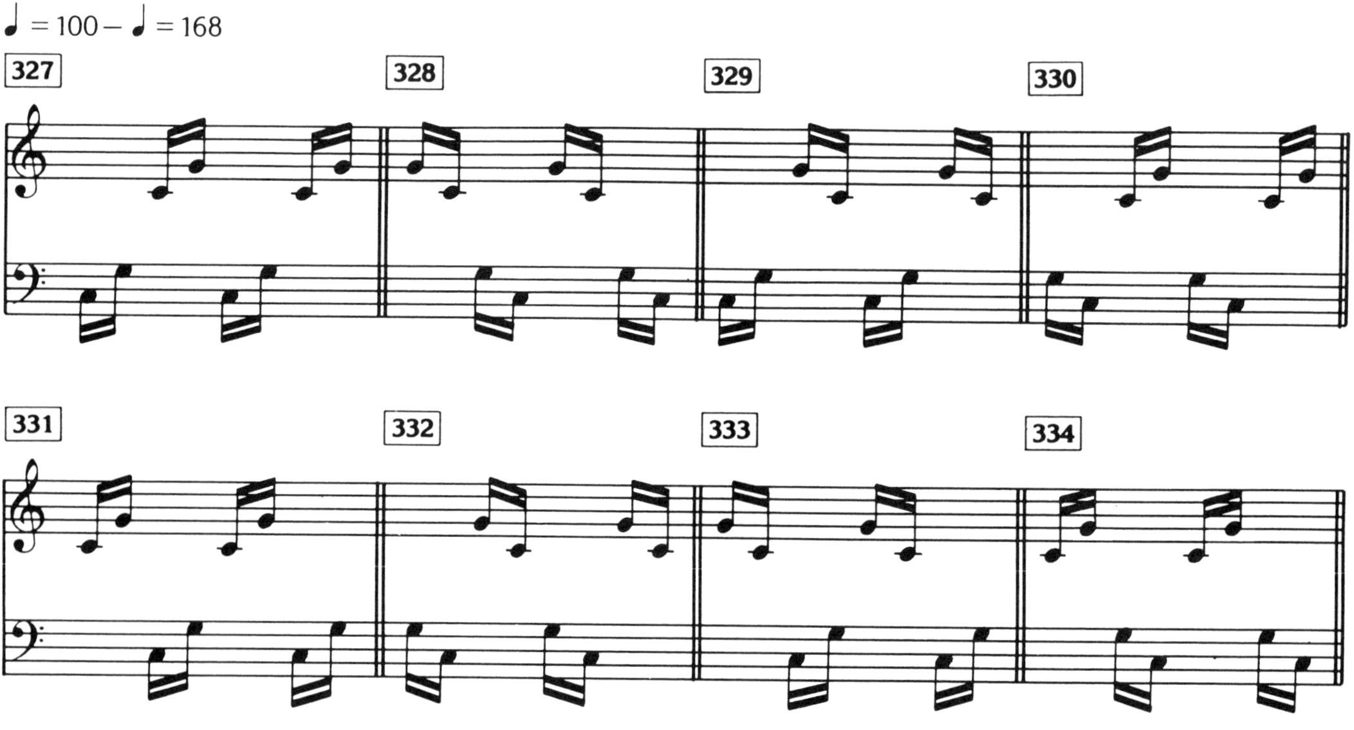

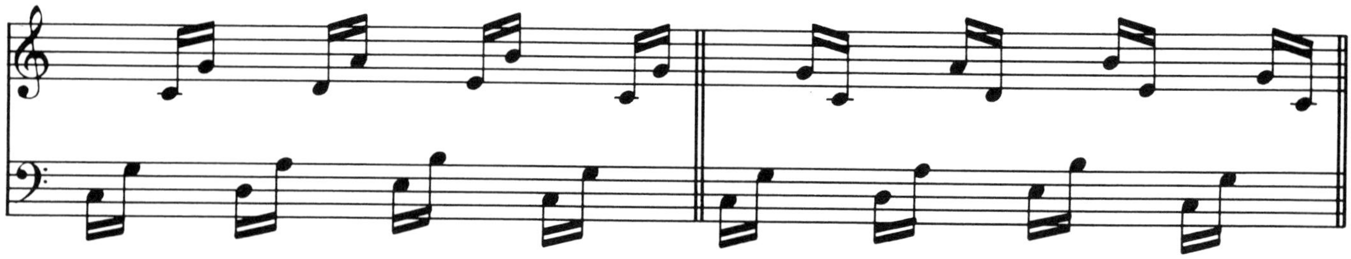

337 338

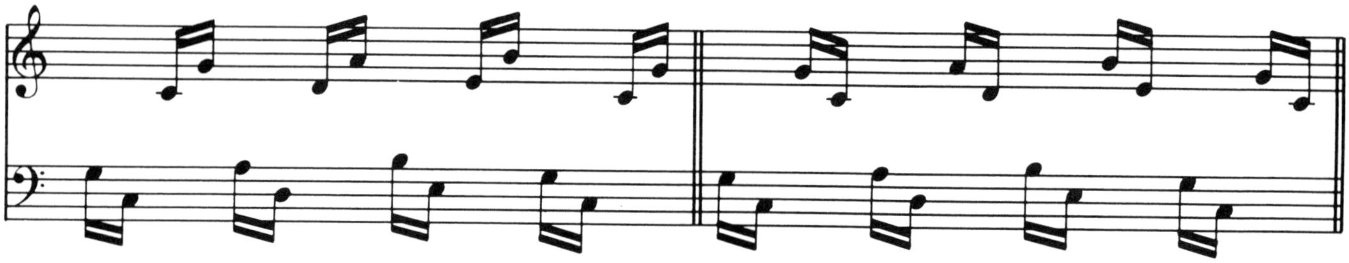

339 340

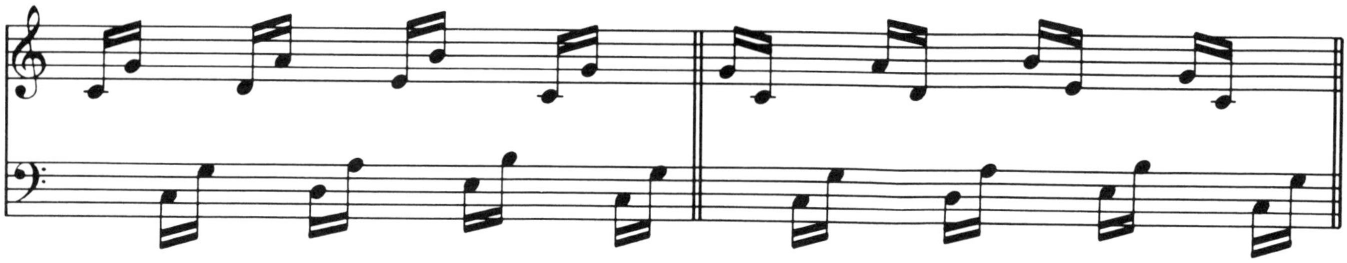

341 342

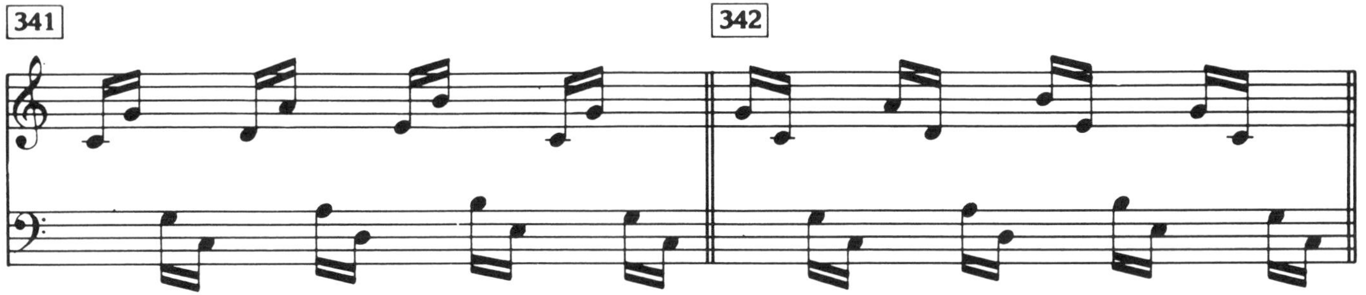

The next eight exercises cannot be transposed a full octave.

343 344 345 346

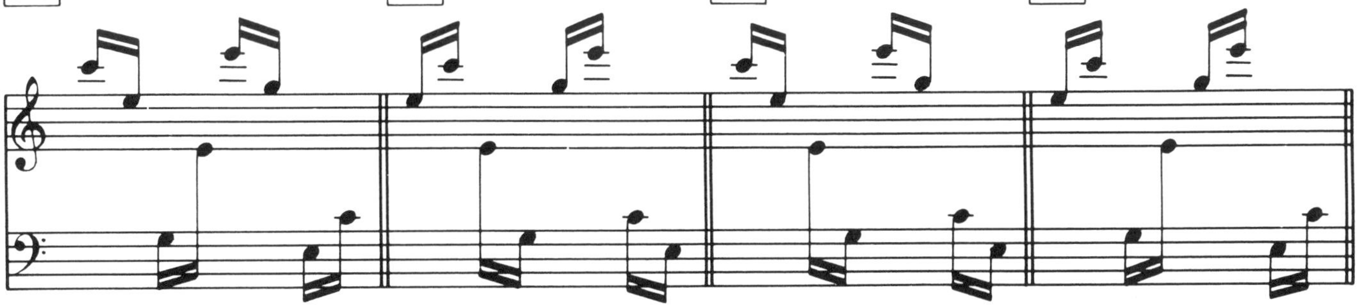

347 348 349 350

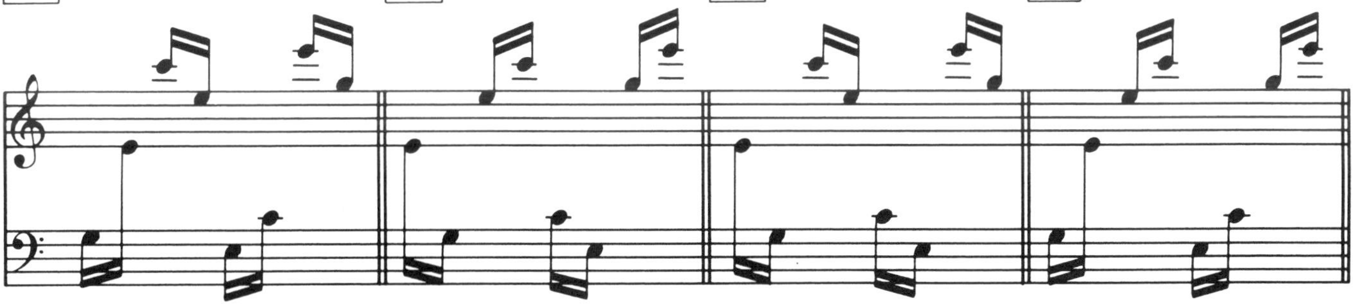

351 352

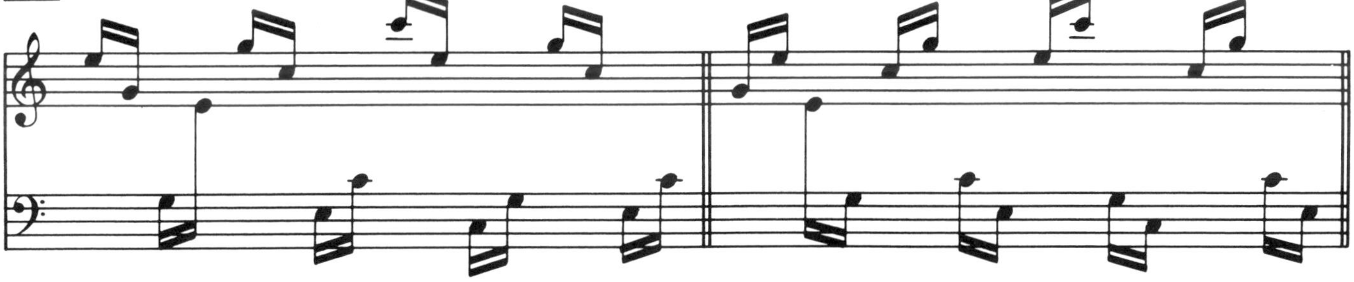

353 354

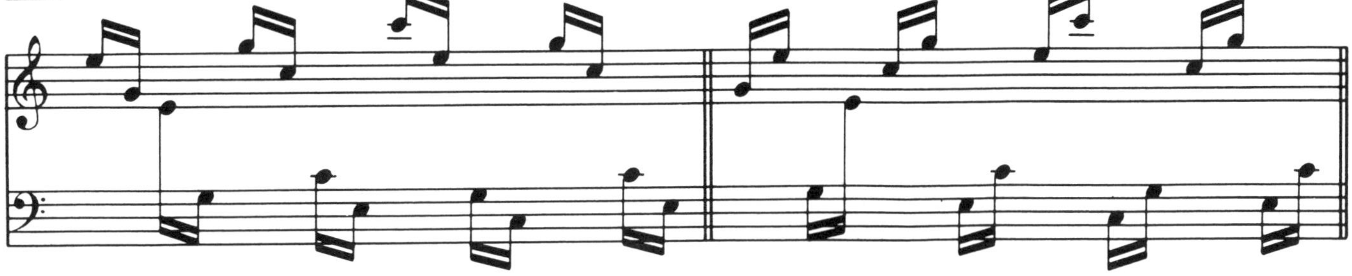

Exercises 359 – 374 are similar to 343 – 358 except the intervals are smaller.

$\quad \downarrow = 100 - \downarrow = 168$

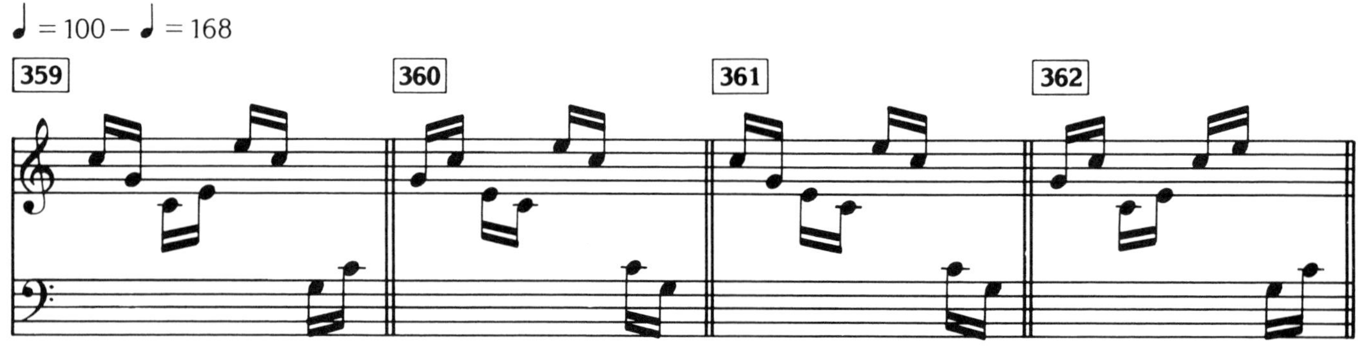

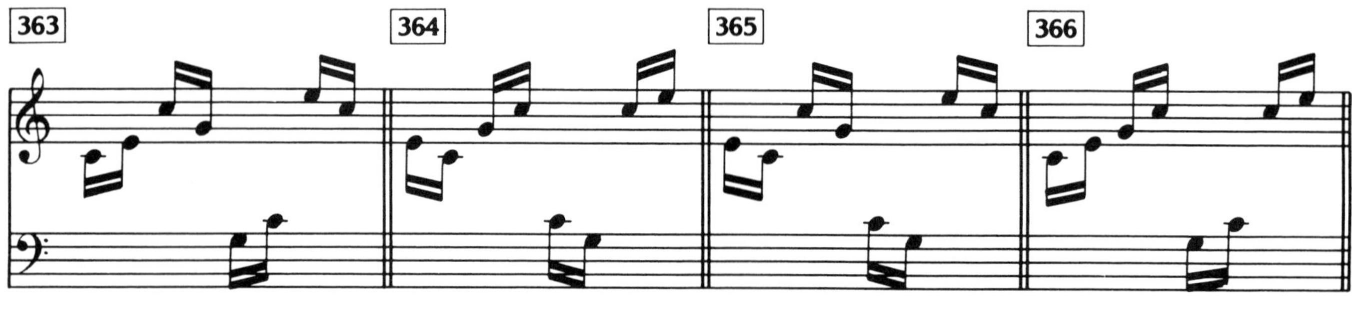

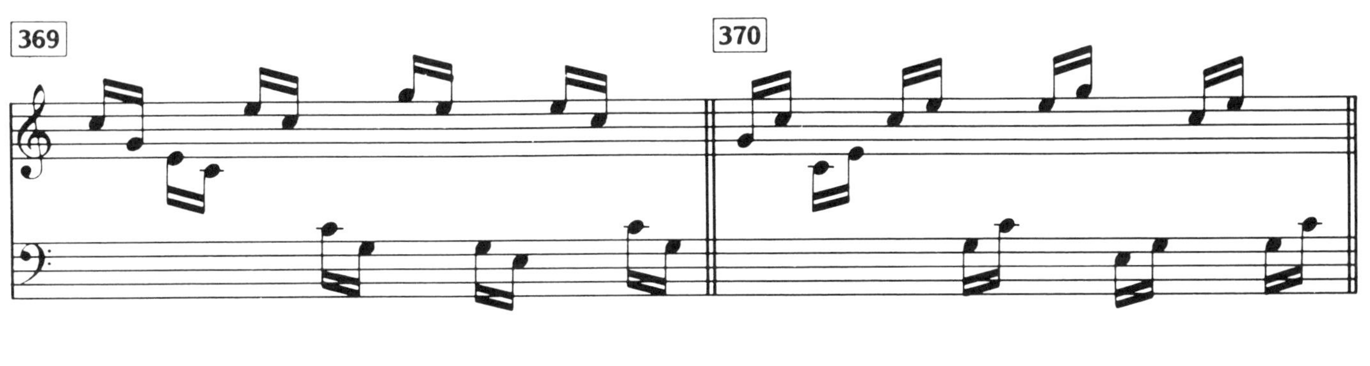

Exercises 375 – 382: The pattern is extended.

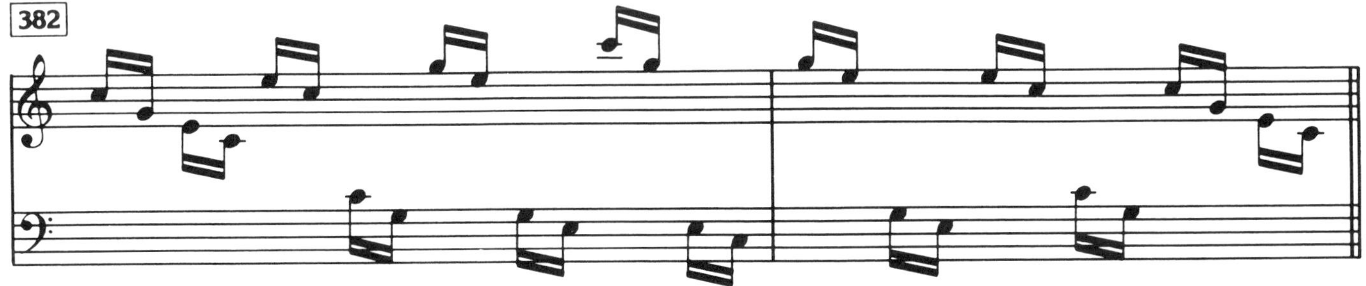

Exercises 383 – 402 are in rhythmic unison. They may be more difficult than the previous sets because of the simultaneous shifts.

♩ = 72 – ♩ = 144

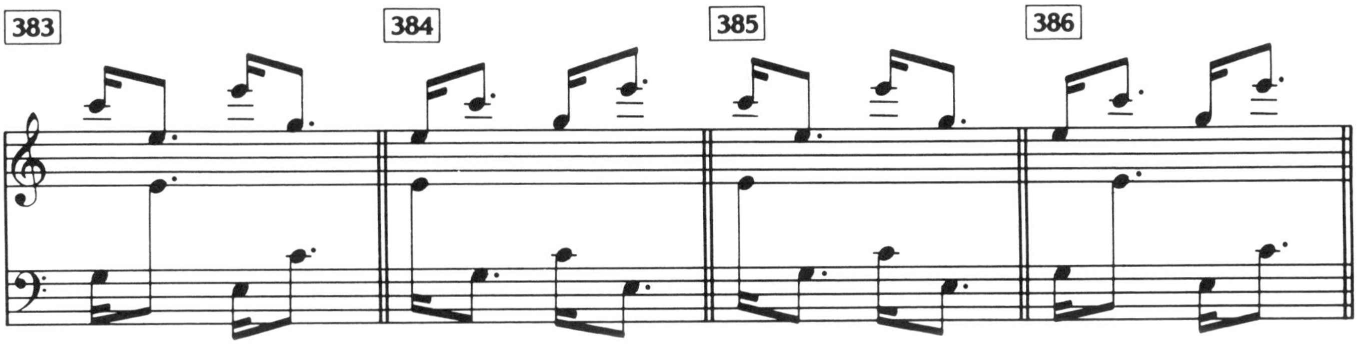

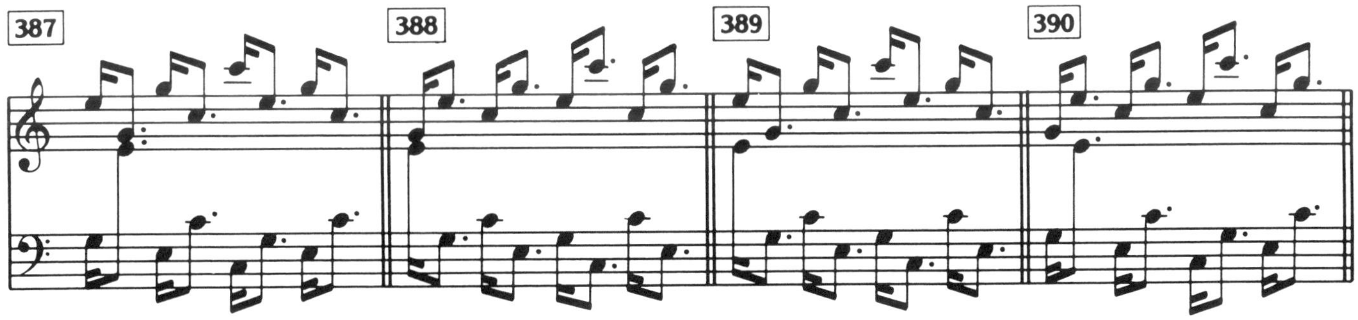

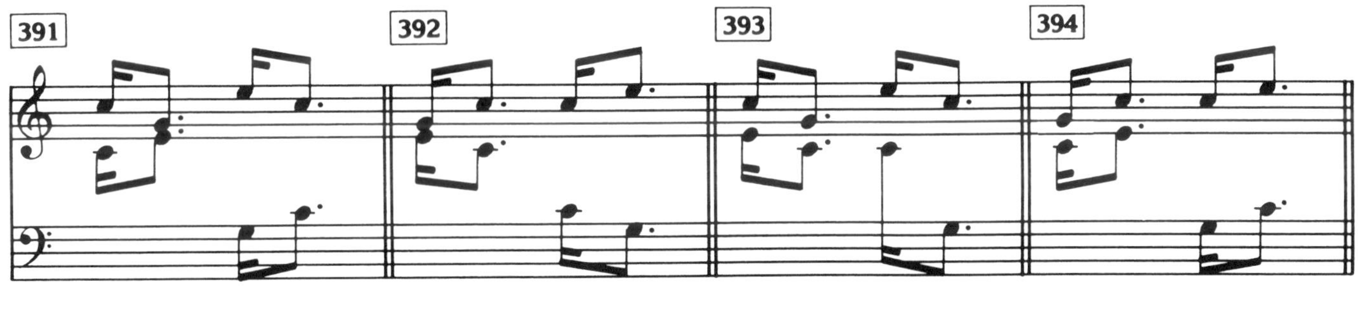

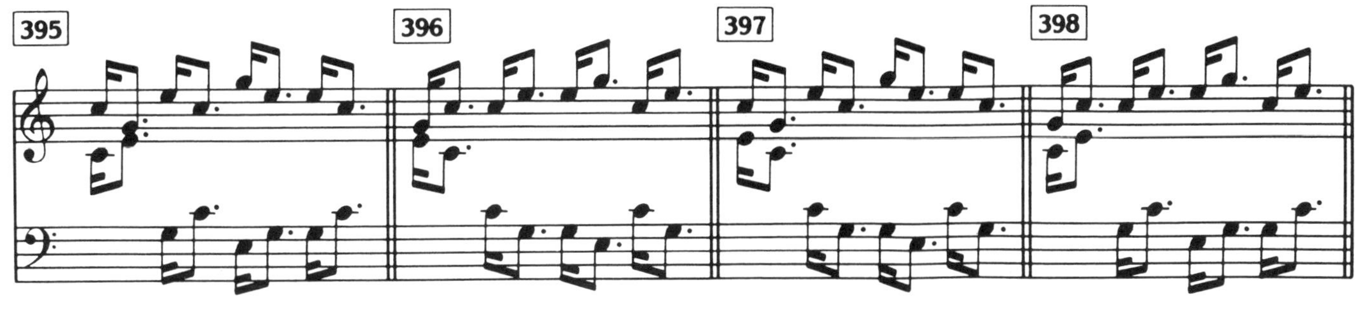

399 **400**

401 **402**

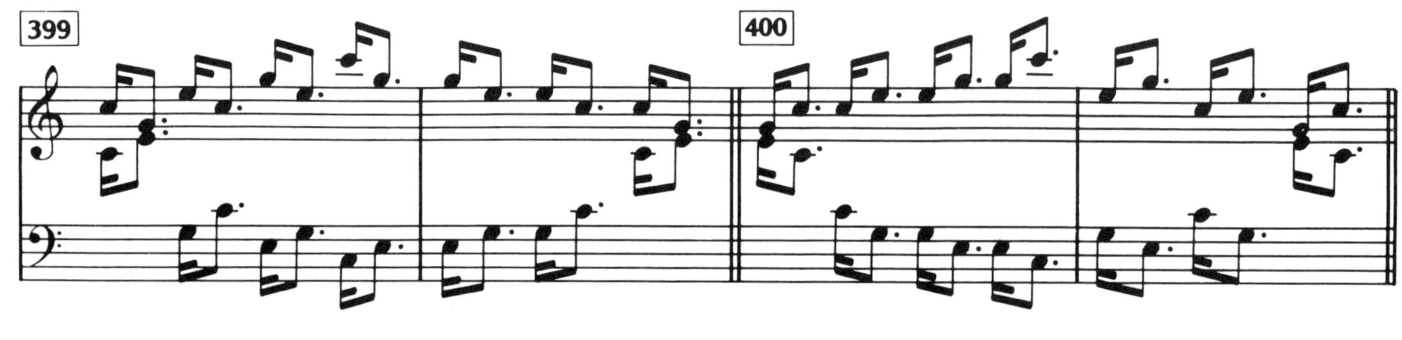

Exercises 403 — 410: Double laterals with large interval changes. Pay close attention to the elbow movements. Do not accent the octaves or allow the small intervals to diminuendo.

♪ = 72 – ♩ = 144

403 **404**

405 **406**

407 **408**

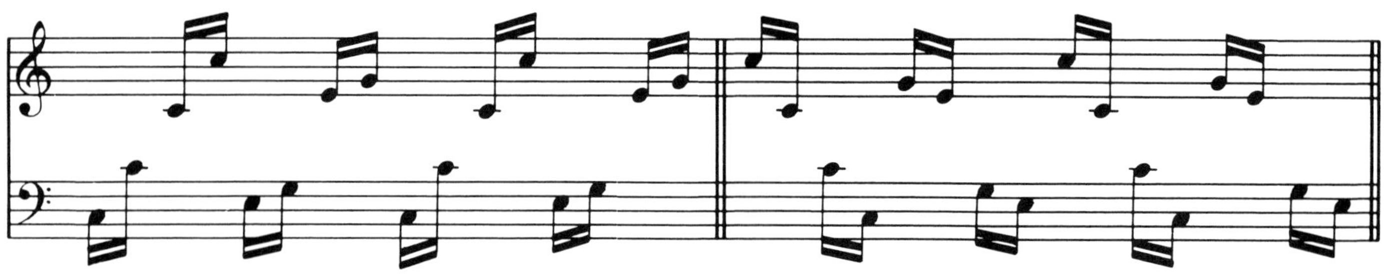

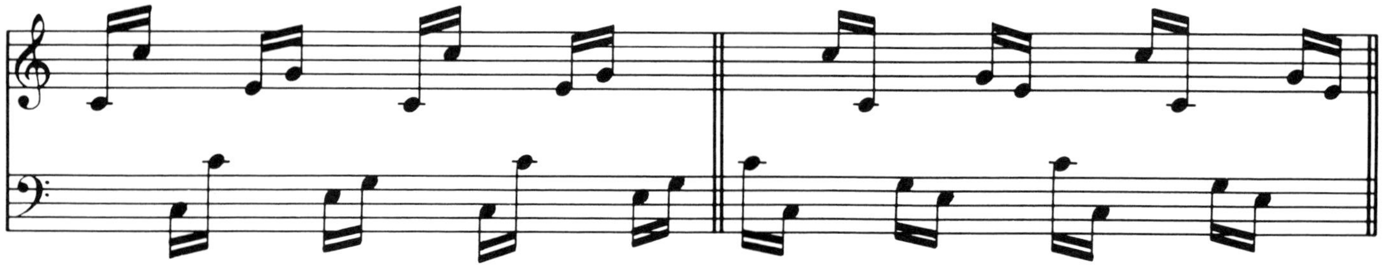

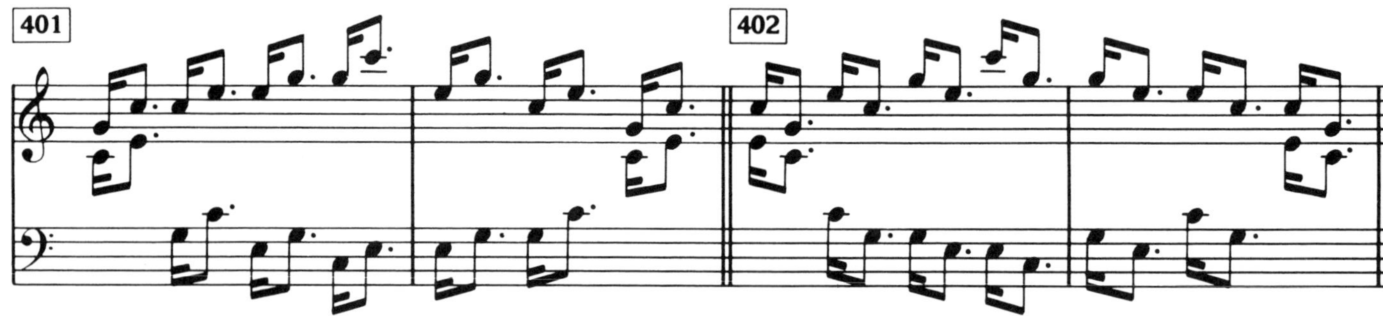

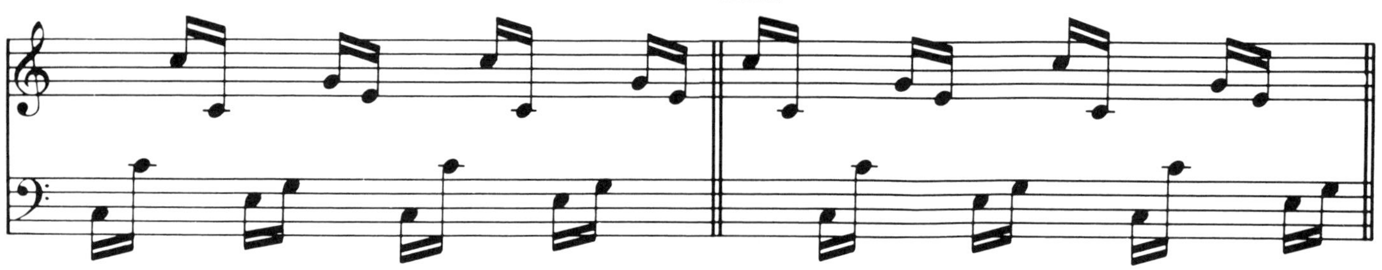

409

410

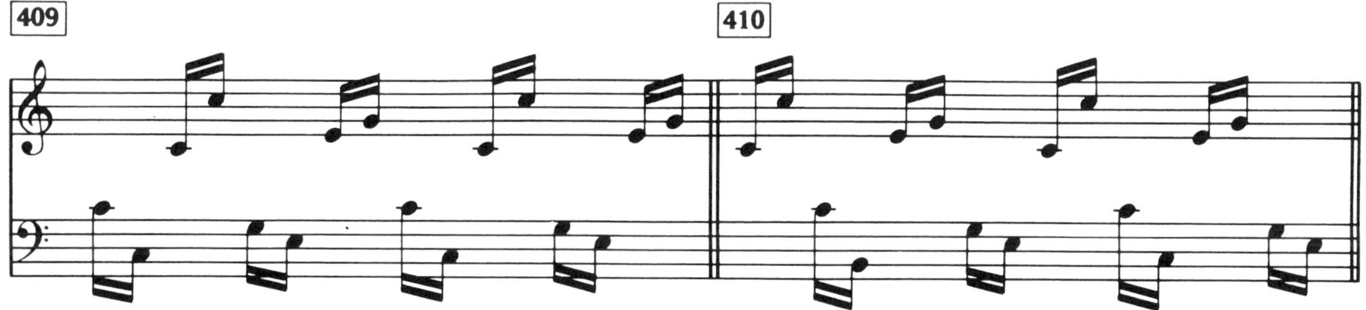

By changing the order of the pitches, the other seven double lateral stroke permutations may be applied to exercises 411 to 414.

♩ = 72 – ♩ = 184

411

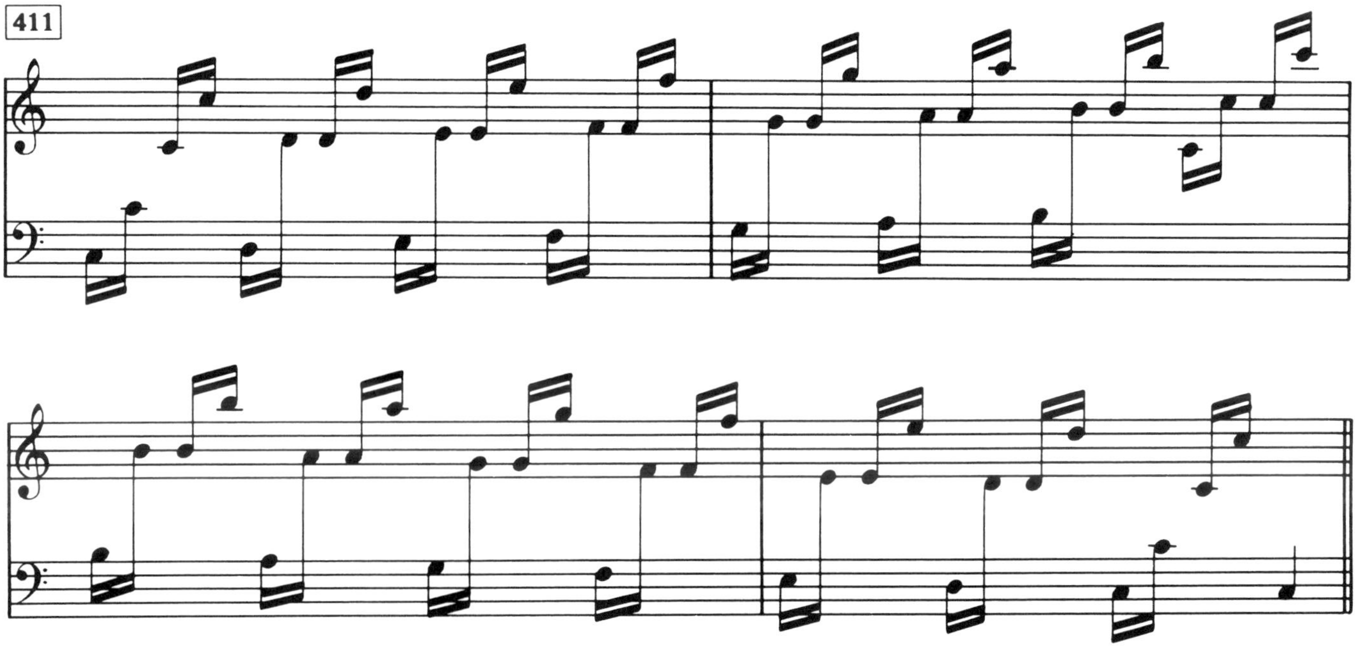

412

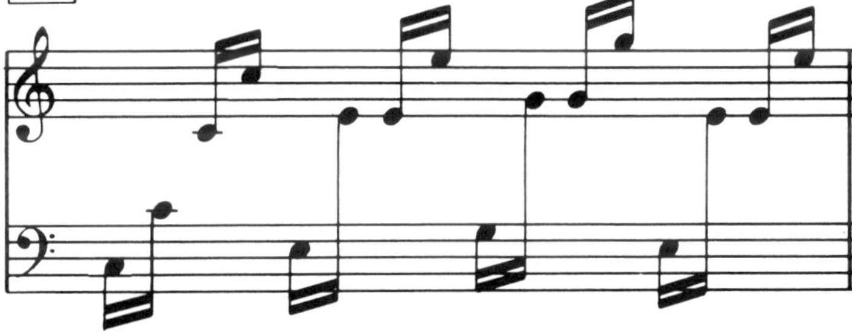

413

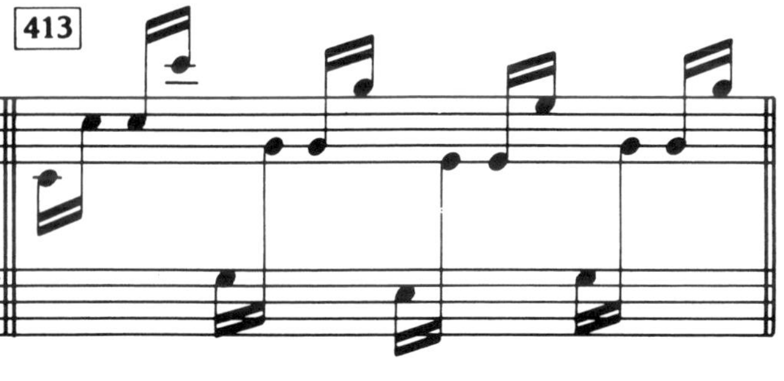

414

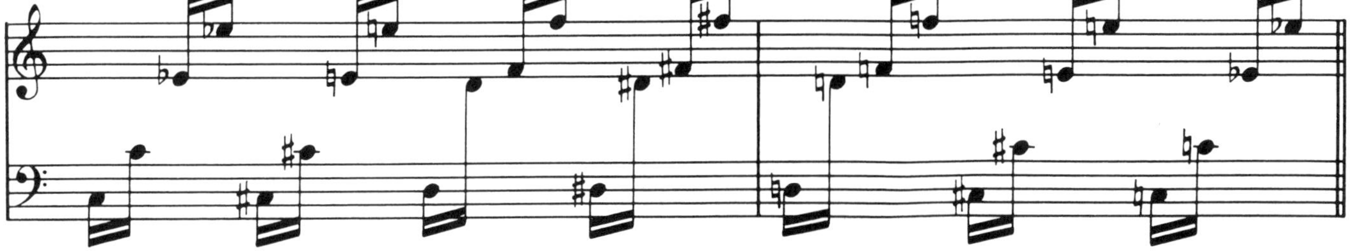

V Mixed Strokes

Exercises 415 — 424: Single alternating and single independent strokes. Exercises 415 — 418 prepare the performance of the changing note double stickings in 419 — 424. For now use the wrist for all the single independent strokes. When reviewing these exercises, add fingers to the wrist motion. Repeat and transpose chromatically through the twelve keys.

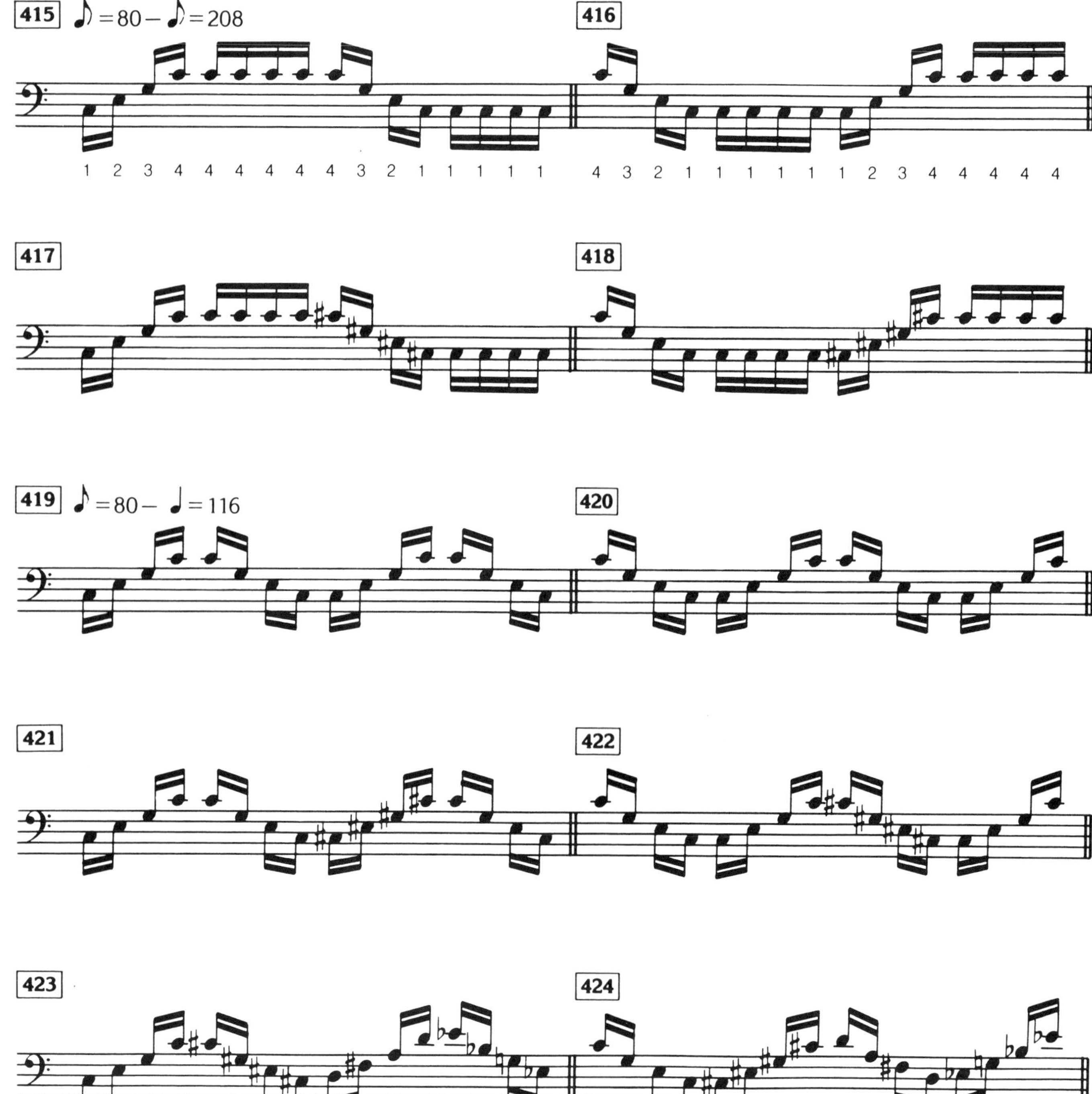

Exercises 425 & 426 are similar to the previous ones except they cover a larger range.

♪ = 80 – ♩ = 104

425

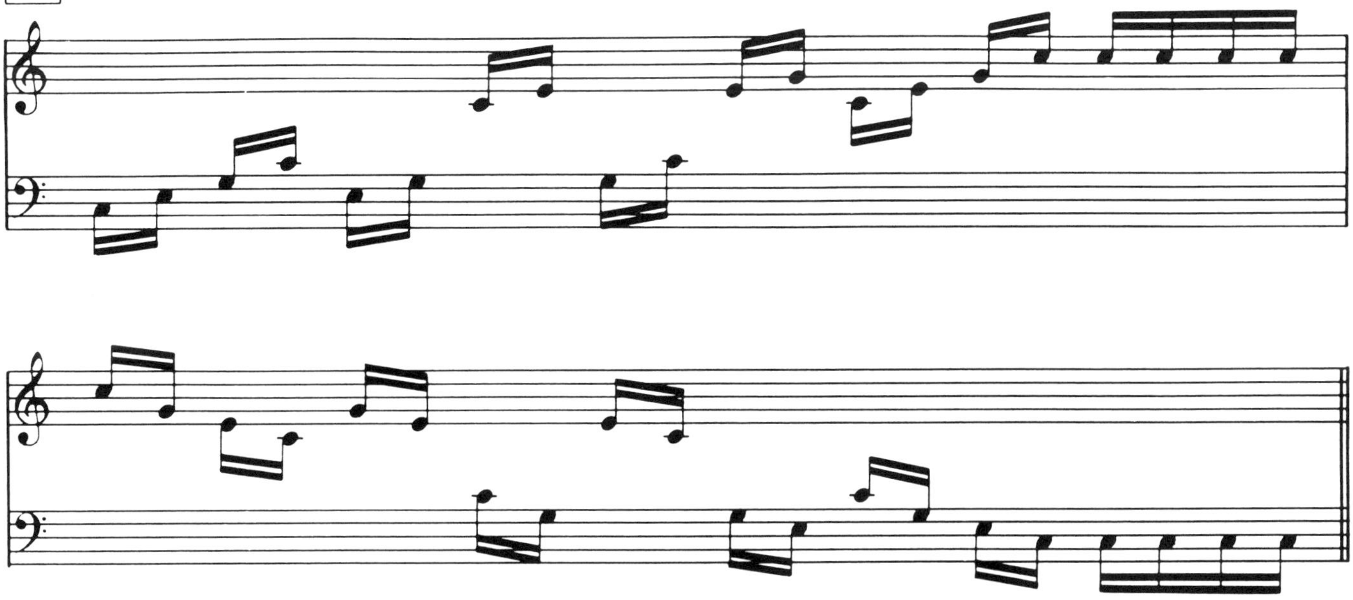

426

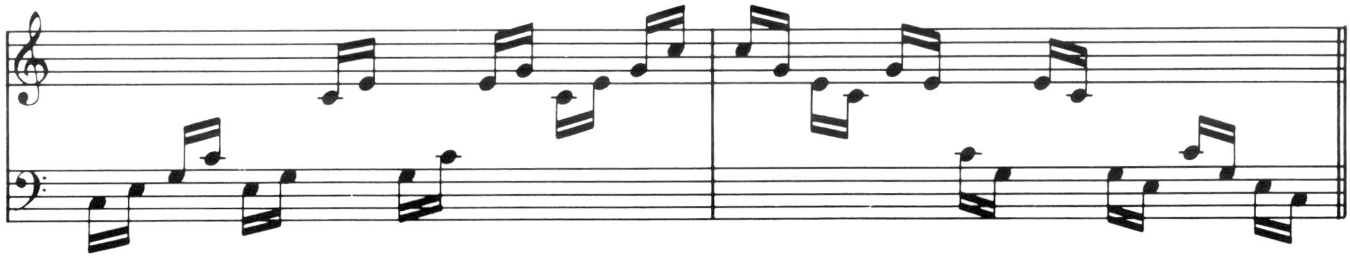

Exercise 427: Apply other sticking permutations.

427

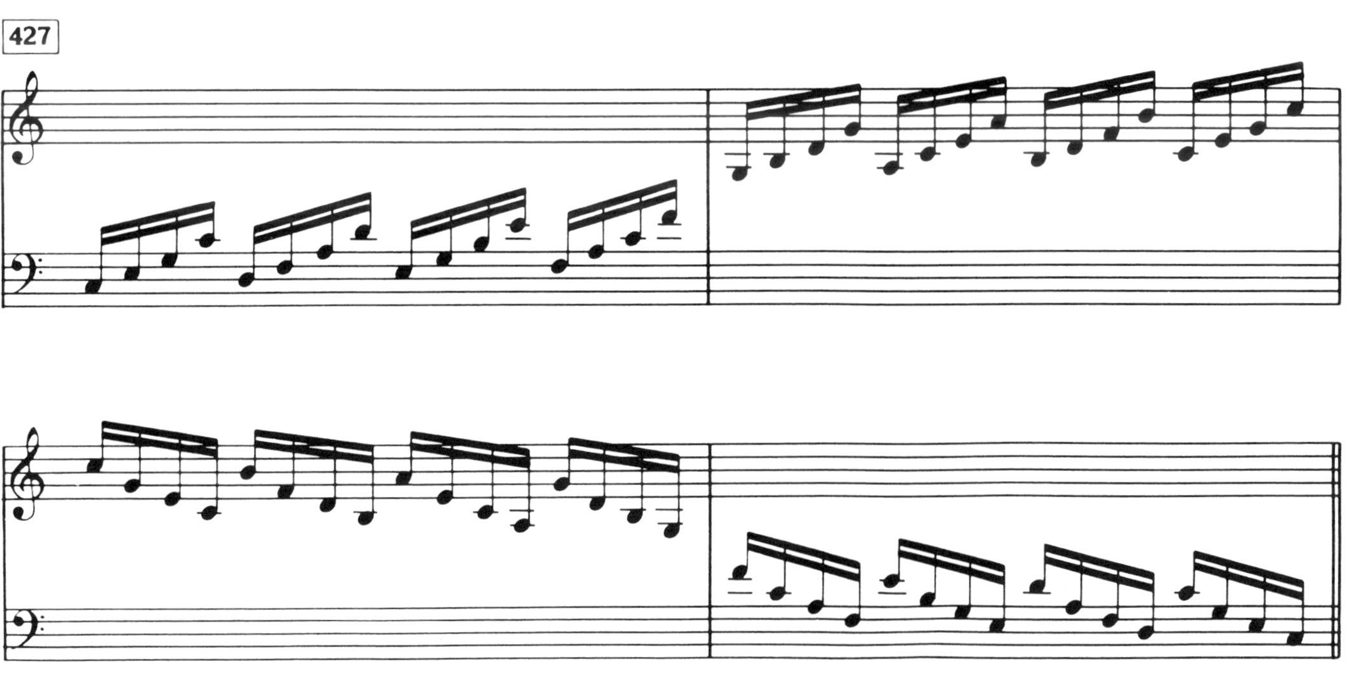

Triplet arpeggios. Exercises 428 & 429 are preparation for exercise 430. The first sticking pattern in Ex. 430 has half as many shifts as the second two patterns.

Arpeggio figures of this type are found in great abundance in Raymond Helble's Grand Fantasy.

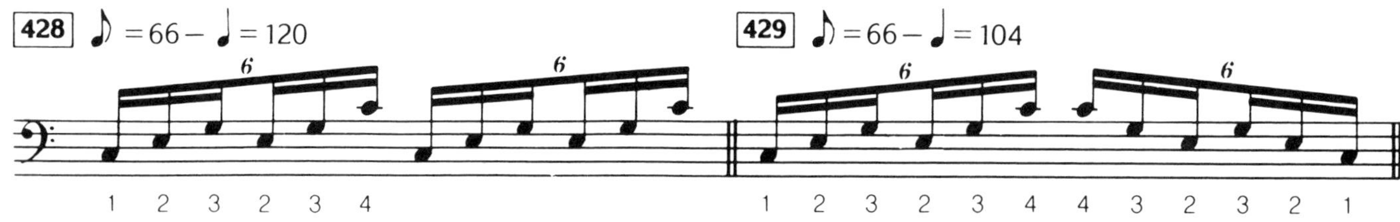

Use only one foot shift ascending and one foot shift descending. Also try 123 ascending and 432 descending. This sticking uses only the easier outside double laterals.

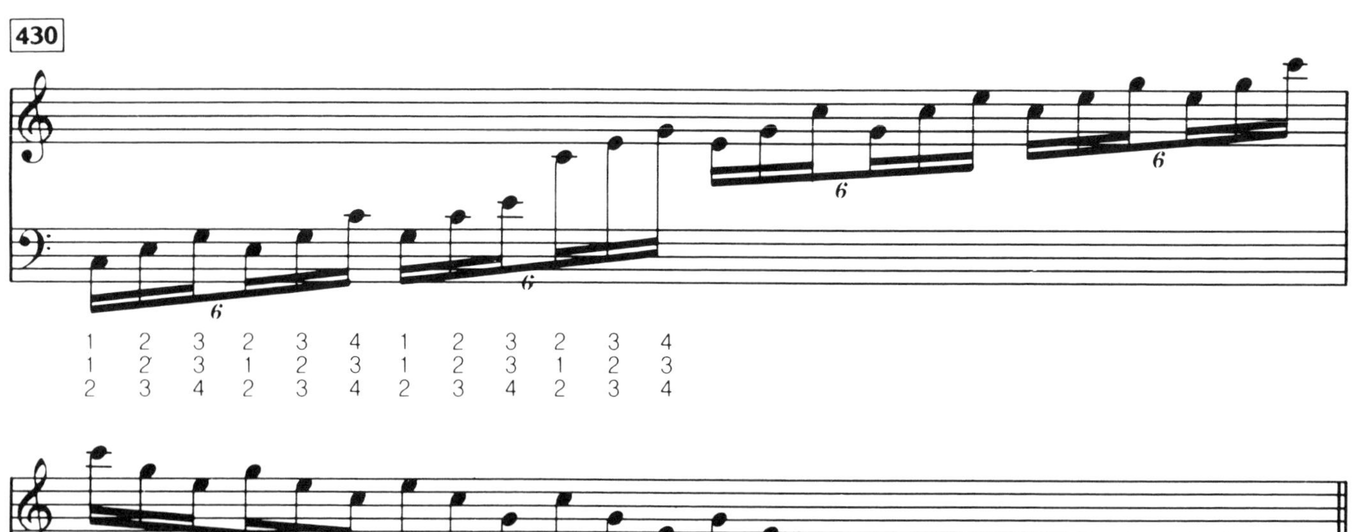

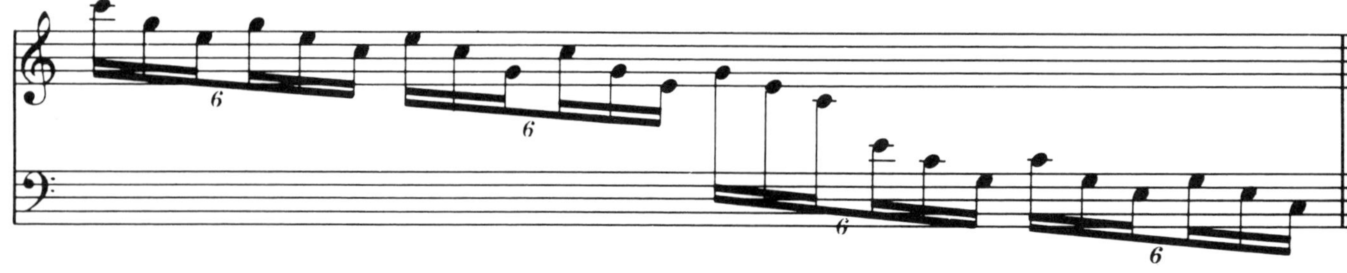

Exercise 431: Two octave arpeggios. The sticking pattern 1234234 works in all keys except B flat major. The other patterns listed are alternate stickings.

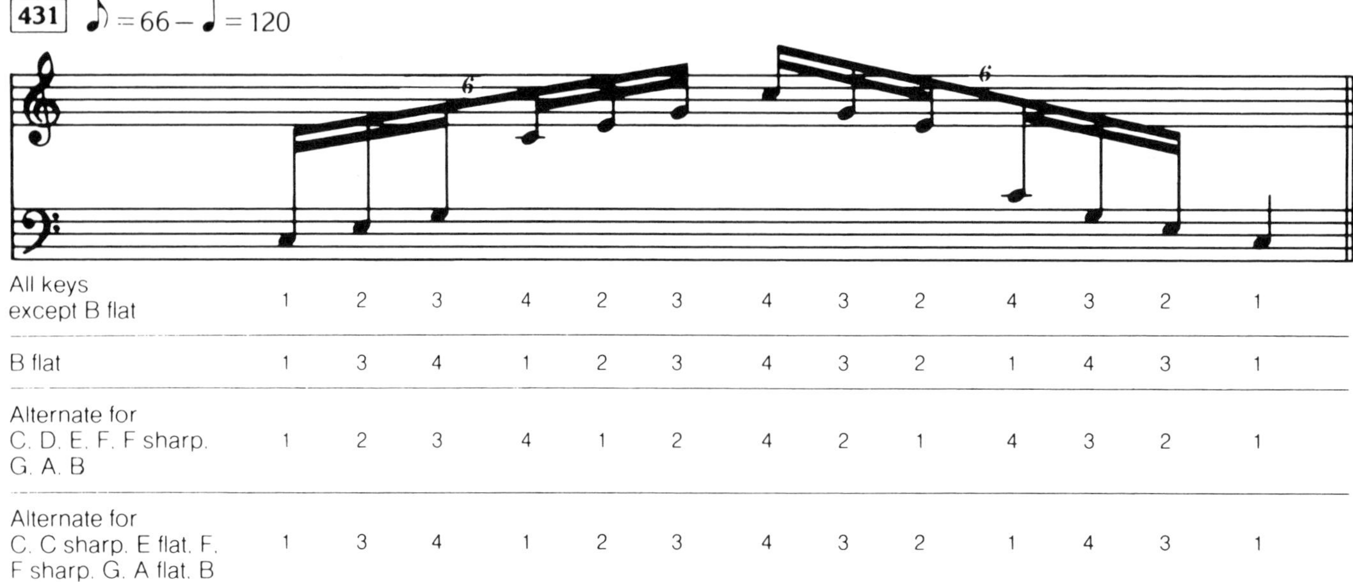

All keys except B flat	1	2	3	4	2	3	4	3	2	4	3	2	1
B flat	1	3	4	1	2	3	4	3	2	1	4	3	1
Alternate for C. D. E. F. F sharp. G. A. B	1	2	3	4	1	2	4	2	1	4	3	2	1
Alternate for C. C sharp. E flat. F. F sharp. G. A flat. B	1	3	4	1	2	3	4	3	2	1	4	3	1

Exercises 432—447: Combined double vertical and double lateral strokes. The double laterals change intervals. In exercise 440 the double vertical stroke starts to change intervals. Pay close attention to the changing **direction** of the double laterals.

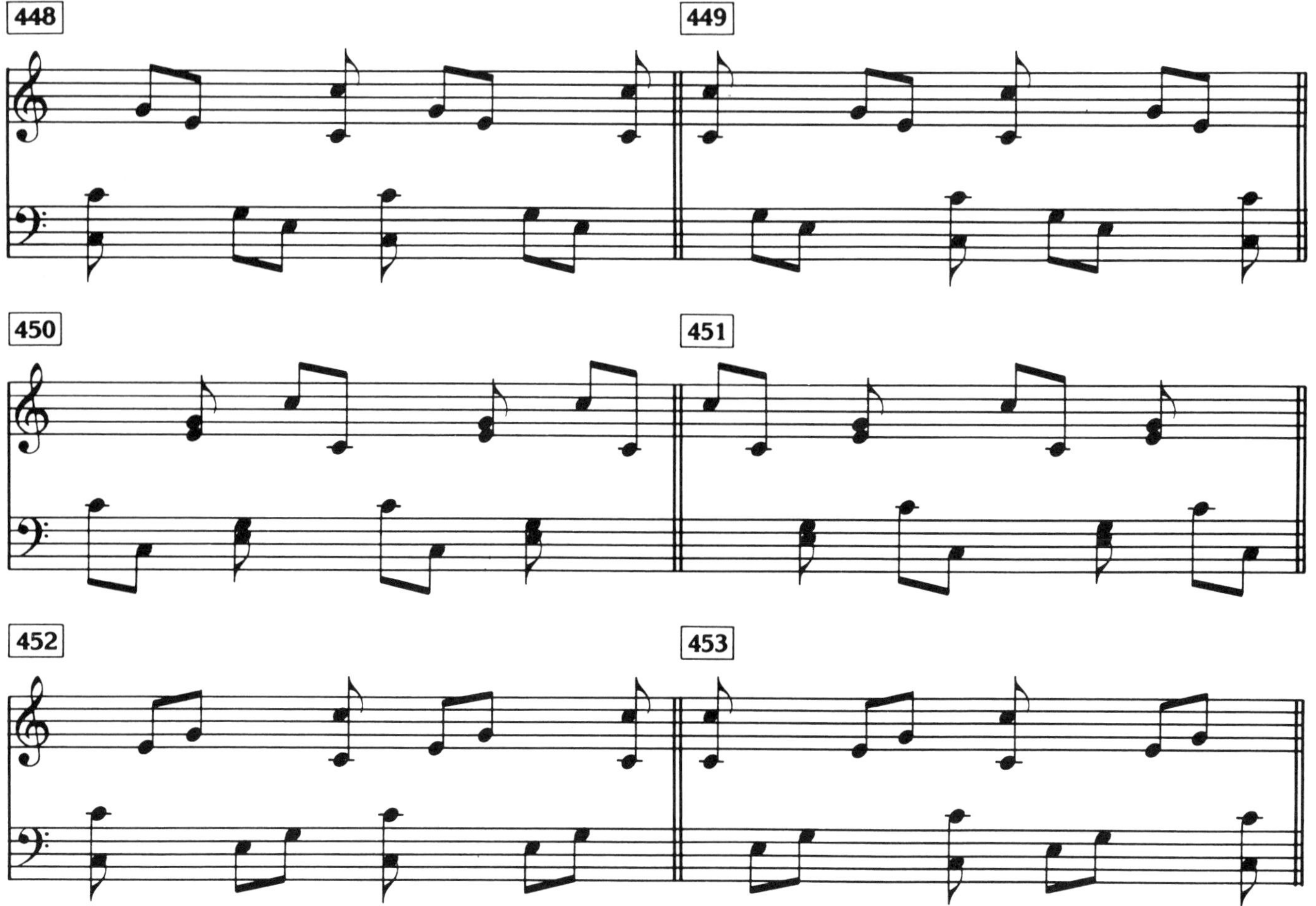

442
443 
444
445 
446
447 
Exercises 448 – 455: Each **hand** alternates double vertical and double lateral.
448
449
450
451
452
453

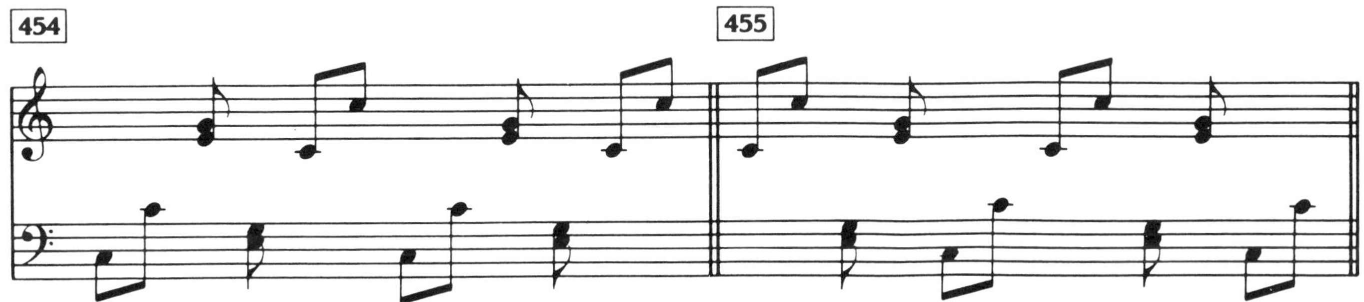

Exercises 456—461: Single, double vertical, and double lateral strokes combined. It would be wise to practice these exercises hands separately until the motions feel natural. One of the main problems is to time the attack of the single stroke on the first beat exactly with the beginning of the double lateral in the other hand.

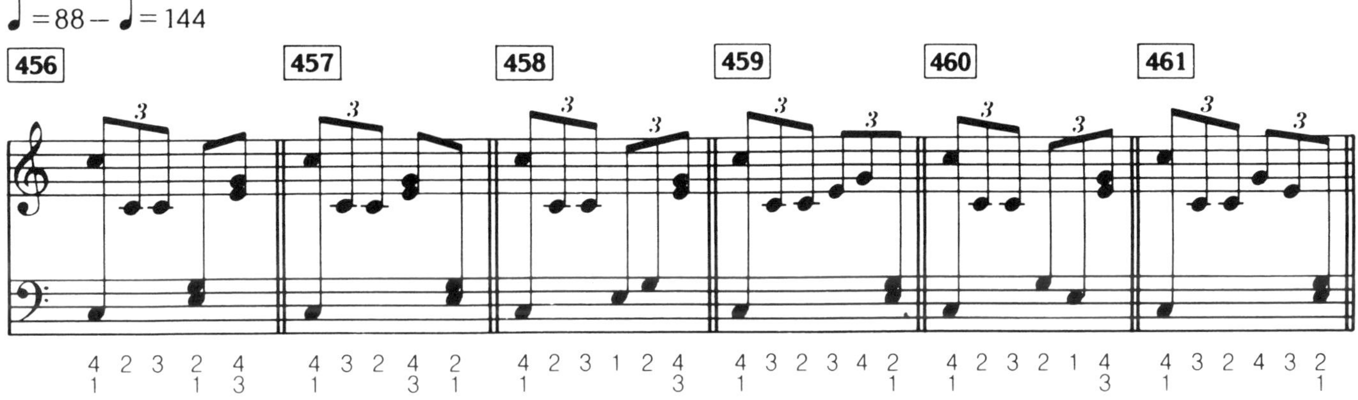

Disjunct double laterals. Exercises 462—477 contain large leaps and large interval changes. Do not confuse the placement of the double lateral stroke. The stroke placement in the moving hand is obvious but not so in the other. The stationary hand starts the pattern with a single stroke and then plays **only** double **inside** strokes.

470 471 472 473

474 475 476 477

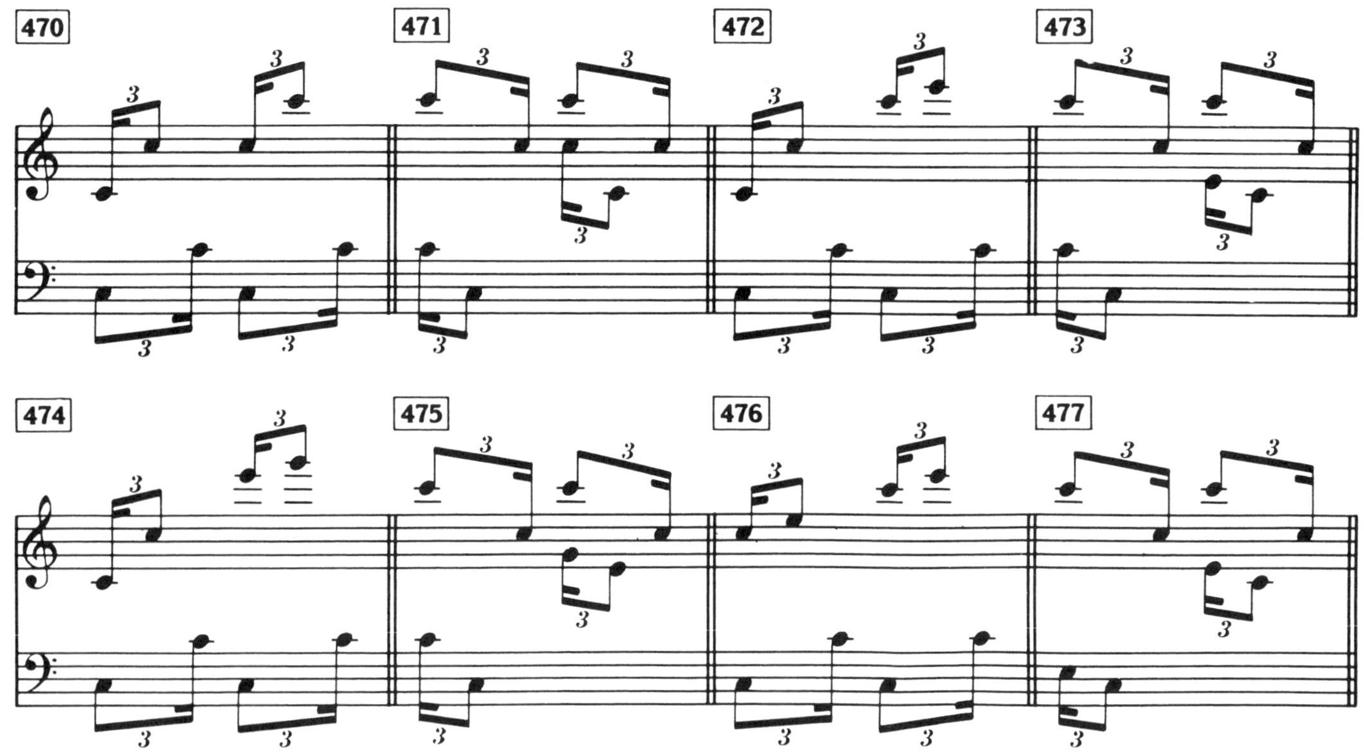

Exercises 478 – 485: Here again is a concealed double lateral stroke. Every third and fourth 16th note of each sextuplet begins a double lateral stroke. The double laterals of each hand are therefore one 16th apart.

♪ = 72 – ♪ = 168

478 479

480 481

482 483

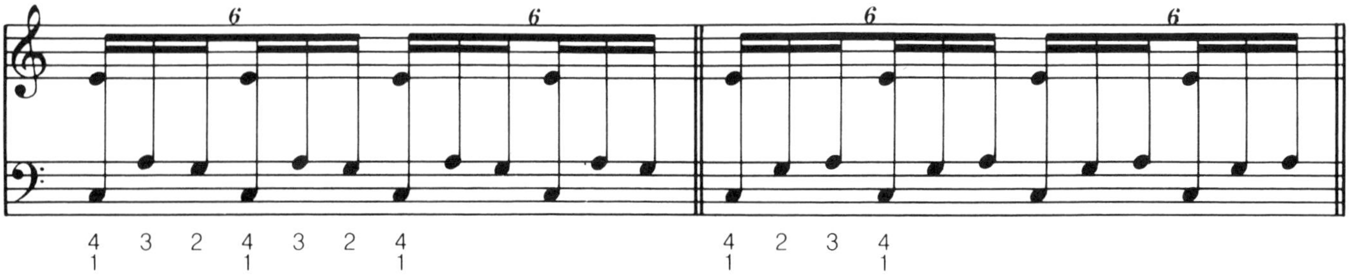

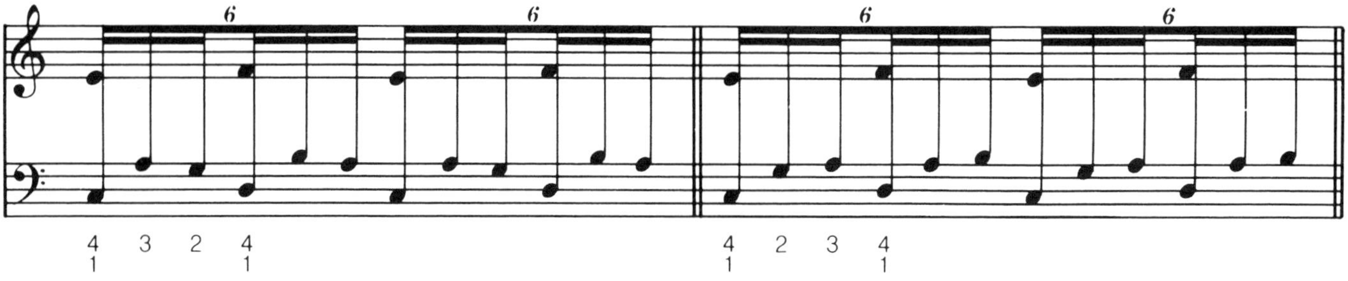

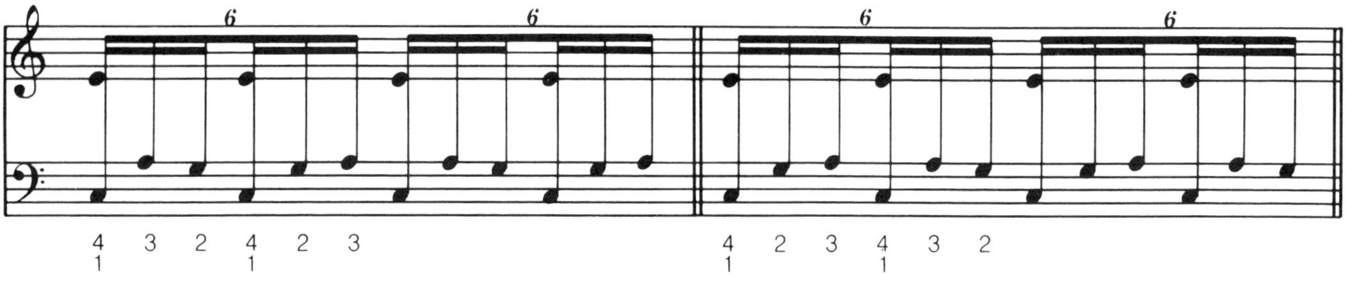

484 **485**

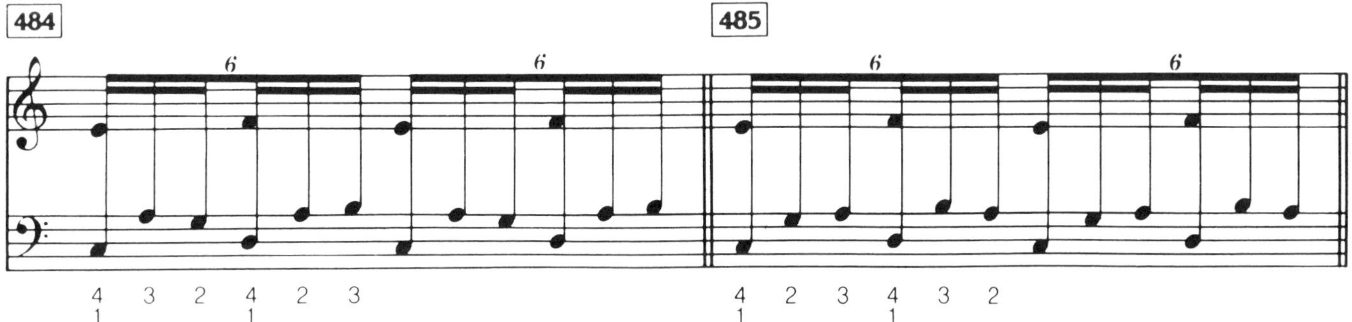

Exercises 486 – 501: Complete exercises 462 – 477 before doing these. This set is similar except the accompaniment contains double vertical strokes. Some of these exercises cannot be transposed a full octave.

♪. = 80 – ♪. = 138

486 **487** **488** **489**

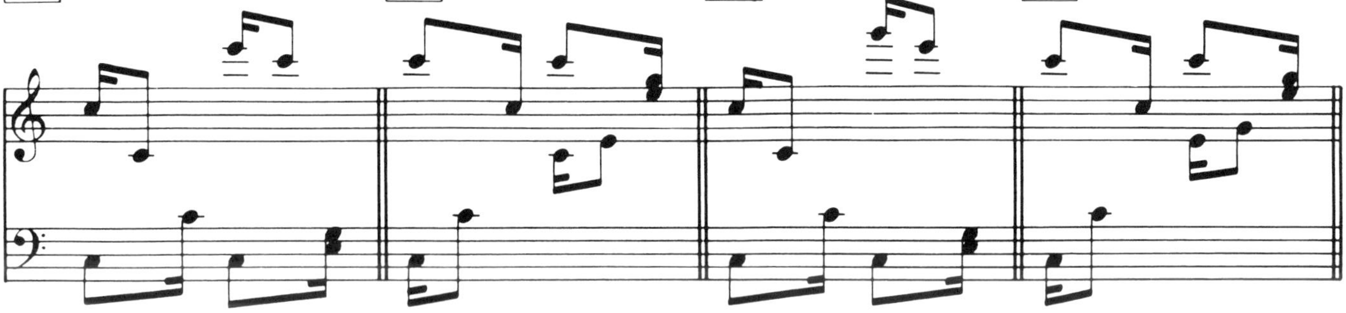

490 **491** **492** **493**

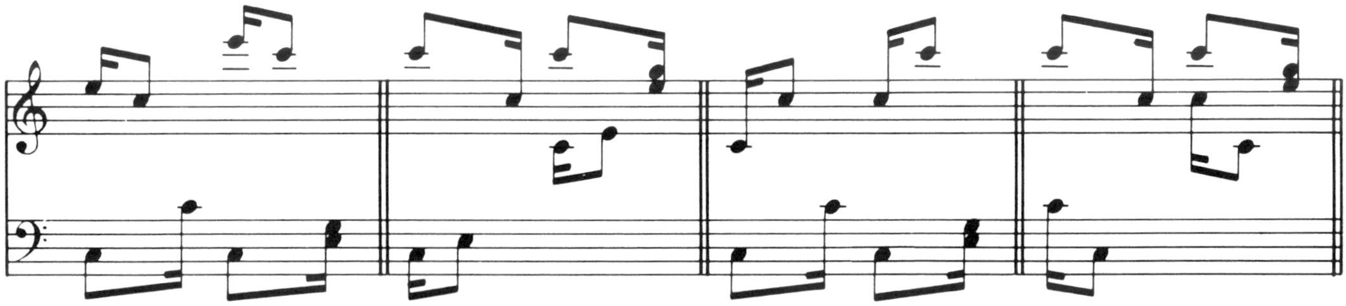

494 **495** **496** **497**

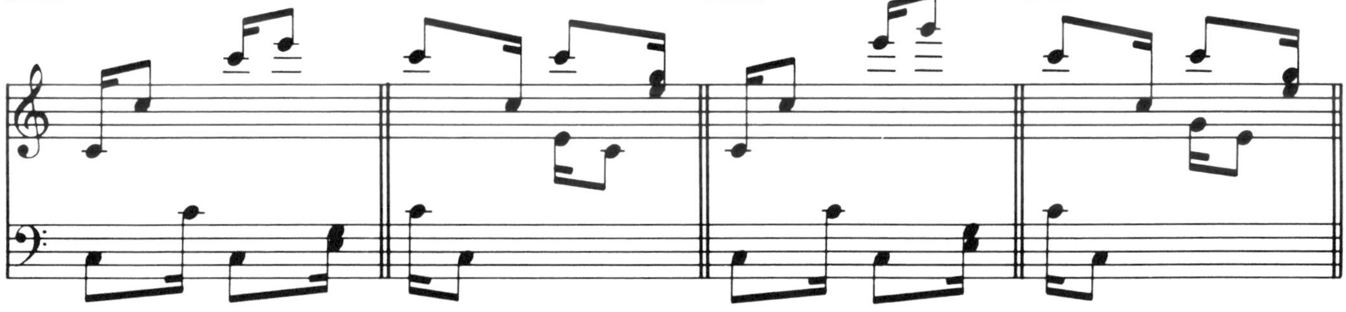

498 **499** **500** **501**

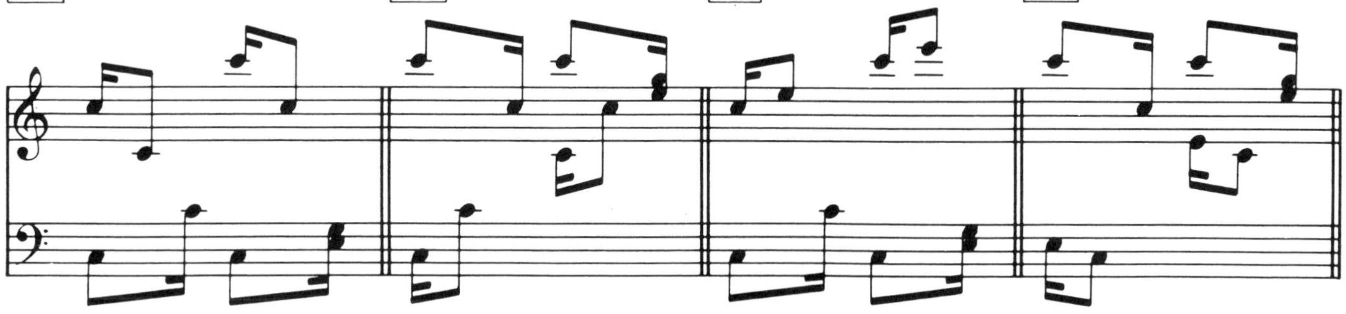

Exercises 502—517: Keep the 8th note pulse clear by
playing the single alternating strokes slightly louder
than the double lateral strokes.

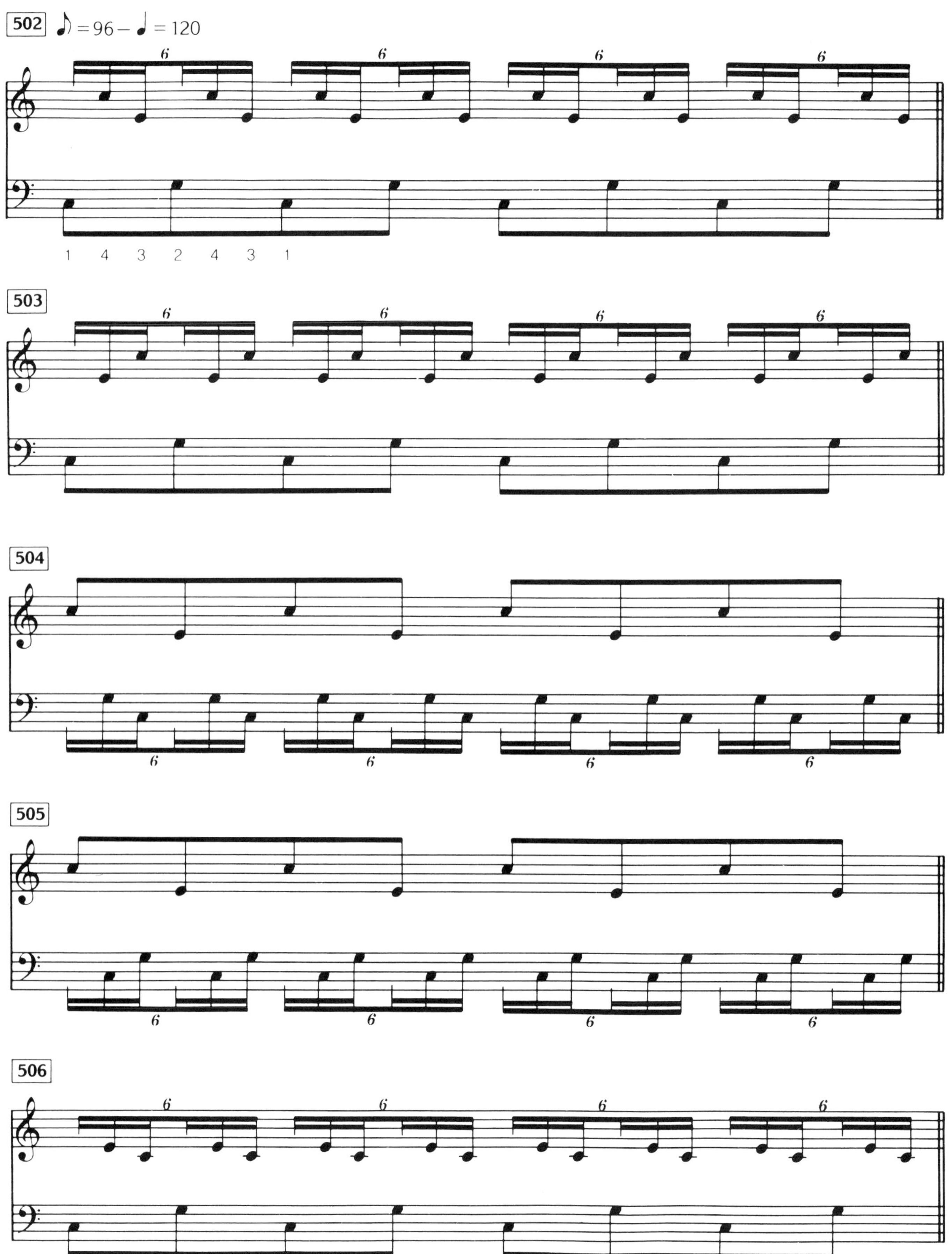

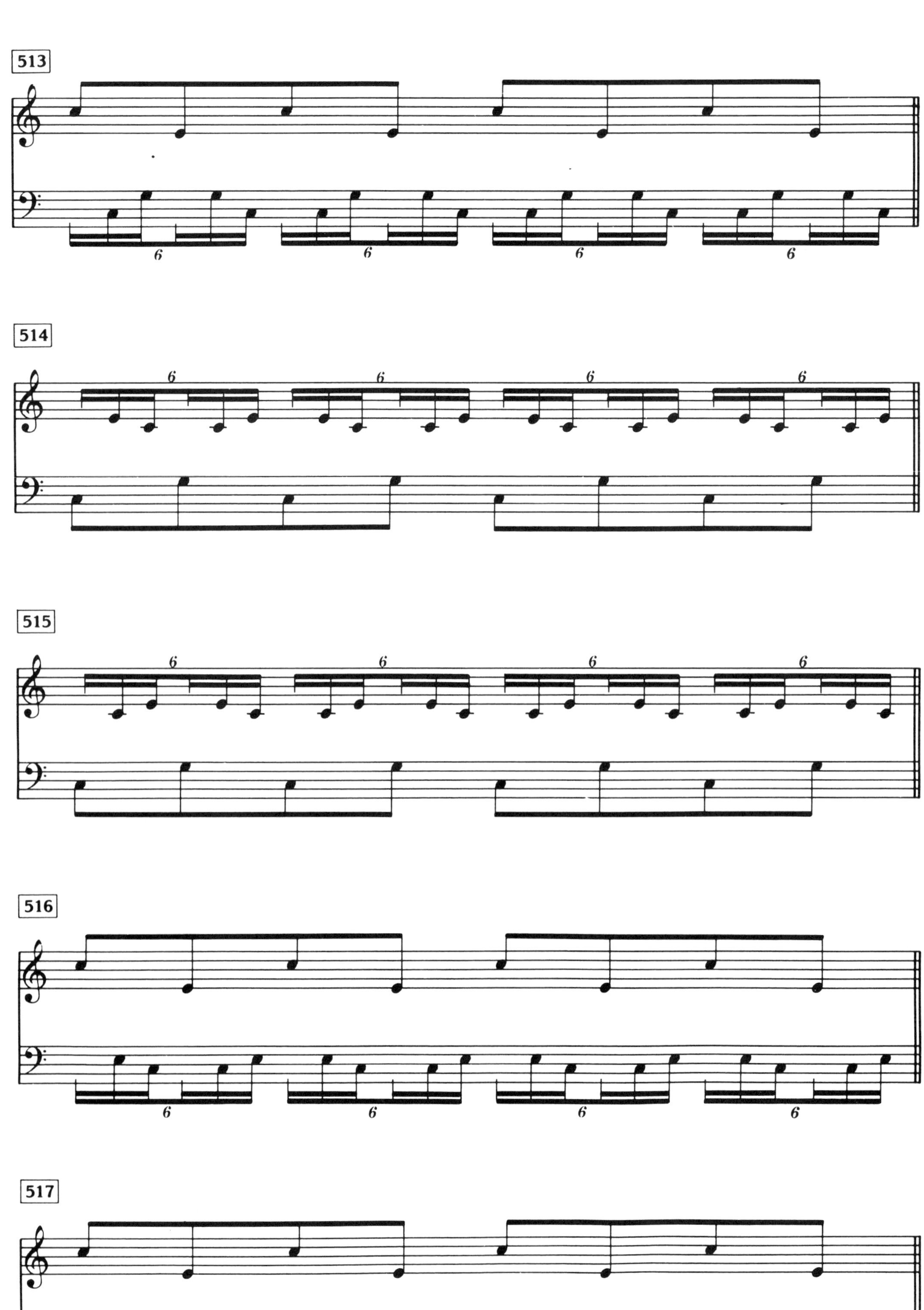

Exercises 518 – 521: The single alternating strokes are replaced now by double vertical strokes in sixths.

518 ♪ = 76 – ♩ = 132

519

520

521

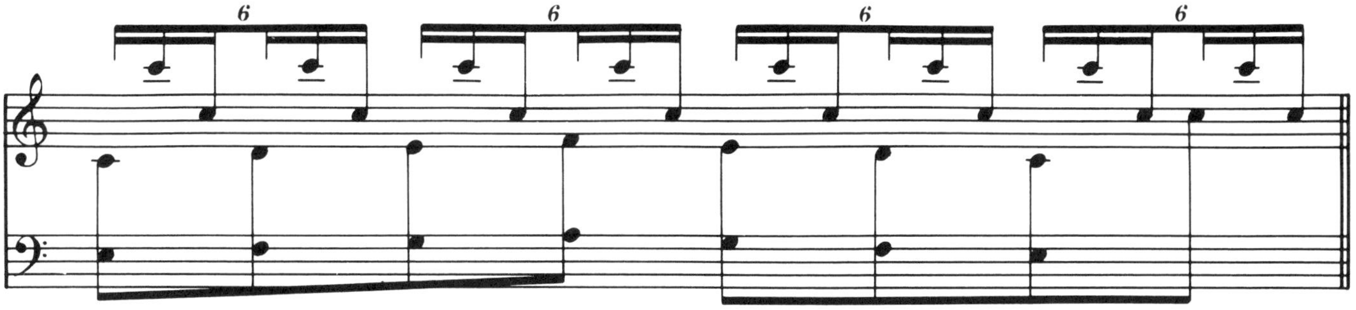

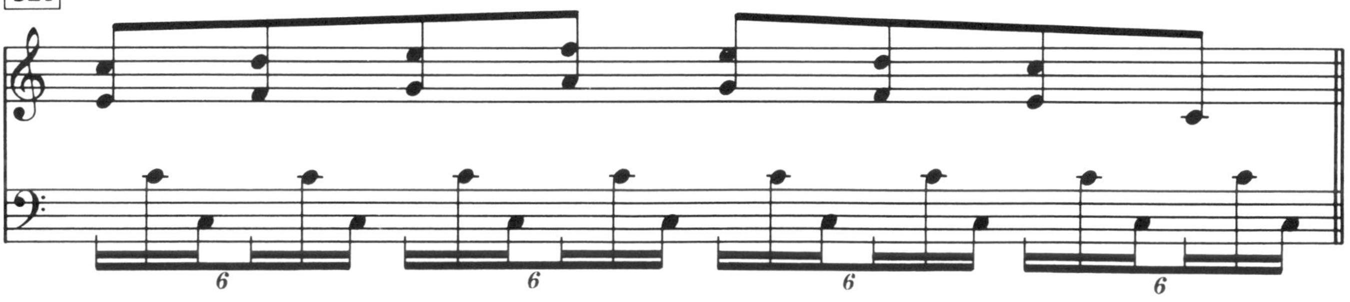

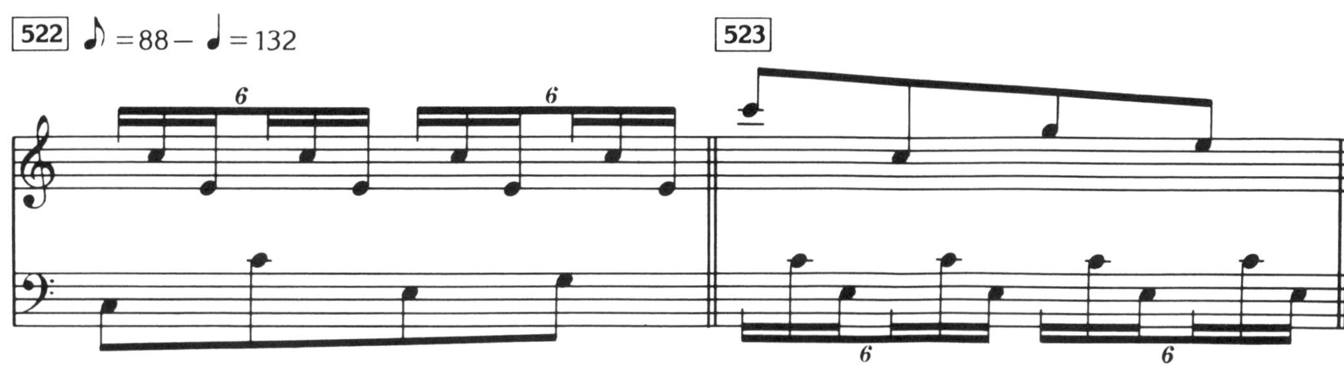

Exercises 522 – 537: The double vertical strokes are replaced with changing interval single alternating strokes. Sometimes the double lateral strokes change directions.

522 ♪ = 88 – ♩ = 132

523

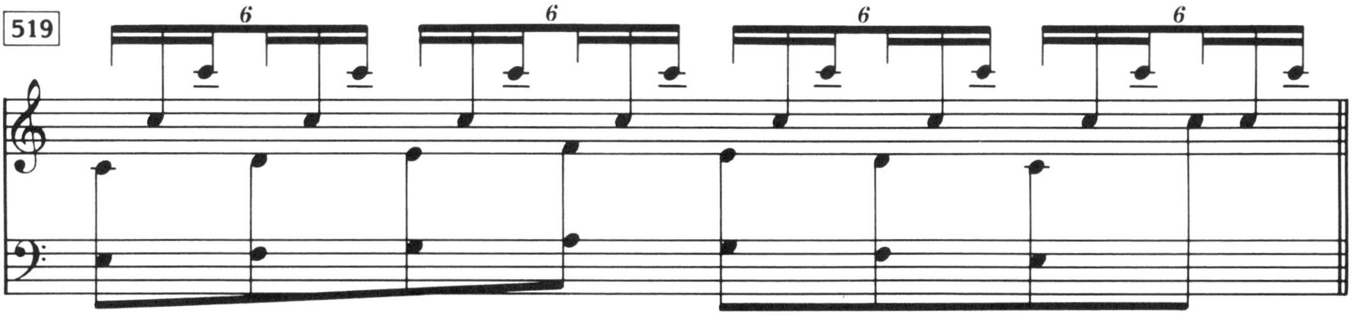

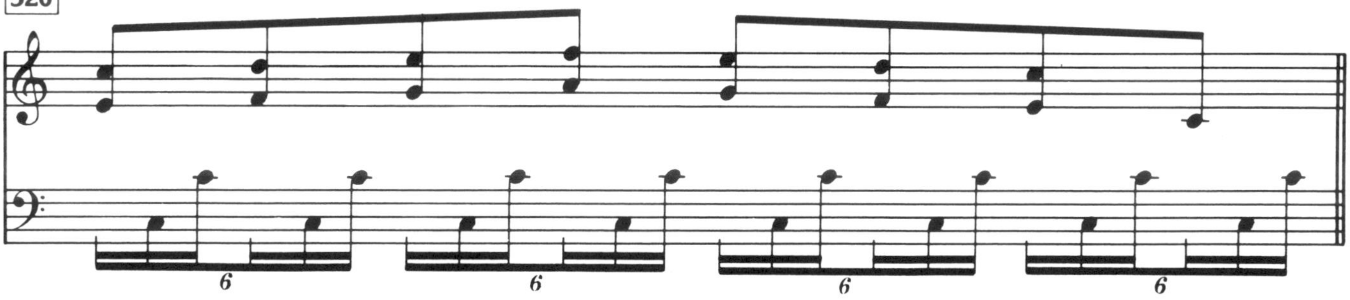

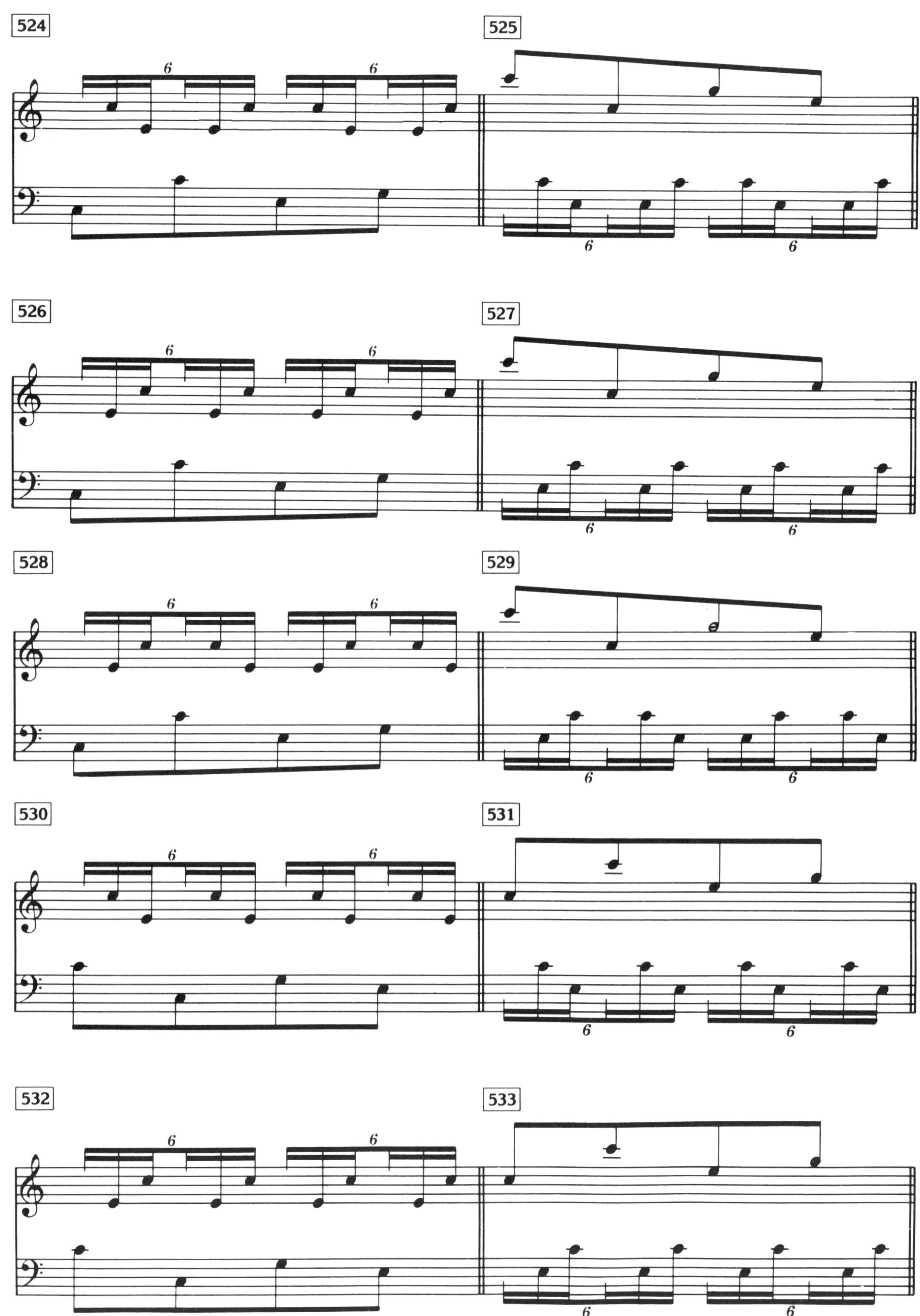

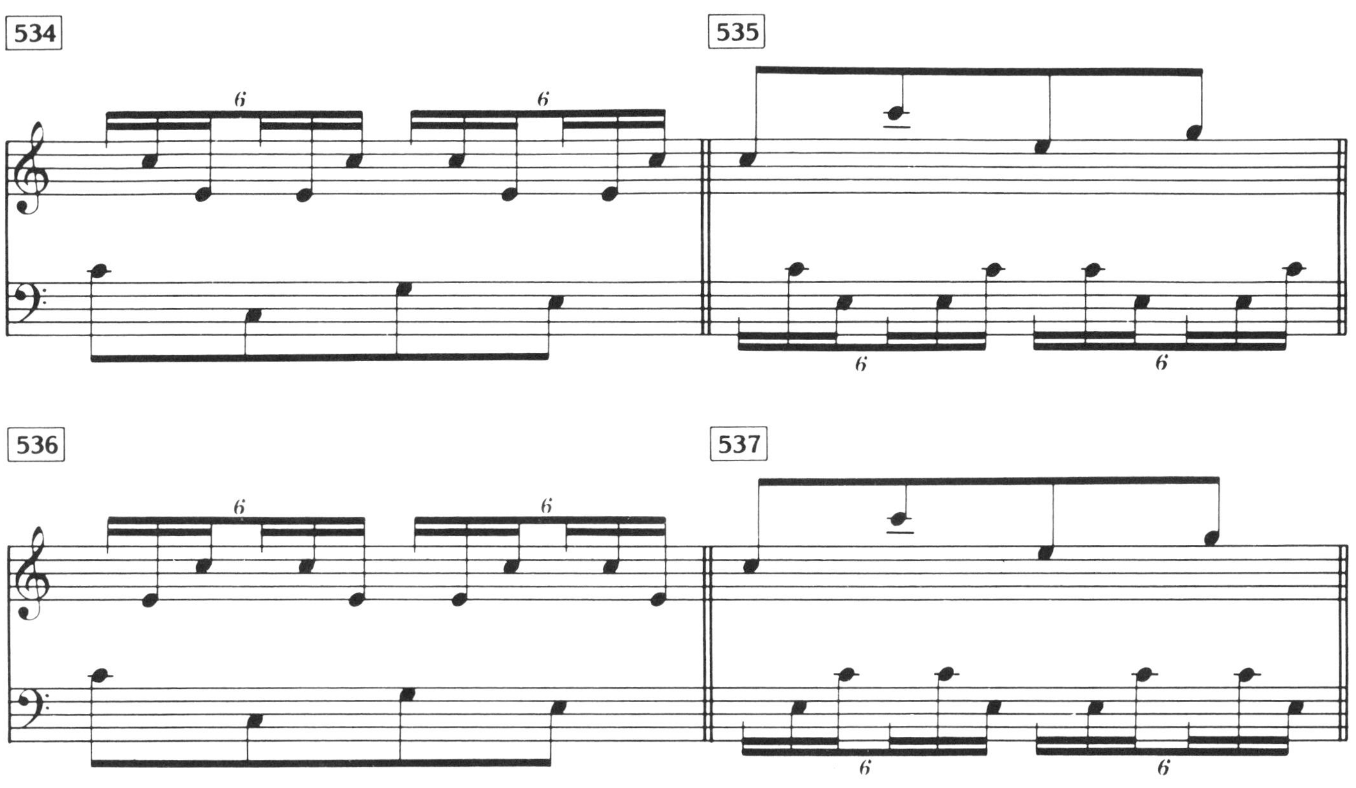

Exercises 538 – 553: Shifts and small interval changes have been added to the double lateral strokes.

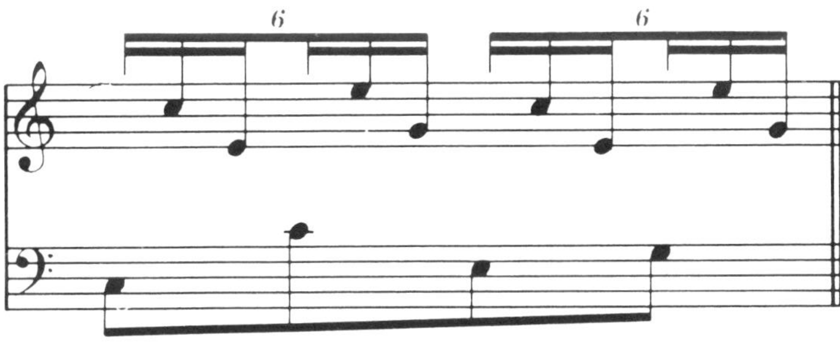

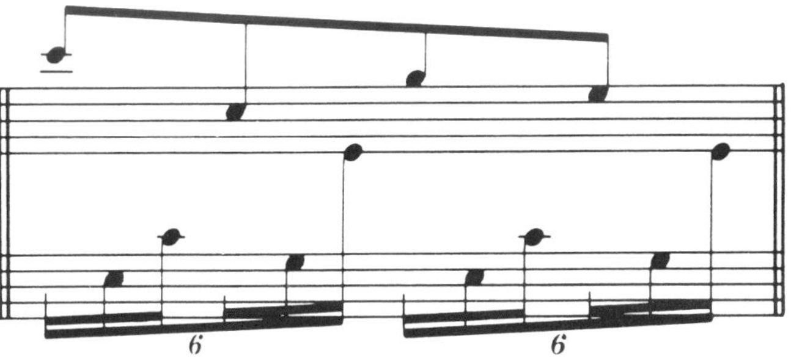

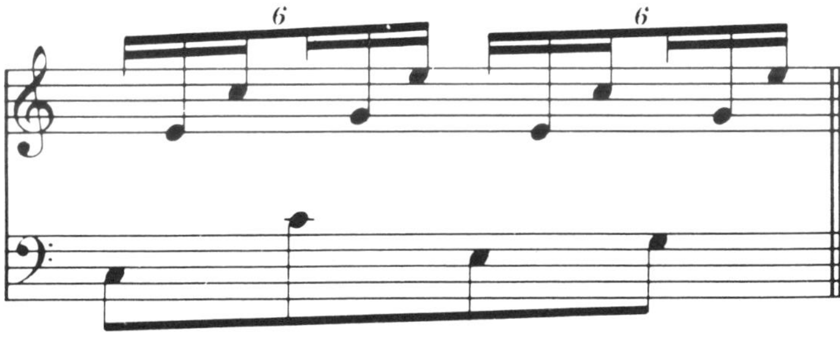

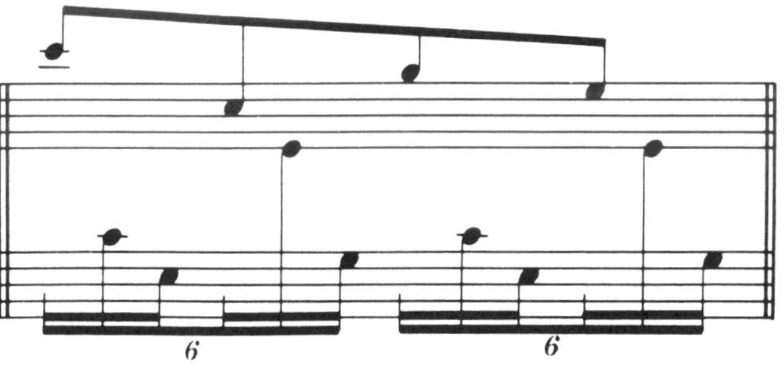

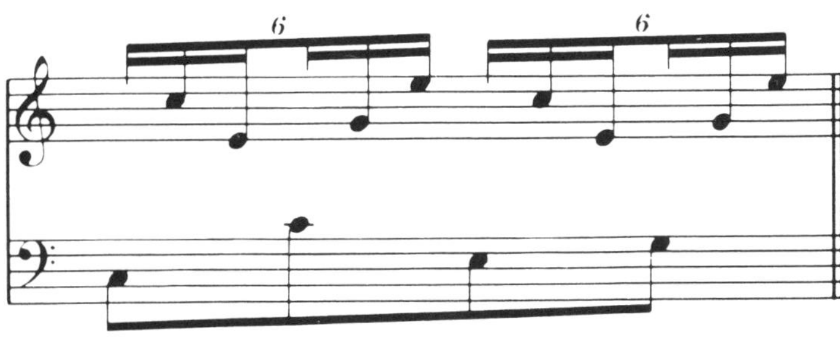

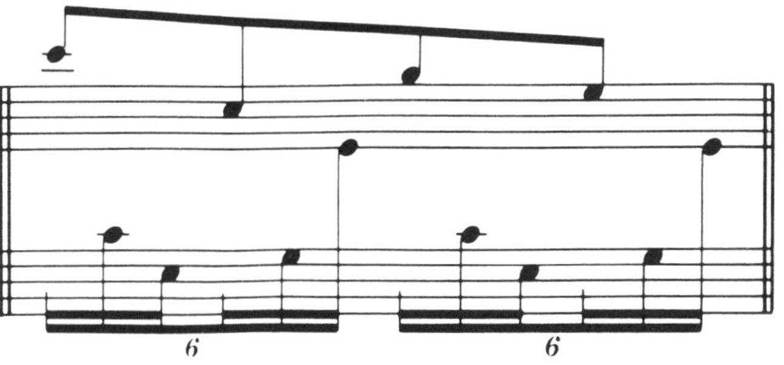

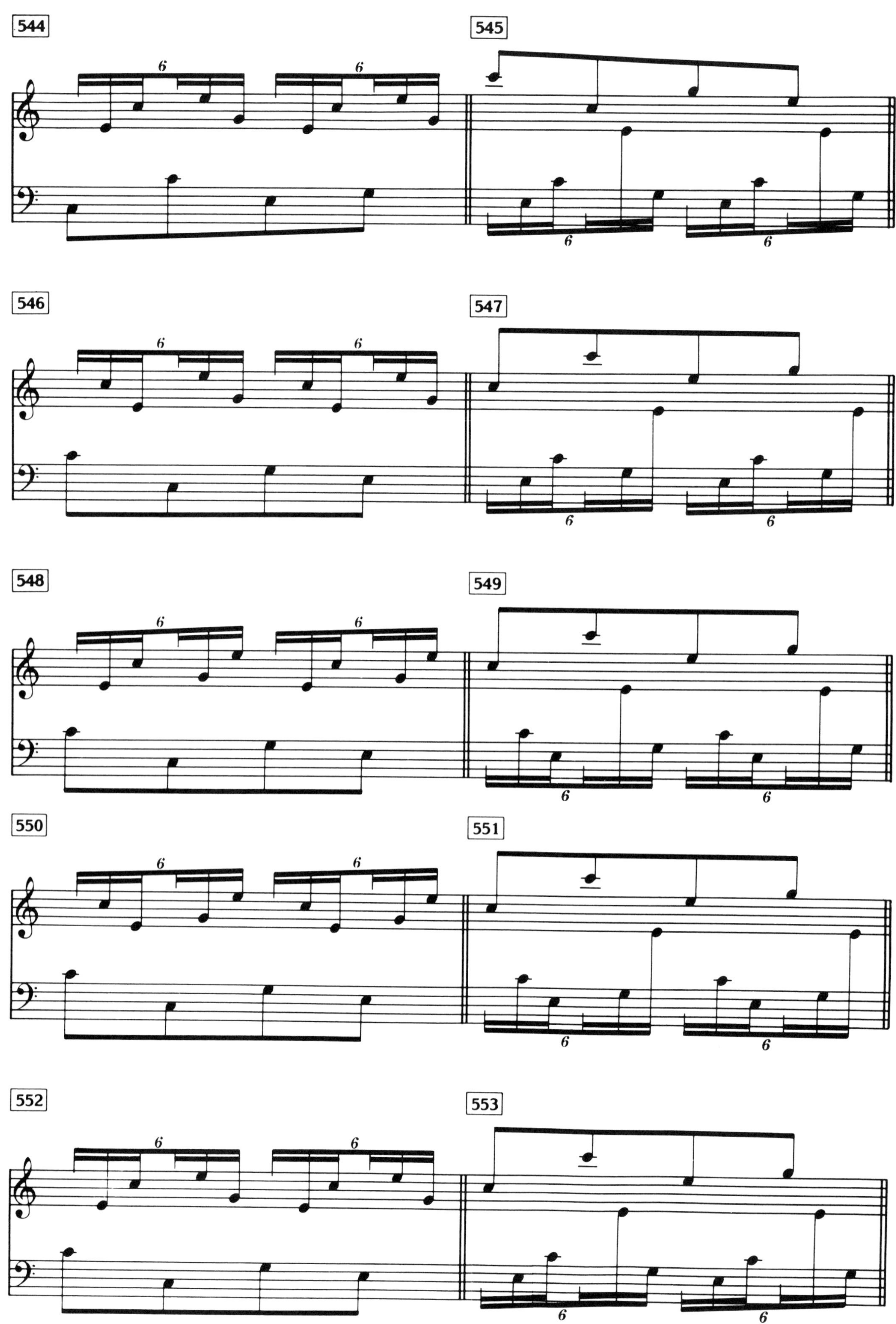
544
545
546
547
548
549
550
551
552
553
6
6
6
6
90

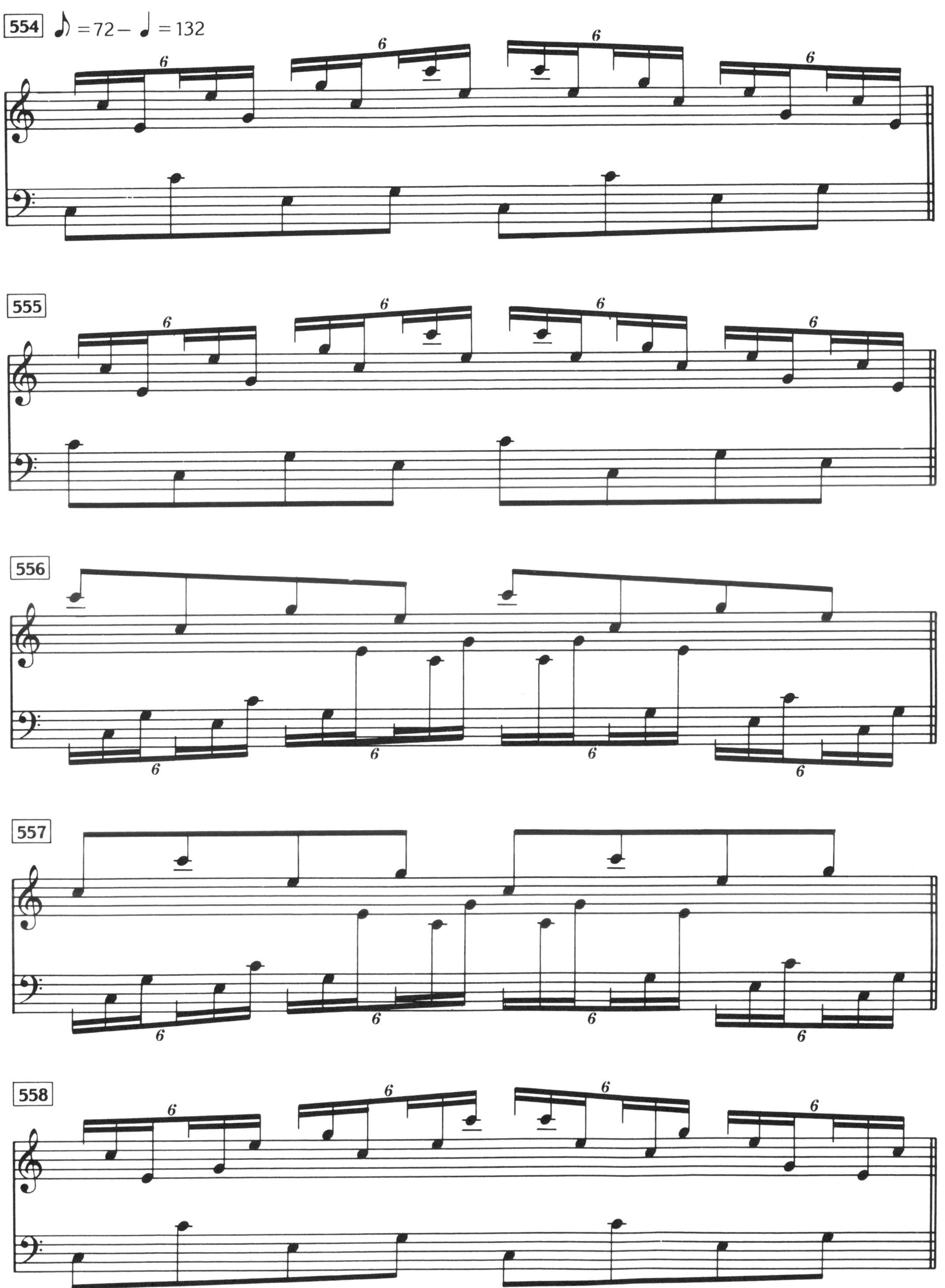
554   ♪ = 72 — ♩ = 132
6   6   6   6
555
6   6   6   6
556
6   6   6   6
557
6   6   6
558
6   6   6   6

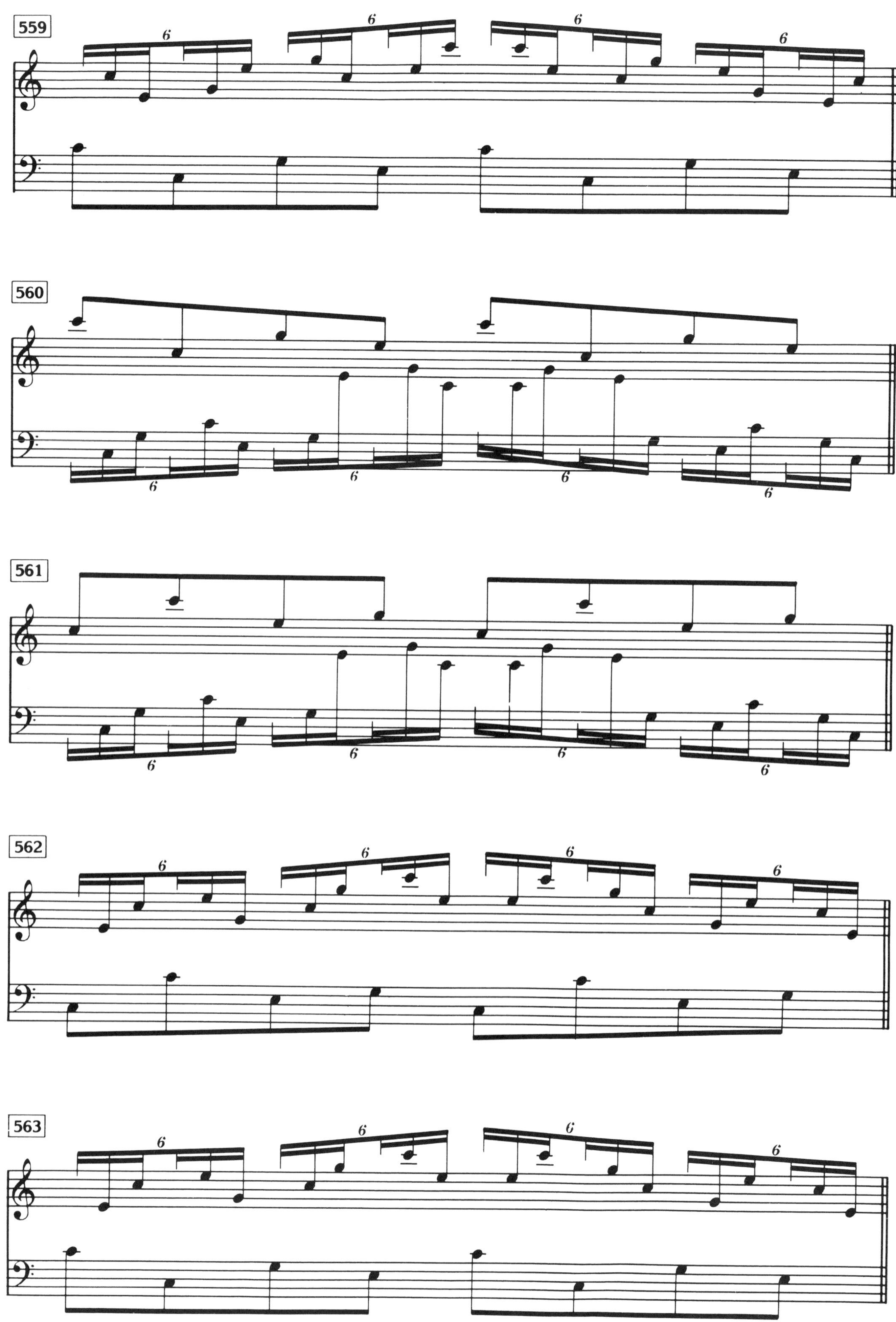

564

565

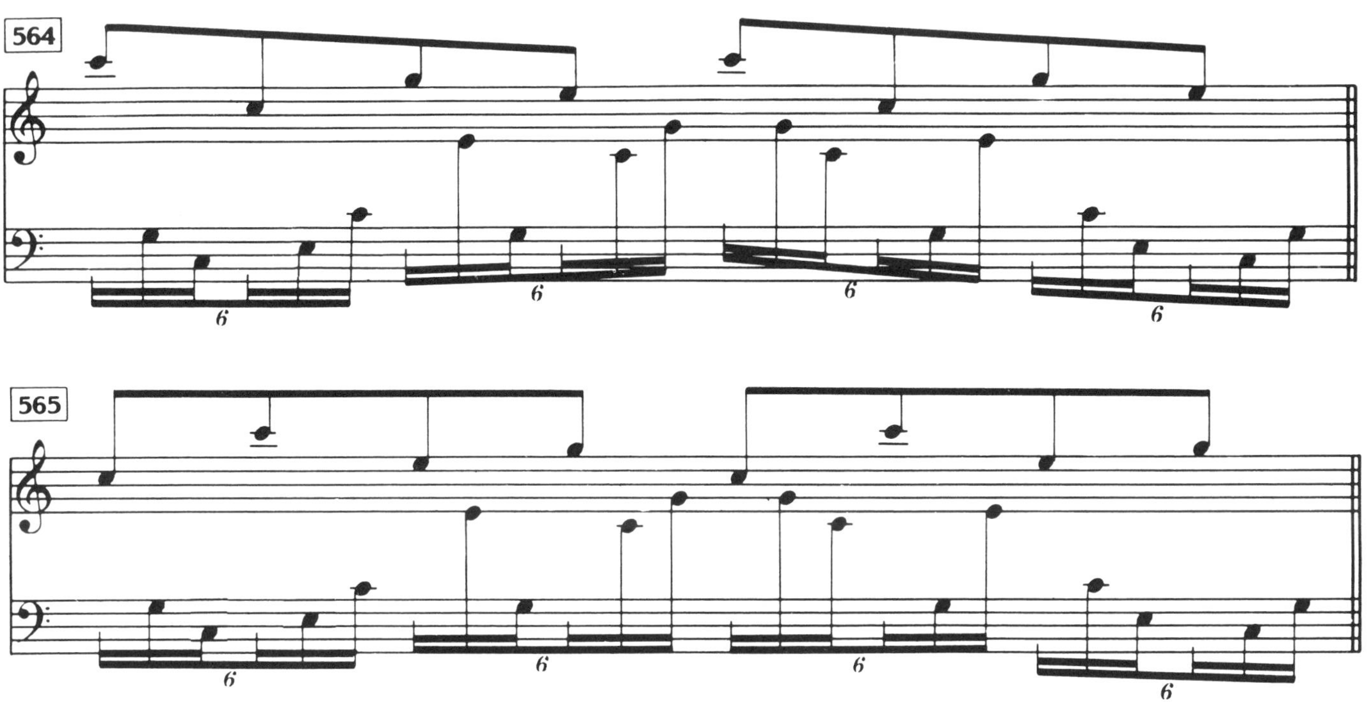

Exercises 566 – 571 are to be practiced hands separately. Start the right hand 8va. The double notes are to be performed with double vertical strokes. All other notes are to be played as single independents.

566 ♪ = 68 – ♩ = 96

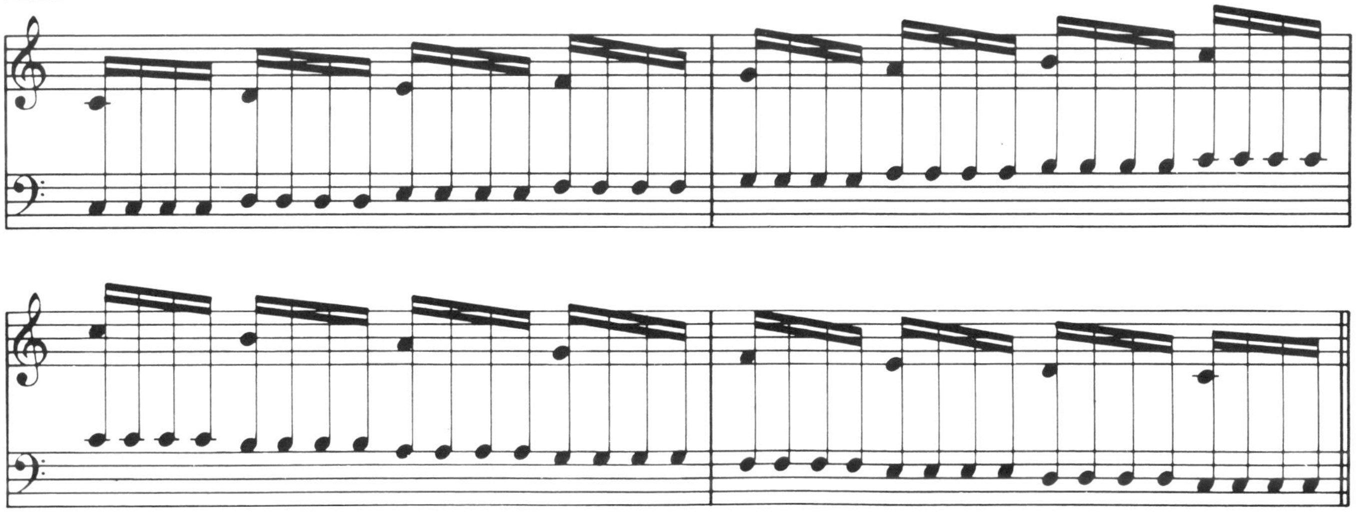

567

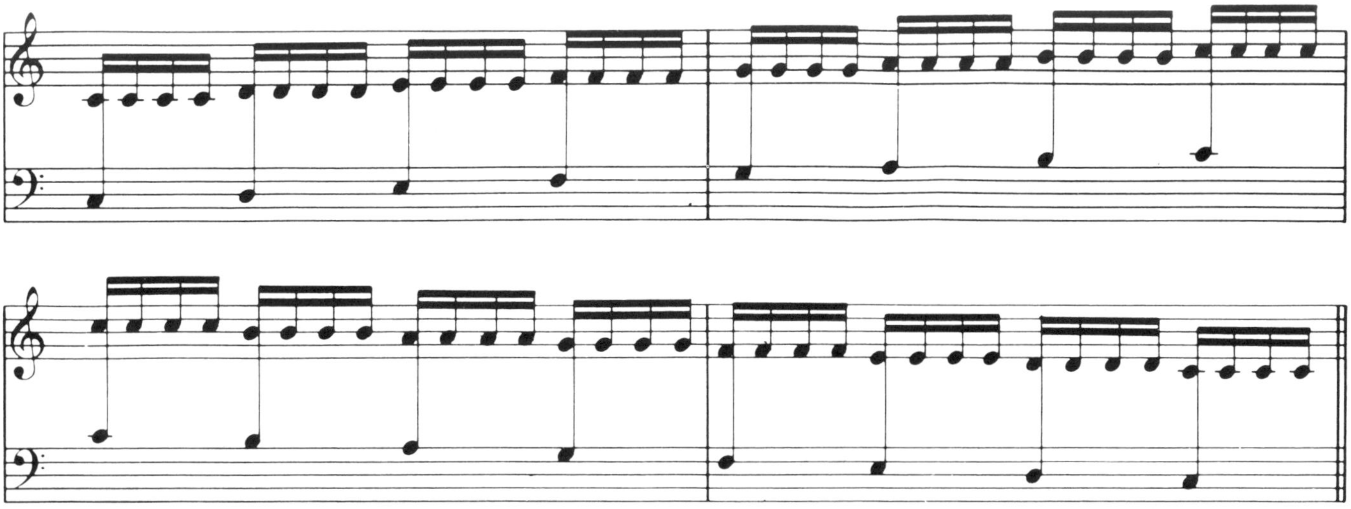

568
♪=68 — ♩=88
569
570
571

Exercises 572—579: Use single alternating and double vertical strokes. Remember to repeat each exercise and to transpose each continuously through all twelve keys.

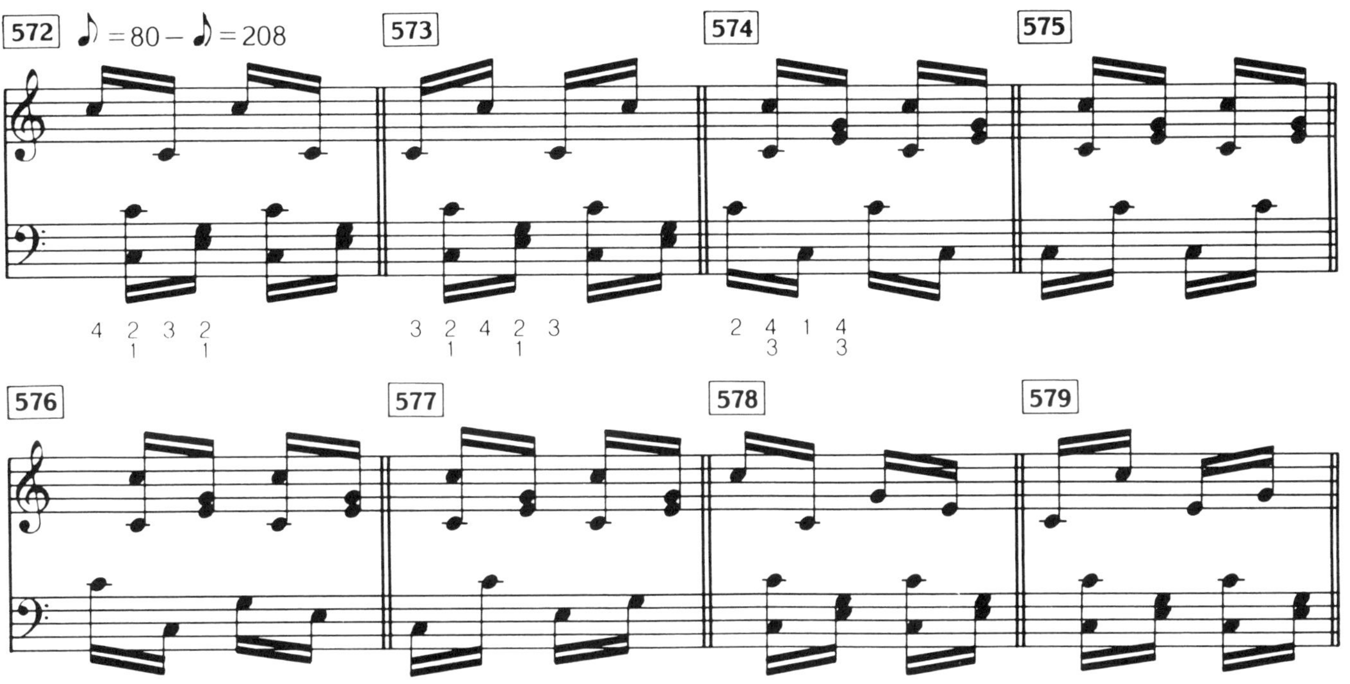

Exercises 580 & 581: All twenty—four permutations may be applied to the single notes. Do not allow the tempo to pull back during the double vertical strokes.

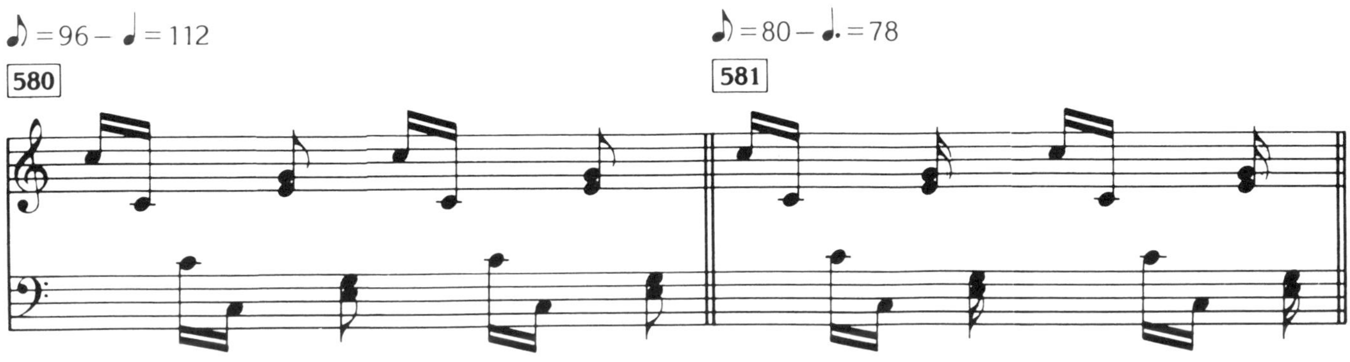

Exercises 582—585: Practice hands separately. Try to match the dynamics of the melodic and harmonic thirds. Start left hand 8 bassa.

Exercises 586 & 587: Review exercises 27 & 28 before starting these. Marimbists with 4 octave instruments should start exercise 586 up a half step.

Exercises 588 & 589: Double laterals with disjunct double stickings. The outer mallet leaps will be more easily negotiated if they are not encumbered by the inner mallet. Release all deliberate pressure on the inner mallet on the note preceding the leap of the outer mallet.

Exercise 590: Scales with sequential sticking. The sticking patterns below work well in all keys except F sharp major. Use the stickings listed below F sharp major as alternates.

590

	2 (1)	3	4	1	2	3	4	2 (1)	3	4	1	2	3	4	2 (1)	4	3	2	1	4	3	2 (1)	4	3	2	1	4	3	2 (1)
	4 (3)	1	2	3	4	1	2	4 (3)	1	2	3	4	1	2	4 (3)	2	1	4	3	2	1	4 (3)	2	1	4	3	2	1	4 (3)
F sharp	1	2	3	4	1	2	3	1	2	3	4	1	2	4	2	4	2	1	4	3	2	1	4	2	1	4	3	2	1
C	1	2	3	4	2	3	4	1	2	3	4	2	3	4	2	4	3	2	4	3	2	1	4	3	2	4	3	2	1
C sharp, D A, A flat	1	2	3	1	2	3	4	1	2	3	1	2	3	4	2	4	3	2	1	3	2	1	4	3	2	1	3	2	1
F	1	2	3	4	1	2	3	1	2	3	4	1	2	3	3	2	2	1	4	3	2	1	4	2	1	4	3	2	1

Third Part
Ten Years Later

1 Other Ways to Use MOM

I have heard **Method of Movement** described as being overwhelming in its detail. At first glance one could be intimidated by all that text, the diagrams and 590 exercises. Teachers wonder how to integrate its concepts and exercises into weekly lessons; students wonder where among its original 96 pages should they begin reading or working; both groups wonder which exercises should be studied while working on a particular piece of repertoire. Notwithstanding the fact that there is already a Chapter I entitled "How to use MOM," I will try to clarify any remaining uncertainty about how to use this book.

Stating the same thing in different words is often helpful when teaching a diverse group of individuals who have different backgrounds. So, before delving into any new material, I will restate in more detail some of the suggestions made in Chapter I.

Reading the book

Read the book. Carefully. From the beginning. Several times. If you don't understand a sentence, back up a few sentences and get a running start. If you begin any of the exercises without the careful application of MOM's ideas and the active participation of the conscious mind, your hands will do whatever they are used to doing. If you begin playing the exercises with your old system, or with no system at all, you are merely embedding bad habits. In order to *improve* your control of the mallets or change your "method of movement" to something more graceful, efficient or accurate, you must consciously repeat the new improved method of motion until it becomes habit. Of course, this is impossible unless you understand *how* your hands, fingers and arms are *supposed* to move. That is why studying the text *before* playing the exercises is so important.

If you are a serious player, every time you work out of MOM you should be trying to develop, build, maintain, refine and refresh the meticulous, efficient and logical habits of movement which you want to have permanently. *There is no other reason to practice technical exercises on a musical instrument.* If you have not understood the text, or if you are not consciously thinking about and trying to control how the stroke or shift is supposed to be performed, you will end up developing, maintaining, refining and refreshing the sloppy, inefficient and illogical habits of movement you probably had before. This is worse than a waste of time; it is counterproductive. In summary, read and understand the text before beginning the exercises.

Doing the Exercises

Let us assume that you are about to begin working on your right hand with an exercise such as 162 in the Double Vertical Stroke section, as recommended in Chapter I. Before you play a single note, go through the following checklist and ask yourself these questions.

1. **Hand position**: Is my hand position graceful, curved and relaxed-looking as described on pages 12-14? Do the mallets feel as if they are "hanging" in the hand?

2. **Height**: Are my mallet heads high enough off the keyboard so that I will be able to go straight down to the bars, without a preparatory "breath" upward, as warned against on pages 16 and 17? Am I high enough to produce the volume I want with a simple down/up piston stroke? Are the mallets higher than they need to be, therefore increasing the chances of inaccuracy as described on page 15?

3. **Recovery**: Do I know the position to which the stroke is going to recover, as described on pages 19-21? The whole stroke will be over in a flash, so if I don't know the position to which the mallets are moving, it will be too late to correct after they start down toward the bars. In the case of exercise 162, all but the last stroke before the transposition recovers straight up. The last recovery in C Major briskly shifts the mallet heads to the ends or centers of C# and G#. This should produce a graceful upward curve, as described on page 19.

4. **Interval Change**: If, instead of 162, I am working on an exercise like 165, I must also think *before* I start the stroke about how and when the interval change will be performed. The change in interval spread must start right after contact with the bars as part of the recovery, but it must not be too late or I will have wasted the stroke recovery momentum, as described on page 18 and 20.

5. **Striking Area**: Where am I about to strike? Is that area of the bar going to produce the sound I want to achieve, as discussed on page 23? For now, I have so much else to think about, I better play near the centers or on the very ends. Later, I may return to this exercise and practice it, for example, with a bright, thin "sol ponticello" timbre, striking every bar 1/2 inch inside of the nodes.

Considering the above points, go ahead and play the first quarter note of exercise 162.

Stop. The mallet heads should now be back in the original "pre-stroke" position, i.e., hovering above the bars. But before playing another stroke, you have a very important job to do.

Think. *Analyze* what you just did. Did your wrist "pop up" and did the mallets feel like they bounced off the bars, as described on p. 33?

Play another quarter note. . . Think. . .

It is the active use of this "thinking space between the gestures," referred to on page 4, that determines whether you are mindlessly repeating your mistakes, or learning from them. When you are certain you are performing the motion perfectly, you can begin to "reduce the thinking space" and begin to speed up the tempo. However, use the above procedure when starting *any new exercise or piece*. I *still* use this procedure on some of my daily exercises and on any complicated passage in new repertoire that I am learning.

II Daily Exercise Routines

You may choose some of your exercises specifically according to the literature you are preparing, as exemplified on the following page, or you may prefer to use the table below. With this approach, you will establish a core of daily exercises which remain constant for perhaps a year or more at a time.

Core exercises to be done daily are in bold face type. When a range of numbers within a particular stroke type is shown, choose one or more exercises from that series. Vary your regimen by adding some of the other listed exercises from that level, or by carrying over core exercises from higher up on the table.

For each of the longer and more difficult routines marked with a +, *add* these new exercises to the core exercises listed on the line directly above it. As you become familiar with each of the exercises, you will be able to judge accurately the time necessary to complete the routine in all twelve keys at your current tempo range.

While the exercise routines initially require about 15 minutes, I believe the serious student of marimba needs to devote an hour or more a day to technical development.

Level/Time	Single Ind.	Single Alt.	Double V	Double L	Mixed
Beginning 15 minute	**1-3**	**50-55**	**162-164**		
Beginning + 30 minute	**31:** (2+3, 3+2 only)	**56-59** **73-74** 134-37	171-177 **225-228**		
Intermediate 30 minute	4-6, 31: (2+3, 3+2)	**60-67** **70-77** 138-41	178-183 **229-232**	279-294	
Intermediate + 45 minute	7-11 **29-31**	**78-93** 138-145	184-193 **271** 233-236	**327-34**	**415-424** 428
Advanced 45 minute	23-26 **29-31**	**68-69** 94-101 146-151	194-97 **203, 271** 211-17 237-240	335-342 **403-10**	**425-427** 429-430 582-85
Advanced+ 1 hour or more	32-49	102-125 152-61	**204-206** 220-224 **241-256** **267-270**	343-382 411-414	**431, 590** 432-455 478-485 502-565

III   Table of Repertoire

The table of repertoire below contains 30 works likely to be performed by college and professional marimbists. The suggested exercises can be worked on concurrently, or they can be used as preparation for the piece. Frequently there are many more appropriate exercises than are listed.

A √ mark before the title indicates that an independent roll is required.

Work	Single Ind.	Single Alt.	Double V	Double L	Mixed
√ Albeniz, Leyenda	30-31		164	403-11	431, 507, 519
√ Bach, Sonatas+Part.	23-26		211-215		582-85
√Bach, Inventions	30	134-161			
√ Burritt, Caritas, Scirocco, Preludes, others		102-109 146-157	263-6,272 271		590, 434-5, 438-9, 442-47, 478-85
Debussy, Child. Cor.	4, 19-20	158-61	207-210, 271	327-334,	425-427
Ewazen, Northern L.		86-89	273-274	343-350, 407-8	590, 518-19
√ Helble, Concerto			263-71,220-224		582-85
√ Helble, Grand F.	29, 31	60-67	187, 203, 214	411-414	425-431, 518-21
√ Helble Preludes 1-3		60-69	237-240,275-76		
√ 4-6	29-49		271	327-34, 359-66,	590
√ 7-9			271, 211-15		582-85
√ Helble Toccata F.	29-31	102-9,152-61	213, 257-262	327, 359-366	430-31
Khachaturian	29-31, 4,16	54,55	208,225-228 207-210	335	
Kurka, Concerto	27-28, 31		273-4, 277-8		586-7
√ Maslanka, MLW		134		329,347,363,411	428
√ Maslanka, Var. LL	25-26, 31	71	263-6, 271-2	428-30	590
Musser, Etudes	29-30	70-77	193-201, 277-8	327-34	
√ Penn, Preludes	1-4, 29-30				590
Peters, Yellow	25-6, 29	73, 78-85			
Sammut, Rotations		102-09, 156-7, 118-19	263-266 215-216	462-470	432-447
√ Schumann, Album		152-61	267-271		
Schwantner, Veloc	6-15, 31		194-97		590, 425-430
√ Serry, Rhapsody	23-26	52-53	271,225-40,209		
Smadbeck, Vir. Tate				327-334	426-427
Stevens, R. Caprice	29		211	329,333,359,363	590
Stevens, Great Wall				329,333,335-6	518-521
Stout, Astral Dance			272	403-411	
Stout, Etudes	23-24, 31	86-101, 126-33	220-23, 263-66 171-73		
Mex. Dances	31	60-69, 257-62	272	295-326, 327-34	478-485
Rumble Strips			273-74	317-322	513-519
Sedimental Struc.					448-455, 478-85
√ Tschaik. Album	23-26	60-7, 134-151	174-7,213-8,243		

IV   Amplifications

The marimbist of today practices and performs in an environment much different musically and technically than existed when MOM was first published. While I have discovered nothing in the intervening ten years that contradicts any principles of good technique described in MOM, I now feel that certain aspects of the method were over or under-emphasized simply due to the context in which the material was conceived and written. The three aspects that I feel need amplification are hand position, inner mallet length and keyboard height.

Hand Position

When MOM was being written it seemed that the tide in favor of a flat-palmed crossed-stick grip was too huge to ever turn. Many of the most progressive percussion teachers of the time were extolling the virtues of "matched grip" because of its applicability to snare drum, multiple percussion, xylophone and marimba. A "thumbs up" vertical hand position, if it was recommended at all, was reserved for timpani playing. As is still the case today, the most influential "classical" teachers in any given area of the world tended to be the orchestral players of the local symphony orchestras, and in general, they had no need for a new four-mallet technique with which to play orchestral excerpts.

Considering the environment into which my four-mallet-marimba vertical hand position ideas were introduced, it is especially astonishing that today the opposite problem exists. Many students resist using any sort of flattened hand position, even when it would be more comfortable to do so. Though pages 33-34 of MOM explain the concept of flattening the hand position, there is still widespread misunderstanding. The following examples from the exercises may help. In both of the cases below, flattening the hand reduces the awkwardness of the wrist position and relaxes tension in the shoulders and arms.

Play exercise 193 slowly in E Major. On the first chord the left hand is "very vertical" because it has an accidental on the inside mallet. The right hand is "normally vertical" because it has two naturals. However, on the second chord (first inversion, E Major), both hand positions flatten because they both have accidentals on the outside mallets and the intervals are relatively small. (If the intervals were minor seconds with the outside mallet on an accidental, instead of major thirds, the hand position would be almost completely flat.)

The hand position also flattens when the hands are spread far apart, even if all the mallets are playing naturals. In exercise 203 played in C Major, the hand positions are slightly flatter in the fourth chord, when the hands are spread out, than they are when they are directly in front of the player.

Whenever the hand position flattens, the thumb and first finger tend to slide apart: the first finger pulls back and/or the thumb moves forward on the stick. This is clearly visible in the picture of the left hand in figure 34.

Inner Mallet Length

Occasionally I hear a student comment that the process of opening and closing a large interval appears to change the length of the inner mallet. This usually calls attention to itself after returning to a small interval, when the inner mallet may feel like it is being held too close to the end. Another manifestation of this same problem is experienced when the end of the inner mallet catches in the palm as the interval opens from small to very large. Both of these awkward feelings can be improved or completely alleviated by the following means.

Imagine that you are going to pop a watermelon pit out from between your thumb and first finger. As you do this, the thumb pulls back toward your palm and the second joint of the thumb bends up. This is exactly the same motion you can use when closing the interval from large to small. The bending of the thumb pulls the end of the inside mallet into your palm for firmer contact, just as if you had "choked up" on the mallet.

The reverse of this technique can be of benefit when opening the interval. Begin with the thumb crooked on a small interval. Flatten the crook of the thumb as you open the interval. As you do this, lift the inside mallet *up* and out with the first finger while pushing down with the thumb. This helps to move the end of the inside mallet through the proper arc in the palm to its goal at the base of the second finger (assuming your goal is to go all the way to a tenth). This same motion, with the emphasis on the movement of the first finger rather than the thumb, is described on page 12, column 2, item 2.

Keyboard Height

The importance of good posture and a natural playing position have been recognized recently in the mainstream of keyboard percussion teaching. It was only a few years ago that six-foot-tall players might have been seen bending almost in half in an effort to lower themselves to the standard height of a marimba keyboard. In the days before the availability of a quickly-adjustable height mechanism, I used to have my students lift the marimba on and off a set of four Manhattan telephone directories. I found this low-tech solution to be more stable than wooden blocks and it had the added advantage of being infinitely adjustable: just flip pages. Today of course, height adjustments are being engineered into the frame itself, as it should be.

Setting aside the question of posture and comfort, there is another important reason to have the keyboard at the proper height. The wrist "pop" associated with a good double vertical stroke is elusive unless the keyboard is high enough. All the pictures in MOM show the handles nearly parallel to the keyboard when the mallet heads are in contact with the bars, but nothing is said about this critical relationship.

If you suspect you are too tall for a standard-height marimba (and most players taller than 5'6" are), determine the feel of a good height relationship by bending at the knees until the handles of the mallets are virtually parallel to the bars at the moment of contact. When you become short enough,[1] the hand will be bent sharply up in relationship to the forearm when the mallets are raised and ready for a large-interval double vertical stroke. At the bottom of the stroke, when the mallets are in contact with the bars and the handles are parallel to the bars, the forearm and top edge of the hand will form a straight line. Once you are familiar with the look and feel of the relationship of stroke, handle, bar and wrist-bend, raise the keyboard experimentally inch by inch until the same relationship exists with a comfortable posture and relaxed shoulders and forearms.

---

[1] How short is "short enough"? At 5'6" I'm a veritable bean sprout compared to Clair Omar Musser, Vida Chenoweth and Keiko Abe. However, with the aid of modern technology (or phone books) you six-footers can experience many of the advantages of being short. Of course, you'll never achieve our "sports-car-like" handling and low center of gravity. . .

It would be difficult to overstate how different the attitudes and assumptions about four-mallet marimba playing were at the time that MOM was written. Since I had been doing an independent roll from the moment I began playing xylophone in 1969, I personally had no appreciation of how "revolutionary" the technique was, but as late as 1976, when I performed at the first Percussive Arts Society International Convention, most percussionists were seeing the independent roll, my "vertical Musser grip," rotary-based strokes and my extended-length birch handles for the first time.

"The Dark Ages"

While most collegiate percussion teachers of the early 1970's could have told you the basics of Musser grip, there were only a handful of teachers in the United States who actually used and taught it. When I wrote to Vida Chenoweth in 1971 to ask her where I could pursue my marimba studies, she wrote back that I would have to come to New Zealand — there were no teachers in the United States that she could recommend!

The few players who played with Musser grip at that time, including Vida Chenoweth, used the "original" Musser grip, which is to say that they,

- frequently used a flattened hand position — except when rolling with four mallets,
- held the outside mallets aloft when playing "two-mallet" melodic lines,
- held the inside mallet aloft to produce a flam-type stroke for the Musser roll,
- sometimes used their thumb and first finger to spread the interval — just as if they were using traditional crossed-stick grip,
- pivoted the inside mallet open and closed from one basic point within the palm,
- "choked up" on the outside mallet.

While my ideas about grip were unquestionably inspired by and based on Musser grip, the technique I teach and use in performance today bears little resemblance to the style described above. All but two of the above techniques are expressly "forbidden" in my system of playing and I recommend the flattened hand position and the flam-type stroke for rolling only in very exceptional situations. I hope this adequately describes the differences between my technique and Musser grip for those players who may never have seen the original.

Going beyond any issue of how I hold the mallets or change intervals, I feel that my *system* of six stroke/motion categories and the way I move around the instrument owe a debt to many influences.

Burton influence

One of the concepts I tried to incorporate was first described by Gary Burton in his <u>Four Mallet Studies</u> published in 1968 by Creative Music. Burton's pivot stroke — keeping the inside right mallet at 90° to the outside, and pivoting the stroke of the outside right mallet around it, in order to keep the unused mallet .still — was a major influence on me. In "classical" music however, the "melody" is as likely to be in the bass, tenor, or alto, as in the soprano. I wanted to be able to play single mallet lines equally well with any of the four mallets. I also wanted to be able to perform "two mallet style" lines with any combination of mallets. My goal was to be able to execute my version of Burton's pivot stroke (limiting the weight and excess motion liability of the unused mallet), with *any* of the four mallets and at *any* interval spread.

Morello influence

In order to achieve this goal, I had to ignore another piece of Burton's advice and not use a straight up-down stroke of the hand, but rather, base these single note strokes on rotary movements of the wrist and forearm. I ended up calling this the "Single Independent Stroke." This rotary action of the wrist and forearm was familiar to me because I already used it for my one-handed roll. An example of earlier use of this style of stroke is the "thumb up" fast-tempo ride cymbal technique used by some drum set players.

I had been studying with Joe Morello, the great jazz drummer, and had learned how critical the fingers were, not only to speed and control, but to volume. (It should be obvious that on a percussion instrument such as marimba, loudness is a product of the speed of the stick, not sheer strength.) A musical instrument technique that does not actively use the most dexterous (and fastest!) appendages on the human body (the fingers), will never rival in subtlety, suppleness, control and potential expressiveness, a technique which does. For that reason I wanted to be sure that true finger control was possible with this new way of holding the mallets. The vertical hand position I adopted and my method of holding and moving the inside mallets, both contributed to the freedom of the fingers to operate.

Guatemalan Influence

The idea for a birch handle mallet came from an Americanized version of a Guatemalan mallet, the now unavailable Jose Bethancourt mallet. In the early 1970's all other keyboard mallets had rattan, plastic or nylon handles, and were generally less than 15" in length. The Bethancourt mallets had thin, wooden handles, tapered to the head, but still stiffer then anything else available at that time.

Some of my peers at the Eastman School of Music may have already quietly suspected that I was only loosely in contact with reality because of my experiments with grip and strokes (and because I worked every day on my one-handed roll — at that time, a technique for which there was no music written). They thought their suspicions well-founded when, in 1971, after a day of experiments, I boiled all my mallet heads, yanked them off and reglued them on extra-long 1/4" diameter hardware-store pine dowels. Two weeks later I repeated the boiling and gluing process on 5/16" birch dowels, and their suspicions about my sanity were confirmed.

I now have a theory that the inherent flexibility of my finger-held grip and technique requires a complementary handle that is <u>in</u>flexible. Adding flexibility to flexibility does not result in a technique that is merely flexible, but one that is floppy, wild and difficult to control. On the other hand, I understand why players who still use a crossed-stick grip feel the need for flex in the handle of the mallet; the relationship of the mallets to the hand is inherently stiffer in this method, so a rattan handle offers some degree of flexibility.

"Method of Gripment"

Although I was careful to refer to my method of holding the mallets as "Musser grip" in the first edition of MOM, not many players or teachers agreed with my designation. Ten years after publication, it is now more common for players who use the book or have studied with me personally to call what they do "Stevens grip." I hope I don't seem like an ingrate, but in terms of having something named after me, I still have my sights set on a hospital wing or highway rest stop, not a grip.

In my opinion, the identification of what I do as "Stevens grip" overlooks the more important aspect of my technique: a "Method of <u>Movement</u>." After all, this book is not called "Method of Gripping." Holding the mallets is surely important, but it does not assure an accurate technique in and of itself. Only when a relaxed finger-actuated grip is combined with a sensible system for the execution of the strokes, interval changes and shifts, (i.e. shape, timing, use of certain muscles, etc.) can the casual "tapping of slats" be transformed into a true "method of movement." Therefore, I think it more appropriate and accurate that my system of grip, strokes, rolls etc. be called "Stevens Technique" or "Stevens Method," not "Stevens Grip."

Conclusion

While the rules of physics and the anatomy of the human body have not changed much in the past fifteen years, the perspective of students and teachers of marimba has been fundamentally altered. I am deeply gratified that my basic method outlined in this book for holding the mallets and striking the bars has been adopted at many of the leading music institutions around the world. Some of my ideas about rolls, mallets, tone production and sticking which I have written about in magazines and taught for many years in lessons and clinics (topics for which there was no room in MOM), have also become accepted as standard procedure. The resultant change in the type of literature written, overall style of playing, sticks used and sound produced has been astonishing. Perhaps the single most telling indicator of change is the fact that many students now enter college with a working version of a one-handed roll. An independent roll is no longer considered a virtuoso technique, but a necessary one.

As the standards of marimba performance continue to rise, and the literature becomes more demanding, the rationality of one's approach to marimba technique becomes more important. It is my opinion that today, even more than when MOM was first written, the success or failure of one's attempt to master this difficult instrument rests on one's understanding and application of the principles of economical movement elucidated in this book.